C000140636

THE AMERICAN EXPRESS POCKET GUIDE TO
ATHENS
AND THE CLASSICAL SITES

Sevan Nisanyan

Mitchell Beazley

The Author
Sevan Nisanyan is a native of Istanbul who studied at Yale and
Columbia. His publications include numerous books on Turkey
and a forthcoming volume of travel notes on Soviet Caucasia.

Acknowledgments
The author would like to thank Louise Oechler, George
Kalogeropoulos and Alkis Kourkoulas for their invaluable help
and advice. A further acknowledgment of debt is due to Peter
Sheldon, some passages from whose *American Express Pocket
Guide to Greece* (now out of print) appear in this book.

The author and publishers are grateful to Penguin Books Ltd
(UK) for their kind permission to reprint the quotations from
A Literary Companion to Travel in Greece (ed. Richard
Stoneman) on pages 45, 61, 85, 97 and 130 and from Pausanias'
Guide to Greece on page 118. The publishers also wish to thank
the American Express Publishing Corporation Inc., New York,
and Gary Walther, Editor-in-Chief of *Departures*, for their
co-operation during the production of this book, and Laurie
Williams for his careful reading of the typescript.

The editor wishes to thank Mike de Mello of Triptych Systems
Limited for his technical assistance during the preparation of this
book.

The *American Express Travel Guide Series* was conceived
under the direction of Susannah Read, Douglas Wilson, Hal
Robinson and Eric Drewery.

For the series
General Editor   David Townsend Jones
Map Editor   David Haslam
Indexer   Hilary Bird

For this edition
Edited on desktop by   David Townsend Jones
Art editors   Castle House Press
Illustrators   Sylvia Hughes-Williams, Jeremy Ford (David
   Lewis Artists), Illustra Design Ltd, Rodney Paull
Jacket illustration   Peter Elson
Gazetteer   Anne Evans

For Mitchell Beazley
Senior Executive Art Editor   Tim Foster
Managing Editor   Alison Starling
Production   Sarah Schuman

Edited and designed by Mitchell Beazley Publishers, part of Reed
International Books, Michelin House, 81 Fulham Road, London SW3 6RB
for the American Express (R) Travel Guide Series

Maps in 2-color and 4-color by Lovell Johns, Oxford, England.
Desktop layout in Ventura Publisher by Castle House Press, Llantrisant, Wales.
Typeset in Garamond and Univers.
Linotronic output through Tradespools Limited, Frome, England.
Produced by Mandarin Offset. Printed and bound in Malaysia.

Contents

How to use this book

How to find it   **(1)** For the organization of the book, see CONTENTS on the previous page. **(2)** Wherever possible, sections are arranged alphabetically, with headings appearing in **BLUE CAPITALS**. The headings are followed by addresses, telephone numbers and other practical details printed in *blue italics*. **(3)** Subject headers, similar to those used in telephone directories, appear in **bold black type** in the top corner of each page. **(4)** If you still cannot find it, look in the INDEX (on pages 137-143).

Cross-references   These are printed in SMALL CAPITALS, referring the reader to other sections or entries in the book.

Using the maps   The full-color maps at the end of the book have a standard grid system, to which the map co-ordinates given throughout the book refer. For example, the Acropolis is on map **1**E3 and Sounion on map **7**F3. A complete list of Athens street names with their map co-ordinates, which includes all streets that fall within the area of our map, appears on page 144.

The method used for spelling Greek names in the text and on maps is explained in the INTRODUCTION on page 6.

Bold and italic type   **Bold type** emphasizes points or topics of interest. As well as being used conventionally for titles, foreign words etc., *italic type* is also used within brackets for addresses, telephone numbers and other practical details.

Abbreviations   These include days of the week and months; N, S, E and W (points of the compass); Ave. (Avenue), St. (Street), Sq. (Square) and the Greek Leof. (Leoforos), Pl. (Platia) and Vass. (Vassilissis or Vassileos); St (Saint); rms (rooms); C (century); and measurements.

Floors   The European convention is used: "first floor" means the floor above the ground floor, and so on.

Price categories   The price ranges quoted below were valid as of late 1990. An inflation rate of 20-25 percent must be anticipated for subsequent years. As a rule, the relative price category is likely to remain more or less the same.

Many hotels, especially those in resort areas, apply an average discount of 20 percent in "half-season" (Apr-May and Oct), and as much as 40 percent in the dead season (Nov-Mar). Conversely, prices during the Aug peak in the most popular tourist destinations become subject to daily supply and demand, and may on some days exceed the posted rates by as much as 50 percent.

Price categories	Corresponding to approximate prices	
	for **hotels**	for **restaurants**
	double room with breakfast in summer	*meal for one with wine, tips and taxes*
▢ cheap	2,000-4,000dr	—
▥ inexpensive	3,500-6,000dr	1,000-3,000dr
▥ moderate	5,000-9,000dr	2,500-6,000dr
▥ expensive	7,500-16,000dr	5,000-9,000dr
▥ very expensive	15,000-32,000dr	—

Key to symbols

☎	Telephone	▭	Cheap
ℝ	Facsimile (fax)	▯▱	Inexpensive
★	Not to be missed	▰▱	Moderately priced
☆	Worth a visit	▰▰	Expensive
i	Tourist information	▰▰▰	Very expensive
▥	Classical site	AE	American Express
⛪	Byzantine church/	◐	Diners Club
	monastery	◖◗	MasterCard/Eurocard/
▨	Fortress/castle		Access
⌂	Traditional architecture	VISA	Visa
▧	Entrance fee payable	♿	Facilities for
◁	Good view		disabled people
✳	Special interest for	▭	TV in each room
	children	≋	Swimming pool
⌂	Hotel	☂	Beach
⇌	Restaurant	♫	Live music/dancing
▤	Air conditioning	▲	Camping

A word from the General Editor
Our authors and editors go to great lengths to ensure
that all the information is accurate at the time the
American Express Travel Guides go to press. However,
no travel book can be completely free of error or totally
up to date. Politicians can announce sweeping new
infrastructure plans; telephone numbers and opening
hours change without warning; and hotels and
restaurants come under new management, which may
affect their standards.

We are always delighted to receive corrections or
suggestions for improvements from our readers, which
where appropriate can be incorporated in the next
edition.

I am particularly indebted to readers who wrote during
the preparation of this book. Please continue to stay in
touch — your feedback is very important to our efforts
to tailor the series to the very distinctive tastes and
requirements of our sophisticated international
readership.

Send your comments to me at Mitchell Beazley
Publishers, Michelin House, 81 Fulham Road, London
SW3 6RB; or, in the US, c/o American Express Travel
Guides, Prentice Hall Travel, 15 Columbus Circle, New
York, NY 10023.

The publishers regret that they cannot accept any
consequences arising from the use of this book or from
the information it contains. The author also wishes me to
point out that his inclusion in hotel information of the
symbol ♿ (facilities for disabled people) is based
primarily on information provided by the Greek National
Tourist Organization.

David Townsend Jones

Introduction

The *American Express Pocket Guide to Athens and the Classical Sites* is intended as a practical handbook for the first-time visitor. In addition to Athens and its immediate vicinity, it covers the great sites of Classical archeology (Delphi, Olympia, Epidauros, Corinth) and many lesser localities located within a 200-kilometer (125-mile) radius of Athens. Also included is an excursion to the no less interesting Byzantine and medieval monuments of the southern Peloponnese. The only Greek islands included are those that lie within little more than an hour's sailing from Athens. Northern Greece is similarly outside the scope of this book.

Some material from the *American Express Pocket Guide to Greece,* by Peter Sheldon, which this volume supersedes, has been incorporated. All the research, however, reflects actual conditions as of winter 1990/91.

The bulk of the descriptive part of the book is devoted to the city of Athens and its suburbs. The Classical and medieval monuments of Athens and the sights of the modern city are treated under separate headings. This is followed by four excursions that correspond closely to the typical sightseeing patterns of most visitors to Athens. Three of the excursions — to Attica, the Saronic Islands and Delphi — can be accomplished in one day each, while the fourth — to the Peloponnese — involves a longer journey.

Spelling

The transliteration of Greek place names has no generally accepted standards. For Classical Greek names, traditional English usage calls for Latinized forms (Delphi and Parnassus rather than Delphoi and Parnassos), although a purist might well insist on Greek forms (Mykenai, Euboia). Until 1976, official Greek documents used the *katharevousa,* a classicizing form of speech that differs from common Greek especially in word-endings (Athine and Halkis rather than Athina and Halkida); pre- and post-1976 forms still coexist happily on road signs. Finally, the transcription of the modern vernacular is subject to much confusion: Nauplia, Nauplion, Navplion, Nafplion, Nafplio all refer to the same place.

We have used common English and Latinized forms in our text where we judge these to be part of the standard cultural heritage of the English language, with modern vernacular Greek forms given in parentheses. So, for example, Mycenae (Mikines) or Piraeus (Pireas).

We have adopted a moderate and not a strict system of transliterating modern Greek, making concessions to common usage at the cost of linguistic rigor. Thus Syntagma rather than Syndagma or Sindagma, but Mistra rather than Mystra, Hydra instead of Idra or Ydra.

Because our larger maps are published in all the numerous foreign-language editions of the *American Express Travel Guides,* we adopt international spellings, rather than common English forms, for place-names on the maps. Readers will therefore notice differences between text and map spellings, although these should present no difficulty. However, spellings on our smaller maps and diagrams conform with the text, as they are designed principally as visual aids.

Accents, which are an essential part of Greek spelling and pronunciation, are generally indicated only in main entries and omitted on place-names elsewhere in the text and on maps.

Before you go

Documents

EC nationals require a passport or valid identity card for a stay not exceeding 3mths. For **nationals of all other countries**, a valid passport is needed. For permission to stay more than 3mths, apply to the **Aliens Bureau** (*Leoforos Alexandras 173, Athens* ☎ *77.05.711*) or the local police.

Drivers from non-EC countries should have an international driver's license, although national licenses from both EC and non-EC countries are generally accepted without fuss. Vehicles need a valid registration certificate (logbook) and either international green insurance card or temporary insurance. The latter can be obtained at border crossing-points.

Health

Foreigners in Greece cannot obtain free **medical treatment**, and a fee is charged by hospitals for outpatients. The **IAMAT** (International Association for Medical Assistance to Travelers) has a list of English-speaking doctors who will call, for a fee. There are member hospitals and clinics throughout Europe, including Athens and several other towns in Greece. For information and a free directory of doctors and hospitals, write to **IAMAT** (*417 Center St., Lewiston, NY 14092*).

UK nationals entitled to full UK health benefits are entitled to the same health cover as Greek citizens upon presentation of form E111, which must be obtained from the Dept. of Health and Social Security before leaving the UK.

For private treatment in Greece, it is important to be insured adequately.

Money

The unit of **currency** is the drachma (pl. drachmes). There are coins for 1, 2, 5, 10, 20 and 50dr, and notes for 50, 100, 500, 1,000 and 5,000dr. Any amount of **foreign currency** over US $500 or the equivalent must by law be declared at the customs entry point, but in practice this requirement is rarely enforced.

Travelers checks issued by all major companies are widely recognized. Major **charge and credit cards** (American Express, Visa and Mastercard/Eurocard/Access; more rarely Diners Club) as well as **Eurocheque Encashment Cards** are accepted in Athens and other common tourist destinations by most shops, travel and car rental agencies, medium-to-better hotels and some restaurants. Bear in mind, however, that some establishments (notably jewelers) will charge a premium of about 7 percent for charge/credit card transactions.

The largest American and British banks, including American Express, Barclays, Chase Manhattan, Citibank, Grindlays, Midland and National Westminster, have offices in Athens.

Costs

‡ Can of soft drink: 100dr ‡ Simple meal at a taverna: 1,000dr ‡ Rock-bottom pension, for two: 2,000dr ‡ Class-A hotel, for two: 12,000dr ‡ Museum entrance: 200 or 500dr ‡ 1 liter super-grade fuel: 140dr

These and all prices quoted in this book reflect the conditions in winter 1990/91. The rate of inflation in recent years has averaged 20-25 percent. The rate of exchange at the time of writing was approximately 150 drachmes to one US dollar, or 300 drachmes to one pound sterling.

Before you go

Customs

Any items intended for personal use may be brought into Greece free of charge. Items that may be interpreted as being for commercial use will cause delays and aggravation at customs. The importation of personal computers, including laptops, is subject to an astonishing amount of bureaucracy.

Through 1992, duty-free allowances on tobacco, alcohol and perfumes will vary depending on whether the goods were purchased at duty-free stores or obtained tax-paid in EC countries. With the completion of the European Single Market at the end of 1992, it is probable that the sale of goods at duty-free prices within the EC will no longer apply, and no duty will then be payable on goods brought into Greece by EC citizens. For up-to-date information, British residents can obtain information from the **Single Market Unit, HM Customs and Excise** (☎ *071-865 5426*). Duty- and tax-free shopping will still be available to travelers departing directly for countries outside the EC, such as the US.

Clothing

Formal clothing will almost never be needed except when staying at luxury hotels or attending official functions. Topless sunbathing is common at practically all beaches; most tourists never wear more than shorts and T-shirts, although visitors are required to enter churches, monasteries and museums in what are deemed to be "decent" clothes. A light sweater is useful even in summer, as the *meltémi,* the regular N wind of the southern Aegean, can get quite chilly.

When to go

The tourist season lasts Apr-Oct, peaking in Aug. Avoid Aug if at all possible, as the combination of heat, tourist crowds, shortened tempers and inflated prices (as much as 40 percent up for accommodations, food and souvenirs) can make it a difficult experience. July is noticeably less crowded than Aug, and June much less so. The most pleasant weather occurs in Apr-May, when many mountains are still snow-capped and greenery and wild flowers carpet the land, although the sea is often chilly. Sept-Oct brings bright warm days and warm sea. Winter is a good time to enjoy the countryside, but Athens is often choked by smog, and most of the islands are depopulated and gloomy.

What to read

Classics: Herodotus, *Histories;* Thucydides, *The Peloponnesian War;* Strabo, *Geography* (Books 8, 9, 10); Pausanias, *Guide to Greece.*

History and archeology: John Chadwick, *The Mycenaean World;* J.C. Stobart, *The Glory that was Greece;* M.I. Finlay, *The Ancient Greeks;* William Bell Dinsmoor, *The Architecture of Ancient Greece;* Fani-Maria Tsigakou, *The Rediscovery of Ancient Greece;* Nicolas Cheetham, *Medieval Greece;* Steven Runciman, *Mistra;* C.M. Woodhouse, *The Greek War of Independence, Modern Greece – A Short History, The Philhellenes.*

Travel and literature: Lawrence Durrell, *Prospero's Cell;* Patrick Leigh Fermor, *Mani;* Robert Graves, *Greek Myths;* Marc Dubin, *Greece on Foot;* Nicholas Gage, *Eleni.*

Further information

The **Greek National Tourist Organization** has representative offices at the following addresses:

645 5th Ave. (Olympic Tower), New York, NY 10022
☎(212) 421-5777
611 W 6th St., Suite 2198, Los Angeles, CA 90017
☎(213) 626-6695
168 N Michigan Ave., Chicago, IL 60601 ☎(312) 782-1084
195-197 Regent St., London W1R 8DL ☎(071) 734-5997
68 Scollard St., Toronto, Ontario M5R 1G2 ☎(416) 958-2220

Getting there

By air
Athens is well served by a wide range of international airlines.
TWA and Olympic each have a daily New York-Athens flight
throughout the year, and Air Canada and Olympic have twice-
weekly flights from Montreal and Toronto. The lowest charter
fare from New York in 1990 was around $450 round-trip.

From Britain, British Airways and Olympic each operate two
daily London-Athens flights. Much less expensive are the various
charter companies and leftover place brokers; they offer a vast
array of options in summer but very little off-season. The lowest
prices in the peak season of 1990 were around £120 for London-
Athens round-trip, subject to various conditions.

Those flying to Greece on discount tickets should be aware that
they may be asked to furnish proof of accommodation. This can
be done by purchasing, from a travel agency, **hotel or camping
vouchers** sufficient to cover the length of stay in Greece.

By train
Trans-European trains are infrequent, slow, very crowded in
summer, and not cheaper than charter flights. A **Eurailpass** or
other discount scheme might nevertheless make the train journey
palatable. For the quickest route from London, take the evening
train from Victoria Station to Cologne, and change for Munich.
There, change to the **Attica Express**, which leaves Munich at
7.24pm and arrives in Athens in about 35hrs.

By bus
There are several companies operating between various Western
European cities and Athens. London-Athens on the **Magic Bus**
costs under £70 one-way and takes three days.

By car
Athens is approximately 3,000km (1,875 miles) from London via
Calais-Strasbourg-Munich-Belgrade. The tedious drive across
Yugoslavia can be avoided by driving down the length of Italy to
Brindisi and taking the ferry to **Igoumenitsa** *(most sailings in
the evening, passage 10hrs, under $17.50/£10 for deck seat plus
$17.50/£10 for car)* or **Patras** *(passage 18hrs, under $35/£20 for
deck seat plus $35/£20 for car)*. Advance reservations are
recommended for cars.

By boat
Regular ferry services link Venice, Ancona, Bari, Brindisi,
Otranto, Rijeka and Dubrovnik to Patras; and Istanbul, Odessa,
Haifa, Latakia, Limassol and Alexandria to Piraeus.

Time zone
Greek time is 7hrs ahead of Eastern Standard Time, 2hrs ahead of
Greenwich Mean Time and 1hr ahead of Central European Time.

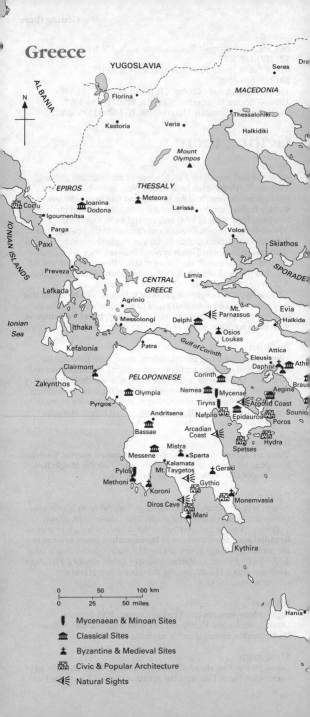

Greece

ALBANIA

YUGOSLAVIA

Seres

Dra

MACEDONIA

Florina

Kastoria

Veria

Thessaloniki

Halkidiki

N

EPIROS

Mount
Olympos

THESSALY

Corfu

Joanina
Dodona

Meteora

Igoumenitsa

Larissa

Parga

Paxi

Volos

Skiathos

Preveza

CENTRAL
GREECE

Lamia

SPORADES

IONIAN ISLANDS

Lefkada

Agrinio

Mt.
Parnassus

Ionian
Sea

Ithaka

Messolongi

Delphi

Evia

Kefalonia

Patra

Gulf of Corinth

Osios
Loukas

Halkida

Attica

Eleusis

Clairmont

PELOPONNESE

Corinth

Daphni

Athe

Zakynthos

Olympia

Nemea

Mycenae

Brau

Pyrgos

Tiryns

Aegina

Andritsena

Nafplio

Argolid Coast

Bassae

Arcadian
Coast

Epidauros

Sounio

Poros

Messene

Mistra

Sparta

Spetses

Hydra

Kalamata

Pylos

Mt. Taygetos

Geraki

Methoni

Gythio

Koroni

Diros Cave

Mani

Monemvasia

Kythira

| 0 | 50 | 100 km |
| 0 | 25 | 50 miles |

Hania

🏹 Mycenaean & Minoan Sites

🏛 Classical Sites

⛪ Byzantine & Medieval Sites

🏰 Civic & Popular Architecture

◁≣ Natural Sights

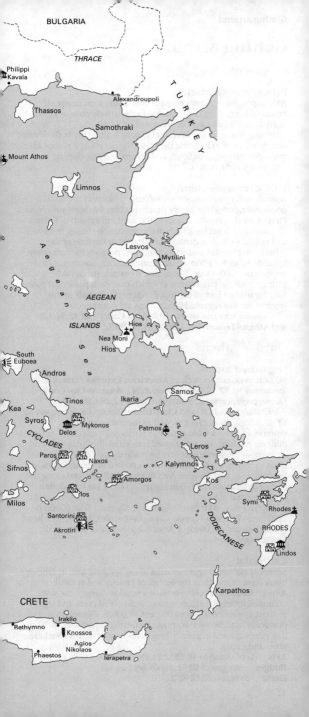

Getting around

In Athens

Private transportation

Although Greater Athens spreads over a vast area, nearly all points of interest are concentrated in a relatively compact central district, which can easily be explored on foot.

Driving your own car in central Athens is generally both slower and much more exhausting than walking, so avoid it except after midnight. Parking is difficult, and drivers as a rule display famously short tempers.

Public transportation

A single urban rail line, sometimes called "subway" because it goes underground for a brief stretch in central Athens, runs from Piraeus via downtown Athens to the northern suburb of Kifissia. The standard ticket for all urban transportation (buses, trolleys and rail) costs 50dr regardless of distance or the time of day.

Taxis are plentiful and remarkably inexpensive: the fare rarely exceeds 300dr for a trip within central Athens; downtown to the airport costs 600-800dr. It is common practice for cab drivers to pick up multiple passengers, in which case each passenger pays fully for his/her part of the trip. Foreigners who balk at this practice are not regarded kindly. Tips are not expected.

Limousine services are available from **Carey** (☎ 32.34.120) and **Athens Limousine** (☎ 32.33.957 ☎ 32.43.401).

Outside Athens

Organized tours

Major tour operators such as **American Express** *(Ermou 2, Syntagma Sq.* ☎ *32.44.975, map 2 D4)*, **Wagons-Lits/Cook** *(Karageorgi Servias 2, Syntagma Sq.* ☎ *32.28.650 and 32.42.281, map 2 D4)* and **Chat Tours** *(Stadiou 4, Syntagma Sq.* ☎ *32.22.886, map 2 D4)*, as well as numerous smaller enterprises, offer a wide variety of packaged tours out of Athens, utilizing modern, air-conditioned buses and also hydrofoils and cruise boats. Reservations may be made directly or through the great variety of travel agencies concentrated in the area between Syntagma Sq. and Syngrou Ave. in central Athens, and along the harbor in Piraeus. The following typical tours are intended to give a general idea:
‡ Delphi, 1 day, with lunch, 7,000dr ‡ Classical Tour (Corinth-Epidauros-Mycenae-Nafplio-Olympia- Delphi), 3 days, with hotel and half-board, 35,000dr ‡ Aegina-Poros-Hydra, 1 day, with lunch, 6,000dr

Car rental

Scores of car rental agencies exist along Syngrou Ave. in Athens; many have branches at the harbor of Piraeus and at Elinikon Airport. Rates for weekly rental of a small passenger car, with unlimited mileage, in high season, inclusive of taxes and legal insurance, vary between 40,000 and 65,000dr. Figures drop drastically, and become surprisingly flexible, in off-season. Note that prices quoted in agency brochures may or may not include taxes and extras.

Avis   Leof. Amalias 48 ☎ 32.24.951
Budget   Syngrou 8 ☎ 92.26.666 ☎ 92.24.444
Hertz   Syngrou 12 ☎ 92.20.102

Thrifty   Syngrou 24 ☎92.21.211 ⊗92.38.964
Staikos   Syngrou 40-42 ☎92.38.941 ⊗(0754) 51.011
Avanti   Syngrou 50 ☎92.33.919 ⊗90.20.095

Car rental is also available at other important entry points (Igoumenitsa, Patras) and tourist centers (Delphi, Olympia, Nafplio and others). Agencies generally insist on having the vehicles returned to the point of rental. Cross-border rentals are not available.

Rail

The Greek rail network is rudimentary. Of the two significant railroad lines run by the Hellenic Railway Organization (**OSE**), the Northern Line to Thessaloniki *(10 trains daily, 8hrs, 3,300dr one-way)* and Alexandroupolis operates from **Stathmós Athinás** (Athens Station), commonly known as **Laríssis** *(☎82.13.882, #1 trolley from Syntagma Sq. or Omonia Sq., map 1 B2)*. The Peloponnese Line to Corinth, Patras, Argos and Kalamata runs from **Stathmós Pelopónnisou**, a short distance s of Larissis *(☎51.31.601, map 1 B2)*. Return tickets are subject to a 20 percent discount.

Bus

There exist two separate systems of long-distance buses.

The Hellenic Railway Organization (**OSE**) operates a parallel network of buses. These depart from train stations, and are much faster but marginally dearer than trains.

Private bus operators are organized in co-operative monopolies (**KTEL**) within each province *(nómos),* and run services among points within the province as well as to and from major centers outside it. In towns served by more than one KTEL, each company may have its terminal in a different part of town, making a multistage bus journey a daunting task indeed.

In Athens, KTEL buses to all points in the Peloponnese, Epirus (NW), Macedonia (N) and Thrace (NE) leave from a joint terminal at **Kifissias 100** *(city bus 051 from Menandrou St., Omonia).* Buses to Central Greece, including Delphi and all points in Thessaly, leave from the terminal at **Liossion 260** *(city bus 024 from Leof. Amalias and Omonia).*

Sea

For many centuries the sea was the principal medium of travel in Greece, and the unique geographical conditions of the country ensure that boats remain one of the more common means of getting from place to place. All Aegean islands and many points along both E and W coasts of the mainland are served by ship from the harbor of Piraeus. Local ferries run between a large number of ports.

Ferry lines are operated by private and rival companies, and as a result the system sometimes displays a spirit of bedlam. Different schedules apply to each of the seven days of the week. No generalized timetable exists for any port other than Piraeus, let alone for the country as a whole *(☎143 for recorded Piraeus timetable, in Greek).* No shipping company or agency will be persuaded to betray so much as an awareness of the services of a rival company. As a rule, there is no reliable way of knowing for certain at point A whether and when a boat goes from point B to point C.

The **Flying Dolphin** hydrofoil service operates between Piraeus and Aegina (departures from Piraeus Harbor), Poros, Hydra, Spetses, Ermioni, Porto Heli, Nafplio, Leonidio and

Getting around

Monemvasia (departures from Zea Marina) *(for information ☎ 45.36.107 and 45.37.107 ☎ 45.35.403)*.

Aegean cruises ranging from one to 14 days or longer are organized by a variety of companies. A wide array of choices is offered by **Sun Line** *(Iasonos 3, Piraeus ☎ 45.23.417)*. **Viking Tours** *(Filelinon 3, Athens)* specialize in smaller boats carrying up to 36 passengers.

Boats can be rented, with or without crew, for sailing alone or as part of a flotilla. Contact **Yacht Brokers Association** *(P.O.B. 30393, Athens ☎ 98.16.582)*, or any travel agency.

Air

Olympic Airways, Greece's only domestic airline, runs services between Athens and some 34 points around the country. Fares are heavily subsidized and therefore quite cheap; examples are Athens-Thessaloniki, 12,000dr one-way (cheaper on night flights); Athens-Mykonos, 9,000dr one-way. Advance reservations are essential on flights to most islands.

The Athens town terminal of Olympic Airways is located at **Syngrou 96** *(☎ 96.16.6161)*. The ticket offices are at **Othonos 6** *(on Syntagma Sq., map 2 D4 ☎ 92.92.555 for international flights ☎ 92.92.444 for domestic flights ☎ 144 for recorded timetable in Greek)*.

The **Elinikon Airport** is divided into two parts. The west terminal serves Olympic Airways only and operates its own bus service to the company's town terminal on Syngrou. The east terminal serves foreign airlines and operates a bus service to Syntagma Sq. A taxi from either terminal to the city center costs less than 1,000dr. There is a connecting bus service between the two terminals, but it is extremely slow and you are generally better advised to take a cab.

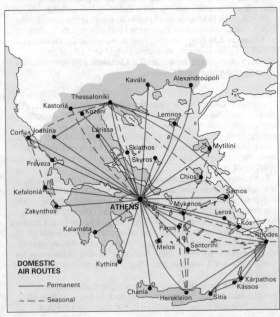

DOMESTIC AIR ROUTES
—— Permanent
- - - Seasonal

On-the-spot information

Tourist information

The **Greek National Tourist Organization (GNTO**, sometimes also called **NTOG**; **EOT** in Greek) is one of the most efficient governmental bodies of the country. It maintains very helpful information bureaus in Athens and other major tourist centers, operates a chain of hotels located in architectural landmark buildings, and is in charge of the management of most museums and archeological sites. GNTO headquarters in Athens are located at **Amerikis 2** (☎ *32.23.1111/9, map 2D4*). GNTO Information Bureaux in Athens are in:

National Bank of Greece, Karageorgi Servias 2, Syntagma Sq. ☎ 32.22.545 and 32.34.130, map **2**D4, open daily until 8pm
General Bank of Greece, Ermou 1, Syntagma Sq. ☎ 32.52.267, map **2**D4, open daily until 6pm

The **tourist police** have the same power as the ordinary police but are also specially briefed to help the visitor. They can be recognized by the shoulder flash *Tourist Police* on their uniforms. Many of them also wear badges indicating the languages they speak. They are often the best source of advice on accommodations — but they are *not* obliged to find you somewhere to stay. For problems and emergencies in Athens call the Tourist Police (☎ *171*).

The **Touring and Automobile Club of Greece (ELPA)** provides various services to drivers. Their headquarters are located in the **Tower of Athens** (*Messogio 2, Athens* ☎ *77.91.615*).

For emergency road assistance ☎ **104**.

Language

English is well established as the lingua franca of tourism throughout Greece. Most road signs, explanatory placards, tickets etc. are bilingual in Greek and English. Nearly all hotel personnel and most service people who come into routine contact with tourists (waiters, shopkeepers, boatmen, museum guards) speak some English. In the SW Peloponnese, for some reason, German seems to be more popular than English.

Speaking a few rudimentary phrases of Greek is of course a sign of goodwill and will be duly appreciated, but bear in mind that an appreciative smile might sometimes be more expressive of your meaning than an *efharistó* (thank you) spoken with an atrocious accent.

Foreign exchange

Most hotels, tourist stores, travel agencies and many individuals will be happy to exchange major Western currencies, but will of course charge a slight commission over the bank rate. Best rates for money and travelers checks are obtained at banks, which are usually open Mon-Thurs 8am-2pm, Fri 8am-1.30pm. On Sun and holidays some banks are open at airports, ports and border crossings.

In Athens, the **National Bank of Greece**, at the corner of Stadiou and Syntagma Sq., remains open for money exchange Mon-Fri until 9pm, Sat-Sun until 8pm.

Shopping and business hours

Shopping hours are a science unto themselves, as there exist different legally stipulated hours for each type of establishment, each day of the week and each season of the year, and these

15

change frequently, too. As a rule of thumb, assume that *nothing* (no company or government offices, no museum or archeological sites) will be open after 3pm, and count yourself lucky if they are. Many shops, especially in areas frequented by tourists, close down for most of the afternoon but reopen in the evening to stay open until 9pm or midnight. Saturday and Sunday are less drastically dead than in most European countries, with many shops in central locations opening half-day on Sundays.

Public holidays

Offices, banks and some shops close on the following days:

Jan 1; Jan 6, Epiphany; Shrove Monday, 41 days before Easter, usually March; Mar 25, Declaration of Greek Independence in 1821; Easter, observed Good Friday through Easter Monday; May 1, Labor Day; Whit Monday, 50 days after Easter; Aug 15, Assumption of the Virgin; Oct 28, Óhi Day, rejection of the Italian ultimatum in 1940; Dec 25-26.

Note that the Greek Orthodox Easter is celebrated according to the Julian calendar, and usually falls on a date from one to four weeks later than it does in Western Christian observance.

Museums and sights

The **standard opening hours** for all museums and archeological and historical sights managed by GNTO are Tues-Sun 8.30am-3pm, closed Mon. This general rule is subject to a bewildering array of variations. The most popular tourist sights are usually open in season until 5 or 6pm, and either do not close at all on Mon or do so only until noon. Some museums proudly display a shield listing different opening and closing hours for every day of the week, not counting holidays and special occasions.

Standard entry charges are 200dr for run-of-the-mill sights, 500dr for major sights such as Delphi and Olympia, and 800dr for the Athens Acropolis.

Post and telephone

The post office (**ELTA**) and the telephone system (**OTE**) are independent of one another.

Post offices *(tahidromío)* are in principle open Mon-Fri 8am-1pm, 3-7pm. The office at Syntagma Sq. in Athens is open Mon-Fri 8am-8pm. Stamps can also be bought in kiosks. There is now a single rate for postcards and letters (100dr to the US, 80dr to Europe). Letters can be posted in yellow mail boxes, which sometimes have two compartments marked *Esoterikoú* (domestic) and *Exoterikoú* (foreign).

General delivery (poste restante) in Athens should be addressed to the main post office at Eolou 100 *(Omonia Sq.)*.

Coin-operated **phone booths** are generally equipped only for local calls, although phones that allow trunk (long-distance) calls are becoming more common. Most kiosks and some cafés offer a public telephone service. Trunk calls can also be made from an OTE office in towns or a post office in villages; in both cases you make your call from a booth and then pay for it at the counter. The telephone system in Athens and major mainland towns is reasonably efficient, but the same cannot truthfully be said about the islands.

In Athens ☎ **134** for general telephone information (in Greek) ☎ **131** for numbers in Athens and Attica ☎ **132** for numbers elsewhere in Greece.

Electric current

The standard throughout Greece is 220V AC (50Hz), which means that appliances bought in North America will require a converter. British appliances need a simple adaptor plug, which, however, is not readily available within Greece. In some very remote places, especially the islands, it is possible to find 110V AC, so ask before you plug in.

Tipping

Restaurant and hotel bills include a 15 percent service charge, so in principle no additional tipping is expected. In restaurants it is customary to leave the small change. In hotels of the better categories (that is, those that usually are not family-owned and operated), it may be appropriate to give a small tip to porters, attendants, etc. Taxi drivers do not expect to be tipped unless they have performed some extra service.

Cabin and dining-room stewards in cruise ships should be tipped in proportion to the duration of the cruise and the quality of their solicitations. On night trains, a 500dr bill slipped to the sleeping-car attendant will work wonders.

Public bathrooms usually employ an old lady who supplies toilet paper and eau de cologne for a few coins; this must be recognized as a form of public charity. Cinema and theater ushers and cloakroom attendants fall into the same category, although with much less charm.

English publications

The English-language newspaper is the *Athens News,* which reports of local news and events within the unfortunate standards of Greek journalism. *The Athenian,* a monthly journal, is useful for up-to-date entertainment and restaurant reviews. *The Week in Athens* is also a reliable source of information for events and carries much local advertising. GNTO publish several leaflets in English on different topics.

Emergency information

The most readily available source of assistance in an emergency is the reception desk of your hotel. The following emergency telephones operate throughout the country:

Police (cities) ☎100
Gendarmerie (countryside) ☎109
Tourist Police (in Athens only) ☎171
Emergency road service (ELPA) ☎104
US citizens emergency aid ☎(01) 72.12.951

Emergency telephone numbers are likely to be standardized throughout the EC from Jan 1993.

Medical emergencies in Athens

Doctors 2-7am ☎105
First aid and ambulance ☎166

The **ELPIS dental hospital** answers emergency calls in Athens between 10pm and 6am ☎64.30.001.

In Athens ☎107 for a list of **all-night pharmacies** *(farmakío),* or look in the *Athens News.* In other areas, a list of late-night pharmacies is displayed in all pharmacists' windows.

17

Consulates in Athens
Australia   Messogio 15 ☎36.04.611/5
Canada   Ioan. Genadiou 4 ☎72.39.511
Ireland   Vass. Konstantinou 7 (map **2**E5) ☎72.32.771
New Zealand   An. Tsoha 15-17 ☎64.10.311
United Kingdom   Ploutarhou 1 (map **2**D5) ☎72.36.211
United States   Vass. Sofias 91 (map **2**D5) ☎72.12.951

Places of worship
St Andrew's American/Protestant Church   Sina 66 (map **2**C4)
St Paul's English Church   Filelinon 29 (map **2**E4) ☎72.14.906
St Denis Roman Catholic Cathedral   Panepistimiou (Venizelou) 24 (map **2**D4) ☎36.23.603
Beth Shalom Synagogue   Melidoni 5 (map **1**D2) ☎32.52.823
Mosque   In Caravel Hotel, Vassilissis Alexandrou 2 (off map **2**D6) ☎72.90.721

There are also churches in Athens belonging to Baptists, 7th Day Adventists, Christian Scientists and Jehovah's Witnesses.

Other Protestant churches exist in Thessaloniki and Patras. There are 21 Roman Catholic churches in Greece, mostly in the islands but also in Thessaloniki, Patras, Kalamata and Nafplio. The only other synagogue is in Thessaloniki.

Disabled travelers
Disabled visitors to Greece should not expect the specially adapted facilities that are becoming common in other Western countries. GNTO have a list of tour operators that may be able to make arrangements for disabled travelers.

Accommodations

Since the early 1970s, tourism has overtaken shipping as Greece's largest industry. Hotels to satisfy the needs and requirements of every class of international visitor therefore exist in abundance in every part of the country, and not only at the major tourist destinations. Almost all of Greece's approximately 5,000 hotels, however, have been built or modified since the mid-1960s, so there are no establishments of great tradition and character such as those found in some European countries. All medium-to-better-category hotels offer modern facilities and uniform standards of design and service, but tend to lack individual character. But modest hotels often compensate for their crumbly looks by the greater charm and friendliness of the personnel.

In Aug it is absolutely essential to have prearranged accommodations in the islands, and advisable to do so in Athens as well. At other times it should be possible to find plenty of room without much difficulty. Many hotels close Nov-Mar inclusive, and in the less popular islands it may be impossible to find any accommodations during this period.

The official hotel classes correspond roughly to our price categories, as follows:

Class	price range		Double room in summer
L	▐▐▐▐	very expensive	15,000-32,000dr
A-B	▐▐▐▐	expensive	7,500-16,000dr
B	▐▐⊐	moderate	5,000-9,000dr
C-D	▐⊐	inexpensive	3,500-6,000dr
D-E	⊐	cheap	2,000-4,000dr

There also exists a vast number of private rooms offering basic service at prices somewhat lower than hotels of comparable category, not so much in Athens but in most other towns and villages in the main tourist regions. They advertise themselves prominently with signs of *enoikiazómenai domátia/rooms/ zimmer;* in a pinch a list may be obtained from accommodation agencies (in major tourist centers) or from local police (in lesser towns).

As a rule, prices for the top three categories of hotels include breakfast, while in the lower categories breakfast tends to be extra. Most beach resorts in the top categories offer half-board.

All hotels in the top two categories and many in the middle categories are air conditioned. All rooms in categories L through C and most in D have private baths or showers, and room telephones. Room TV and minibars are rare except in category L. All hotels in categories L, A, most in B and a few in C take major charge and credit cards; almost none does so in the lower categories.

Two state-run hotel chains deserve separate mention. **Xenia** hotels, operated by a semi-governmental agency, exist in most towns and at significant tourist destinations. Their architecture and style of management reflect the slightly chilling touch of public administration, but they all offer reliable standards at reasonable prices. The newer network of **GNTO** guesthouse/ hotels consists of impeccably restored historic buildings and architectural landmarks, run generally by young and highly educated personnel, with an excellent esthetic sense compensating for any management deficiencies that may crop up.

An alternative that in recent years has become increasingly popular in Greece is self-catering (efficiency) villas and apartments. These are scarcely more expensive than comparable hotels, and may prove an especially attractive option for families or small groups planning to stay in one place for a week or more. One specialist rental agency in Athens is **Accommodation Center** *(Filelinon 3, map **2** D4 ☎ 32.20.00).*

Campers can choose from more than 100 organized campsites, those operated by **GNTO** being the best. Lists and information may be obtained from GNTO or tourist police. Camping in the open is prohibited by statute, though the ban is only enforced in and around towns.

Our hotel listings

For Athens, we have included a broad and representative listing of hotels in every price range. For localities covered in the excursions, the listing always includes the generally recognized "top" hotel of the locality, and one or two representative hotels in categories C and above (usually the largest hotel in each category). Hotels in category D or pensions are occasionally included when they have been found by personal experience to be especially attractive or well-managed establishments.

Food and drink

Taverna food

The heart and soul of Greek food culture is the *taverna:* a simple restaurant with that invariably rickety look, with more tables out on the sidewalk or garden than inside, clustered together in the main square, along the harbor walk or at a beauty spot at the edge of town. Its next of kin include the *psistaría,* a taverna specializing in barbecues, and the *ouzerí,* an establishment primarily for drinking *oúzo* but serving a range of appetizers as well. For Greeks, dining out is a social affair. The taverna performs a function similar to the English pub or German *Kneipe.* Eating, in other words, is incidental to holding forth with a group of friends or enjoying the spectacle of the world passing by.

The culinary claims of the taverna are therefore, inevitably, modest; what counts first is such things as the quality of the setting (good view, lovely pergola, lots of action) or the charm of the host (sassy, friendly). It is easy to find fault with the culinary dimension of things. The choice, for example, is astonishingly limited, with *all* tavernas across Greece offering the almost identical menu. Food is invariably edible and occasionally quite tasty too, but very often drowned in olive oil and sometimes smothered in tomato paste as well. Seafood is generally fresh and tasty, but special care should be taken to ensure that it is not fried in burned or reused oil. Sauces are almost unknown. Experimenting in unorthodox tastes is as rare and shocking as a church painter fooling around with his icons.

As a rule one orders food after inspecting the wares in the cook's display, or even checking the boiling pots in his kitchen. A preview is especially important when ordering fish, which varies enormously in size, quality and price; it is safest to investigate the fridge and have your choice weighed and priced before you commit yourself to any seafood.

Standard taverna fare includes "Greek salad," which Greeks call *horiatikí,* or "peasant salad"; *tsatsíki,* a yogurt and cucumber mix laced with garlic; *melitsánosaláta,* a creamy eggplant (aubergine) dip; fried squid, or *kalámaria;* octopus, or *ohtopódi,* usually prepared as a salad; *mousákka,* a casserole of eggplant and minced meat; and *pastítsio,* a macaroni casserole. In addition, there is the usual variety of grilled meats and fried fish. *Souvláki* is lamb or pork bits grilled on a skewer. *Biftéki* is not what the name suggests but a sort of breaded and fried meatball.

Coffee, if at all available, is either instant or "Greek coffee," a murky concoction sipped from tiny cups. Filtered coffee is unknown except in the classiest establishments. Desserts do not form part of traditional taverna fare, although some tavernas have lately taken to including *baklavá* or ice cream on their menu. For a wider selection of desserts you move on to a *záharoplastío,* or pastry store, large numbers of which exist in every town.

A typical taverna meal involving an hors d'oeuvre, salad, main course and table wine will almost always cost between 1,000 and 1,500dr. In Athens and Piraeus as well as other major tourist destinations there also exist numerous "upscale" tavernas catering primarily to tourists. Apart from over-solicitous waiters and garish decor, these rarely offer anything more or better than an average taverna, but cost from two and three times as much.

Restaurants

The *estiatório,* an eating establishment more in tune with Western concepts of a restaurant, is a phenomenon more or less confined in Greece to the cities of Athens and Thessaloniki — not counting, of course, the restaurants of better-class hotels that serve standardized "Greek and international cuisine" all around the country.

Restaurants offering the best and most imaginative in traditional Greek cooking are generally those owned by Greeks who emigrated in the 1920s and '50s from Constantinople (Istanbul) and Alexandria. In addition, Athens now has a variety of restaurants with original and interesting menus, only marginally "Greek" in character. These tend to cater mainly to the yuppiedom and resident aliens, and are rarely visited by tourists.

About a dozen national cuisines are represented in Athens by one or two restaurants each. Apart from the occasional pizza-and-spaghetti parlor or hamburger joint, non-Greek eating is virtually unknown in the provinces.

Drink

As with so much else in Greece, so with wine: entirely acceptable and perfectly enjoyable wines exist in great abundance, but none really deserves to be singled out for special praise. Regional character is mostly a matter of speculation; vintage is rarely indicated and rarely matters; and grape variety is practically unknown. Greeks themselves show a preference for house wine over bottled brands; this turns out to be excellent advice, especially in the sw Peloponnese and on some islands.

Rétsina, the best-known Greek wine, obtains its resin flavor from the pine casks in which it is aged. It must be drunk well-chilled. Demestica, the most common nonresinated brand, comes in white, red and rosé. Cambas and Boutari are reliable, good, dry wines. Cava Clauss, a full-bodied dry red (rare and expensive), and Chateau Clauss are considered the best of the Greek wines.

Two brands of lager, Amstel and Heineken, brewed in Greece under license, dominate the beer market. There are no small local brewers, and imported brands are a rarity.

Oúzo, a colorless aniseed liquor that turns white when mixed with water, is the most popular aperitif. It is always served with *pikilía,* simple snacks served at the waiter's whim, or *mezés,* more substantial appetizers, which at their best remain a Cypriot and Constantinopolitan specialty. It is generally believed that the best way to cure an ouzo hangover, or for that matter any hangover, is *patsá,* a gelatinous white soup made of sheep's trotters and/or tripe. This is admittedly an acquired taste, but once acquired it tends to stay with you.

Breakfast

For most Greeks, breakfast consists of a cup of strong coffee and a pack of cigarettes. Hotels make a concession to foreign ways by adding bread, butter and a half-spoonful of bad jam; this procedure is euphemistically called a "continental breakfast." If you want eggs and limp bacon, ask for "English breakfast"; it costs 500-700dr.

Time chart

Earliest times

BC

5000-3000	Neolithic settlements on the mainland, especially Thessaly.
3200-2000	Cycladic culture in the Aegean islands. "Pelasgian" fortified towns on the mainland.
2000-1375	Minoan "Palace" civilization in Crete (Middle and Late Minoan period); high point in 1700-1450.
2200-1800?	Greek language introduced by invading Indo-European tribes from the N.

Time chart

1600–1200	High point of Mycenaean civilization. Royal palaces in Mycenae, Tiryns, Pylos.
c.1220	The Trojan War: coalition of Mycenaean princes attacks Troy in Asia Minor.
1200–700	Greek Dark Ages. Invading tribes from N (Dorians) destroy Mycenaean culture.
c.1000	Greeks colonize W coast of Asia Minor (Ionia).

Archaic and Classical Athens

Before 1200?	Legendary king Theseus unites the clans of Attica under Athenian leadership.
680–640	Landowning nobles eliminate kingship; two *archons* (chief magistrates) elected annually. Earliest written record: Cylon, a winner of the foot-race at Olympia, attempts coup d'etat.
621	Draco reforms Athenian law, establishing a criminal code to discourage private revenge and setting "draconian" penalties.
594–593	Solon appointed *archon.* He reforms social and economic laws, broadens Athenian citizenship, establishes coinage, standardizes weights and measures, and sets up Council of 400.
560s–527	Peisistratus, an enlightened tyrant, seizes power and rules with popular support. He initiates major building projects, codifies Homeric poems and introduces the cult of Dionysus. Athens becomes an important city under Peisistratus.
530s	Temple of Apollo at Delphi built by political enemies of Peisistratus (aristocratic faction of the Alcmaeonids).
527–510	Dictatorial rule of Hippias and Hipparchus, sons of Peisistratus.
508–500	Reforms of Cleisthenes inaugurate Athenian democracy. City and Attica divided into 10 *demes* (clans), each electing 50 representatives to the Council of 500. Ostracism: any citizen can be exiled for 10yrs by popular vote.
490	First Persian War. Athenians and Plataeans defeat Persians at Marathon.
480s	Themistocles, the leader of the democratic party, dominates Athens. Policy of naval build-up; port of Piraeus established and fortified.
480–479	Second Persian War. Vast Persian army under Xerxes breaks Greek defenses at Thermopylae, occupies Athens and destroys the Acropolis. The Persian navy is defeated at Salamis, and the Persian army finally defeated at Plataea. The Athenian navy expels Persians from Asia Minor.
477	Cimon exploits Athenian naval power to create the League of Delos, an alliance of most Aegean city-states. Members pay tribute to a common fund controlled by Athens. Attempts to secede from the League are suppressed forcibly by Athens.
462–429	Pericles, leader of the democratic party, dominant in Athens. The city reaches peak of political power and cultural brilliance.
460–451	First war against Sparta. Sparta resists the expansion of Athenian hegemony over the mainland.
c.450	Start of massive rebuilding program on the Acropolis, ruined since the Persian invasion. Construction of the Parthenon. Classic age of Doric temple architecture.

22

431-404	Peloponnesian War between Athens and Sparta. The war ruins Greece and exhausts Athens economically.
429	Death of Pericles in a plague epidemic.
415-413	Sicilian expedition of Alcibiades ends in disaster.
405-404	Athenian navy wiped out by Spartans at Aegospotami. Athens capitulates. The League of Delos dissolved. Regime of terror (30 Tyrants) in Athens under Spartan aegis.
403	Moderate democracy restored by Thrasyboulos.
399	Socrates put to death on charges of corrupting the youth.
371-362	Epaminondas of Thebes breaks the ascendancy of Sparta after a series of battles (Leuctra, Mantinea). Theban success allows Athens to pursue expansionary policies.
368-357	Second League of Delos, a narrower and weaker alliance than the first. It collapses when the allies are lured away by Philip II of Macedon.
359-336	Rise of Philip, a brilliant diplomatist and general, as the dominant force in Greek politics. Demosthenes, in famous speeches (known as Philippics) urges Athenians to lead Greece against Macedonian ascendancy.
338	Battle of Chaeronia establishes Philip's mastery over Greece. City-states remain autonomous, but Macedonian military presence leaves little room for independent policy.
334-323	Alexander, son of Philip, conquers Asia Minor, Syria, Egypt, Mesopotamia, Persia and northern India. Rapid Hellenization of the Eastern Mediterranean world.
322	Final Athenian revolt against Macedon ends in failure. Demosthenes commits suicide.
	Hellenistic and Roman Greece
323-281	Alexander's generals fight over the spoils of his empire. Antigonus Gonatas emerges victorious in Macedon and Greece; suppresses revolts by various alliances of Greek cities.
279	Gauls (Celts) invade Greece, but turn back at Delphi after a miraculous intervention of Apollo (reputedly a violent thunderstorm).
199	Philip V of Macedon defeated by Romans at Cynoscephalae (N of Lamia). Roman consul Flamininus announces the liberation of Greece at the Isthmian Games in 196. Rome becomes the arbiter of Greek affairs.
146	Romans destroy Corinth and suppress the Achaean League, an alliance of Peloponnesian states. Greece subjected to the Roman province of Macedonia (afterwards separate province of Achaea in the s with Corinth as capital). Athens and other loyal Roman allies remain nominally independent.
88-86	Athens sides with Mithridates against Rome; defeated and plundered by Sulla.
60s-31	Greece suffers heavily in the civil wars of republican Rome. Strabo describes it as a ravaged and depopulated land, with many ancient cities reduced to ruins. Athens remains alive and important because of its philosophical schools. Cicero, Caesar, Antonius and Augustus visit it as tourists.

Time chart

AD

54	St Paul preaches in Athens and Corinth. Dionysius the Areopagite becomes the first Athenian convert to Christianity.
66-67	Nero spends a year traveling in Greece, amassing a vast collection of ancient Greek art. He participates in the Olympic, Pythian and Isthmian Games, winning in 1,808 categories.
117-180	Period of revival under Antonine emperors. Hadrian promotes ancient Greek culture, rebuilds temples and reactivates ancient games (117-138). Herodes Atticus, a wealthy Athenian, endows public buildings throughout Greece in the reign of Antoninus Pius (138-161). Marcus Aurelius (161-180) reorganizes the Athenian schools into a university.
c.170	Pausanias visits Greece and writes the earliest known traveler's guide to its antiquities.

Byzantines, Franks, Venetians

331	Constantine transfers the capital of the Roman Empire to Byzantium, renamed Constantinople. Major works of art carried off to the city. Christianity becomes state religion. Steep decline in all provinces including Greece.
391	Edict of Theodosius: all pagan temples closed down and oracular activities prohibited, and Olympic Games discontinued after 1,000yrs.
395	Goths under Alaric invade Greece and sack Eleusis.
529	Edict of Justinian: the Athenian schools, final bastions of paganism, dismantled. Parthenon becomes a church. Athens sinks thereafter into historic insignificance.
c.580	Slavs invade Greece and sack Athens.
747	Great plague depopulates Greece. Slavs settle in the Peloponnese. Greek language and Christianity disappear except in some fortified towns.
c.860	Byzantine attempts to convert Slavs. Earliest monasteries in Greece.
c.1020	Reassertion of Byzantine authority in Greece.
1054	Final schism between Rome and the Byzantine Orthodox church.
1204	The Fourth Crusade captures Constantinople and expels Byzantine emperors (until 1261). European knights acquire feudal domains in southern Greece. Principality of Achaea in the Peloponnese (Geoffroi de Villehardouin), with 12 subordinate duchies. Duchy of Athens and Thebes (Othon de la Roche, Guy de Brienne). Parthenon becomes a Roman Catholic cathedral.
1311-86	Athens captured by Catalan mercenaries, becoming a property of the kingdom of Aragón.
1386-1456	Athens acquired by the Florentine banking family of Acciaiuoli (1386), who subsequently come under Venetian protection. Attica resettled by Albanians.
1349-1460	The Peloponnese recaptured by the Byzantines, who set up a semi-independent government (despotate) based in Mistra.

Turkish rule

1456-60	Ottoman Sultan Mehmed II captures Athens and various Italian, Frankish and Greek possessions in southern Greece. Greeks allowed communal

	autonomy under the rule of the Orthodox church, headed by the Patriarch of Constantinople.
1499, 1540	Last Venetian strongholds on the Greek mainland fall to the Turks.
c.1600	25 percent of Greece's population estimated Muslim (Turkish or Albanian). In Athens the Acropolis houses Muslim and Jewish quarters, while Greeks live downhill. Parthenon becomes a mosque, with the addition of a minaret.
1687	Venetians under Morosini capture the Peloponnese. Athens besieged without success; Parthenon heavily damaged by Venetian shelling.
1715	Turks reoccupy the Peloponnese.
1764-66	Society of the Dilettanti undertakes the earliest European archeological expedition to Greece.
1799-1815	Napoleonic wars awaken British interest in Greece both as strategic asset and as travel destination.
1801-03	Lord Elgin purchases the Parthenon friezes, which are later placed in the British Museum.

Modern Greece

1821	Germanos, Bishop of Patras, raises the flag of Greek revolt in Kalavryta on Mar 25. Athens captured and Turkish inhabitants massacred in 1822. Philhellenic sentiment in Europe: Lord Byron joins the Greek war of independence.
1825-27	Ottoman counterattack under Ibrahim Pasha, commander of a private Egyptian army. Greek revolt effectively crushed with the capture of Missolonghi and Athens.
1827	Britain, France and Russia intervene on behalf of the Greeks. Turkish navy destroyed at Navarino.
1830	London Protocol declares Greece (comprising southern Greece and the Cyclades) a sovereign monarchy. Prince Otto of Bavaria appointed king in 1832, with Nafplio as his capital.
1834	Athens, a town of 5,000, becomes the capital of Greece. European architects begin to rebuild the city.
1863	Otto overthrown in a revolt. Prince George of Denmark appointed king after Allied intervention.
1881	Thessaly granted to Greece by European powers.
1897-1949	Greece experiences "six major wars, four foreign invasions, two civil wars, all manner of coups d'etat and pronunciamentos, several revolts, three serious revolutions and a succession of economic catastrophes" (Harold Nicolson).
1912-13	Greece obtains Macedonia and Epirus in the Balkan wars.
1915	*Dichasmos* (discord) between royalists and followers of Venizelos divides Greek politics for a generation.
1919-22	w coast of Turkey granted to Greece by the victors of World War I. Greek invasion of Asia Minor results in disastrous defeat by the Turks. The Treaty of Lausanne repatriates nearly all Greek inhabitants of Turkey (1.5 million) to Greece, causing huge social problems.
1924-35	King George II deposed by republicans; returns 11yrs later after a monarchist referendum.
1940	Mussolini invades Greece. One-word reply of General Metaxas to the Italian ultimatum of Oct 28: *óhi* (no).

1941	Hitler invades Greece after Italian failure.
1944	Britain, aided by local partisans, forces German army to retreat in Oct. First civil war in Athens between partisans and British-supported government forces.
1946-49	Second civil war, with vicious fighting between communist-led partisans and US-supported government forces. The wounds of the civil war fester until the 1980s.
1951-63	Conservative governments under A. Papagos and Constantine Karamanlis.
1963-65	Center-left government of George Papandreou unleashes political chaos.
1967	Military coup of Colonel Papadopoulos. King Constantine II goes into exile.
1973	Student uprising at the Athens Polytechnic forces Papadopoulos out. New junta under General Gizikis.
1974	Coup and Turkish intervention in Cyprus. Military regime collapses; Karamanlis returns from exile and elected prime minister (1974-81). Monarchy abolished by referendum.
1981	Greece admitted to the EC.
1981-89	Pan-hellenic Socialist Alliance (PASOK) government under Andreas Papandreou. Economic crisis and allegations of corruption bring PASOK down.
1990	Constantine Mitsotakis, leader of center-right Nea Demokratia, comes to power after three inconclusive elections. Karamanlis elected President.

The ages of Greek culture

Cycladic (3200-2000BC)

The discoveries of James Th. Bent in 1883-84 revealed first traces of this hitherto unsuspected civilization, which flourished in the Aegean islands of Paros, Naxos, Melos, Delos, Amorgos and others. Its most characteristic products were the remarkably graceful **marble idols**, which ranged from tiny to life-sized. The

best collections are at the Goulandris Foundation's Cycladic Art Museum and the National Archeological Museum in Athens, and at the British Museum in London.

Traces of **walled settlements** from this period have been found on the mainland (for example, the Athenian Acropolis). Ancient Greeks knew these early inhabitants under the general name of "Pelasgians." Their masonry of heavy, irregular stone blocks was attributed to the Cyclopes, the one-eyed monsters of legend.

Minoan (2000-1375BC)

The excavations of Sir Arthur Evans (after 1900) brought to light the civilization of the legendary King Minos of Crete. The **frescoes** discovered at Knossos and other Cretan royal palaces revealed an exceptionally elegant, pleasure-loving and sophisticated society. More recent discoveries showed Minoan presence or influence at many points around the southern Aegean, especially in the island of Santorini, at the peak period before 1500BC.

The Minoan culture used the so far undeciphered "Linear A" script. Its language is unknown. The palaces lost their momentum after the volcanic eruption of Santorini c.1500BC, and were subjugated by Mycenaean invaders from the mainland a century later.

All important works of Minoan art and architecture are kept in Crete, excepting the Santorini frescoes, which are at the National Archeological Museum in Athens.

Minoan fresco: *The Prince of the Lilies.*

Mycenaean (1600-1200BC)

The earliest "Greek" civilization has been named after the royal stronghold of Mycenae, where Heinrich Schliemann discovered in 1874-76 its first and so far most important material remains. The Greeks of Classical Antiquity knew of this period as the Heroic Age, whose vaguely remembered history formed the basis of the Homeric legends.

The foundation myths of the various royal dynasties of the Heroic Age suggest a complicated pattern of cultural give-and-take. Thus, a Phoenician (Kadmos) founded Thebes, an Egyptian (Danaos) started the royal dynasty of Argos, some Cretans founded Delphi, and a Lydian (Pelops) fathered most late-Mycenaean rulers of the Peloponnese.

Architecture: The major surviving examples are the royal palaces of Mycenae, Tiryns and Pylos, of which the first two are heavily fortified. The *megaron,* a royal hall consisting of a rectangular throne room, an open vestibule in front and two columns supporting the porch, formed the basis of Greek temple architecture in subsequent ages.

Art: By far the most important collection of Mycenaean art is at the National Archeological Museum of Athens, and includes golden death-masks, bronze ornamented weapons, bronze and gold cups and jewelry. Their "barbaric" quality contrasts with the graceful elegance of Minoan art.

Writing: A script known as "Linear B" was adapted from Crete around 1400BC and used for inventories and official transactions. This has now been fully deciphered as an early form of Greek thanks to a large collection of tablets discovered at Pylos. Examples exist in many museums.

"Geometric" (1200-700BC)

A series of ill-understood events destroyed Mycenaean civilization around 1200BC. The Dorians, a warlike Greek tribe from the N, invaded the Peloponnese, whose earlier inhabitants ("Achaeans" and "Ionians") either migrated or were enslaved. Knowledge of stone architecture and writing disappeared for over 500yrs. Toward the end of this period, Homer compiled the oral traditions about the Heroic Age into the epics of the *Iliad* and the *Odyssey.*

27

Greek culture

The only tangible relics of this dark era are **ceramic pots**, which are generally decorated with simple geometric patterns. Some splendid specimens exist at the National Archeological Museum of Athens.

Archaic (700–480BC)

Urban culture revived rapidly in the 7thC, at first on the w coast of Asia Minor (Miletus, Ephesus, Samos), followed by the mainland itself. Old aristocracies were replaced by the so-called tyrants, popular leaders who came to power by coup d'etat. Greek colonies were planted around the Mediterranean world, notably in Italy and on the Black Sea coast. The Greek alphabet was adapted from the Phoenician script. The disciplines of philosophy (Thales, Heraclitus), mathematics (Pythagoras, Euclid), historiography (Hecataeus) and lyric poetry (Sappho) flourished.

Architecture: The earliest Greek temples built of stone came into existence around 550. Temples on the Greek mainland adopted the **Doric Order**, while those in Asia (including the eastern Aegean islands) developed the **Ionic**. Traces of these early structures are prominent beneath or near most temples of later date, but few survived the following century, and with the exception of Corinth's largely ruined Temple of Apollo, none survives today.

Sculpture: Sculpture moved quickly from depicting gods in human form to depicting men of godly bearing. The most common types of statue are those called **kouros** (young man) and **kore** (young woman), characterized by a stiff hieratic pose and a strange, distant smile. Magnificent examples are in the archeological museums of Athens, Delphi, Piraeus and Thebes.

Detail from Athenian black figure vase, c.540BC, by Exekias.

Pottery: Some of the finest art of the Archaic period was executed on clay vases, a field in which Athens emerged c.550 as the undisputed leader. Earlier pottery employed the **black figure** technique, where figures were painted in black glaze and detail was added by incision. By the year 500, Athenian artists perfected the **red figure** style, in which unpainted figures stood out against a black background and were detailed by brush. Examples of both styles abound at the National Archeological Museum of Athens as well as various local museums throughout the country.

Classical (480–330BC)

Broadly used, the term "Classical" covers all of pagan antiquity from the early Archaic age to the downfall of Rome more than 1,000yrs later. In a narrower sense it refers to the 150yr period following the Persian Wars, or even its middle part (450-404) alone, into which the greatest achievements of Greek art, architecture and literature were crowded.

Athens was the dominant political power of Greece in the early part of this epoch, followed by Sparta (404-371) and Thebes

(371-362). The country collapsed into chaos in the 4thC as a result of protracted wars.

Culture: In 472, the City of Athens voted to stage Aeschylus' tragedy *The Persians* for the annual festival of Dionysus. Just 8yrs earlier, Athens had narrowly won a bitter defensive war against the Persians in which the playwright himself had been wounded. The tragedy, however, presented the war entirely from the viewpoint of the Persian king, and dwelled in extraordinary human detail upon the fears and agonies of his female relatives. The underlying message, to be sure, was one of boasting, but this particular way of expressing triumph is unique in world history.

Pericles himself expressed the Athenian ideal in his funeral oration for the victims of the Peloponnesian War:

> "We are lovers of the beautiful, yet simple in our tastes, and we cultivate the mind without loss of manliness....
>
> We regard a man who takes no interest in public affairs, not as a harmless, but as a useless character. The great impediment to action is, in our opinion, not discussion, but the want of that knowledge which is gained by discussion preparatory to action....
>
> While our government is a democracy, the claim of excellence is also recognized; and when a citizen is in any way distinguished, he is preferred to the public service. There is no exclusiveness in our public life, and in our private intercourse we are not suspicious of one another, nor angry with our neighbor if he does what he likes....
>
> And we have not forgotten to provide for our spirits many relaxations from toil; we have regular games and sacrifices throughout the year; our homes are beautiful and elegant; and the delight which we daily feel in these things helps to banish gloom."

Architecture: The Greek **temple** reached its zenith during a wave of building activity toward the middle of the 5thC. Many Archaic temples that lay in ruins after the Persian War were rebuilt on a more ambitious scale. The Temple of Zeus at Olympia, completed in 456, was the first great work of the period. At the Parthenon of Athens, completed in 438, architects Ictinus and Callicrates achieved a level of refinement rarely equaled since.

The Greek temple (see illustration on page 30) was intended only to accommodate the image of the deity, while public worship took place at an altar that was placed outdoors. The emphasis in temple architecture was therefore on the external aspect.

With few exceptions, such as the Erechtheum of Athens, all temples in mainland Greece were built in the Doric Order, ideally suited to a severe and monumental style. Most major temples were **peripteral hexastyles**, consisting of an inner sanctum *(cella)* with halls in front and back *(pronaos and opisthodomos),* surrounded by a single row of columns *(peristyle)* with six on the short side. Arches being unknown, the roof was held by wooden beams, which have disappeared in all instances.

The **agora**, which was the hub of public life in cities, was adorned with **stoas** (porticoes), which were colonnaded vestibules intended equally for commerce and for socialization.

The custom of building open-air **theaters** in stone appeared toward the middle of the 4thC. The fully preserved theater of Epidauros dates from this period, as does the reconstruction of Athens' Dionysus Theater in stone. Theaters were built to

Greek culture

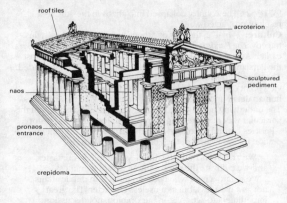

Temple of Aphaia, Egina: cutaway reconstruction.

Labels (clockwise): roof tiles; acroterion; sculptured pediment; crepidoma; pronaos entrance; naos

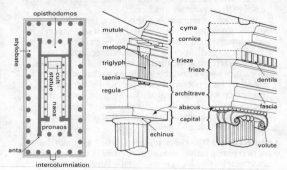

Typical elements of a **Greek temple**, located on a ground plan. Entry is through the pronaos.

Labels: opisthodomos; mutule; cyma; cornice; metope; frieze; frieze; triglyph; dentils; taenia; architrave; regula; abacus; fascia; capital; stylobate; echinus; volute; anta; intercolumniation

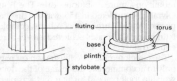

Elements of the **Doric** (left) and **Ionic** (right) Orders. The proportions and the details differ but the fundamental divisions are constant.

Labels: fluting; torus; base; plinth; stylobate

accommodate the entire adult male population of cities, and were designed for maximum acoustic effect. Uses included public assemblies and parades as well as dramatic performances.

Sculpture: The expression of human beauty in marble, bronze and ivory reached a level of extraordinary eloquence in the works of Phidias and Polyclitus. The severe nobility of these sculptors of the Periclean age was replaced by the gentler, more individual style of Praxiteles and Scopas in the following century. With the possible exception of the *Hermes* of Praxiteles (at Olympia — see illustration on page 127), none of the masterpieces of the great sculptors have come down to us in the original. The excellence of such anonymous works as the Trident-hurling *Poseidon* and the *Anacythera Youth* (both at

Athens' Archeological Museum) and the *Delphi Charioteer* (at Delphi) can only hint at the quality of the far more famous works that have been lost.

Surprising for the modern eye accustomed to the bare marble surfaces of Classical sculpture was the fact that both free-standing statues and reliefs were originally painted in full color. Some traces of paint are still visible, for example, on temple friezes at the Acropolis Museum.

Painting: Free painting developed into an important branch of art in the 5thC, and the paintings of Polygnotus at the Pinakotheke of the Athens Acropolis, of Paeonius at the "Painted" Stoa of the Athens Agora, and of Polyclitus at the Heraeum of Argos drew admiring visitors. None of these works survives. Pottery painting, on the other hand, no longer attracted great talents as in the Archaic age, and generally declined in quality.

Literature: The traditional "goat songs" *(tragoidia)* of the Dionysian festival were developed into an art form by Aeschylus (524-456) in the 470s. In the austere and aristocratic drama of Sophocles (496-406) and the psychological realism of Euripides (480-406), ancient tragedy reached its high point. Aristophanes (446-388) lampooned contemporary Athenian manners in his comedies.

Philosophy: The Ionian traditions of philosophy were carried to Athens in mid-5thC by Anaxagoras, who taught both Pericles and Socrates. Socrates (died 399) influenced a whole generation of Athenians by his relentless questioning of fundamental values. Plato (427-347) and Aristotle (384-322) founded in the next century two rival schools of philosophy that defined the opposing poles of Western thought until the modern age.

Hellenistic (330-30BC)

The Hellenistic Age, which was a period of great economic and artistic vitality elsewhere in the Eastern Mediterranean, found Greece exhausted by war and emigration. Cities were depopulated, and many ceased to exist. Thebes (336) and Corinth (146) were ruined, the cities of Arcadia and Messenia were deserted, and only two minor towns continued to exist in Boeotia. Works of art left from this era are accordingly few in Greece and of no great significance.

Architecture: The brief ascendancy of Corinth in the 3rdC was associated with the elaborate **Corinthian Order**, which embellished its column capitals with stylized acanthus leaves. It became the most popular form of temple architecture during the Roman era, although surviving examples are rare in Greece. Similarly, the brilliant reinterpretation of the Ionic Order introduced by Hermogenes in Asia Minor in the 3rdC found no echo in Greece.

Sculpture: In the transition from Classical to Hellenistic, Lysippus carried the work of Praxiteles one step further with his precise realism, light touch and technical virtuosity. The compositional mastery of the bronze *Horse with Child Rider* at the Athens Archeological Museum is typical of the period. In the 3rdC, Pergamum in Asia Minor captured the leadership in this field with its entirely new school of sculpture.

Philosophy: Philosophy was one field in which Athens maintained its lead through the Hellenistic era. Two new philosophical schools, Stoicism (founded by Zeno, 336-263) and Epicurianism (Epicurus, 342-271), emerged in Athens. Both turned away from public issues to emphasize the private fulfillment of the individual.

Roman (146BC-AD395)

The early centuries of Roman rule perpetuated the barrenness of the Hellenistic period. While the 2ndC AD witnessed an era of widespread revival under the Antonine emperors, Greece never really recovered a position among the richest and most advanced provinces of the Roman empire.

Culture: The Antonine revival was consciously antiquarian in spirit, in the sense of a renewed interest in the past glories of the Classical age. Hadrian rebuilt temples in the style of 400yrs earlier. Pausanias, with his enthusiasm for ancient traditions and historic monuments, was a typical author of his age. The philosophical schools of Athens clung to the traditions formulated in the 4thC BC.

Architecture: The major technical advance of the Roman era was the **arch**, which formed a prominent feature in all types of public building. New and characteristic architectural forms included the public bath, the aqueduct, the monumental fountain *(nymphaeum)* and the triumphal arch. Roman-period theaters added elaborate stage-building with arched entryways. New types of temple architecture that developed in Italy, Syria and Asia Minor found no echo in Greece, where the only significant temple erected in the Roman period was that of the Olympian Zeus in Athens.

Sculpture: In the field of realistic portraiture, Roman-age sculptors developed a level of mastery rarely equaled by any other age. High demand for the portraits of emperors, governors and wealthy citizens created a type of commodity art with generally superb standards of workmanship but hardly any outstanding names.

Byzantine (330-1460)

Under the Byzantine Empire the center of Greek culture shifted definitively to Constantinople (Istanbul), while Greece itself entered an era of unmitigated disaster. What remained of its cultural vitality was sapped by the outlawing of pagan cults and temples by Theodosius in 391 and the closing of the Athenian schools in 529. A succession of barbarian invasions devastated the land. By the 9thC, Slavic tribes predominated and the Greek language and Christian religion disappeared from the countryside.

Monasteries played an important role in recivilizing Greece after the return of Byzantine authority in the 11thC. Democratic in structure and popular in background, they enjoyed immense influence among common folk and often voiced the sentiments of the people as against the court.

Court culture experienced a period of late flourish in the 14th-15thC, when close contacts with the Latin West, especially the Italian city republics (Venice, Genoa), produced a mutual cross-fertilization. In Greece this was reflected most of all in the southern Peloponnese, which was ruled in 1349-1460 by a feudal Byzantine principality (Despotate of Morea) based at Mistra.

Architecture: Early Byzantine churches (4th-6thC) were in the form known as *basilica,* which consisted of an oblong hall with a semicircular recess (apse) in the E wall and two parallel rows of interior pillars supporting the roof. No church from this period survives in southern Greece except in the form of barely recognizable traces.

In the Middle (9th-12thC) and Late (13th-15thC) Byzantine periods, the **cross-in-square** construction became the standard. Churches consisted of a cross-shaped hall with a dome usually surmounted on a cylindrical drum, preceded by an entrance hall *(narthex)* and occasionally an outer hall *(exonarthex);* the sanctuary *(bema)* was separated from the nave by a solid curtain decorated with icons *(iconostasis)*. Classic examples in Greece are the monastery churches of Daphni and Osios Loukas. Later churches generally opted for five domes instead of one, and experimented with increasingly complex compositions.

Painting: Church painting followed a rigidly conventional scheme with regard to both subject and disposition within the church. Each saint and each biblical scene had its precisely defined pictorial conventions. The banning of church images in the iconoclastic period (8th-10thC) had the effect of further consolidating Orthodox sentiment about the immutability of the holy pictures. Mosaic was generally abandoned after the 11thC in favor of the cheaper fresco.

An artistic revolution got under way toward the end of the 14thC, which had its main centers at Crete, Constantinople and Mistra. The best Byzantine artists developed a boldness of expression and a wealth of color that was reminiscent of the early masters of the Italian Renaissance. The ultimate outcome of this trend was El Greco, who was born Kyriakos Theotokopoulos in Crete. Excellent examples of late Byzantine painting can be seen at Mistra, as well as at the Byzantine and Benaki Museums of Athens.

"Frankish" and Venetian (1204-1715)
The Byzantine Empire was temporarily overthrown in 1204 by the armies of the Fourth Crusade. Within a few years Greece was taken over by an assorted pack of European knights: Geoffroi de Villehardouin, a Burgundian nobleman, conquered the Peloponnese; Othon de la Roche, another Burgundian, took Attica and Boeotia, while three Veronese gentlemen shared Euboea. There was a French barony at Salona, near Delphi, and an Italian marquisate near Thermopylae. The Catalans, the Genoese, and even some Flemings entered the fray later on, and feudal domains changed hands with astonishing celerity and inconsequence. By the late 14thC the republic of Venice emerged as the only Western power to own well-entrenched strongholds in mainland Greece. These were lost to the Turks piecemeal between 1456 and 1540, partly recovered in 1687 and lost again in 1715.

The "Frankish" legacy in Greece consists of scores of **castles**, which are particularly common in the Peloponnese. All are in various degrees of ruin, though they command magnificent views. The best preserved examples are to be found at Mistra and Clairmont (Hlemoutsi, near Kyllini).

Venetian fortifications are usually **citadels**, either enclosing a town or capable of accommodating its inhabitants during a siege. The finest examples are the strongholds of Methoni and Koroni. Nafplio preserves a wide range of Venetian civil architecture.

More indirectly, the Byzantine "Renaissance" of Mistra displays a strong element of Frankish and Italian influence, both in the feudal foundations on which it rested and the Westernizing forms of art that its court favored.

Greek culture

Turkish (1456-1828)

Toward the end of the Byzantine era, the common people, the church and the provincial nobles of Greece had for a variety of reasons come to prefer "the turban of the Turk to the miter of a cardinal." The court, which alone pursued a pro-Western policy, was repudiated. The Turks allowed Greeks broad communal autonomy under the Orthodox church. Monasteries kept their domains and privileges. Peasants were taxed more equitably than under their Frankish or Byzantine feudal masters; the most enterprising of them generally converted to Islam. Any hint of private power or privilege, however, was ruthlessly stamped out by an all-encompassing bureaucratic state. What little remains of the Turkish era reflects this background.

Religious art: After the Italian-influenced vivacity of the 15thC, Greek church art froze into a rigid conservatism. Painting was reduced to increasingly crude reproductions of Byzantine originals; the term **post-Byzantine** is used to describe this trend. Only naive folk painters — such as Georgios Markos, who painted many churches in Attica in the 18thC — achieved some originality, perhaps because of their ignorance of the models.

Architecture: The only noteworthy examples of Greek civil architecture are in the islands, which enjoyed a certain administrative autonomy and became relatively rich through trade. The pirate villages of Mani are another original case of architectural activity that grew beyond the dead hand of the *pax turcica*. Turkish relics consist of purely functional, small-scale public works, such as mosques, public baths, fountains, poorhouses and schools; a great many of these were destroyed during or after the War of Independence.

Turkish fortresses were generally reconstructions or improvements of earlier strongholds. In a few cases such as Karababa (Halkida) and the fortresses of Rio and Antirio, one can observe new forms introduced by the needs of artillery warfare (squat, sloping walls, projecting bastions).

Modern (1821-)

The War of Independence: From the 1770s, Russia adopted a policy that aimed to weaken the Ottoman Empire and set up an Orthodox power in Constantinople. Meanwhile, leading Greek intellectuals, influenced by the ideals of the French Revolution, contemplated a revival of ancient Greece.

The collapse of Turkish authority in the 18thC left Greece in the hands of Albanian lords and roving bands of brigands called *klephts*. Attempts by the reforming Sultan Mahmud II to reassert Turkish rule precipitated a general rebellion in 1821 in which *klepht* leaders (Kolokotronis, Mavromichalis) and the pirate fleets of various Aegean islands (Hydra, Psara) played a prominent role.

After initial successes the uprising was mired down in internecine fighting. The intervention of Britain and France in 1827, which saved the rebellion, was motivated by considerations of grand strategy as much as philhellenic sentiment. Western powers determined the status of the new country by the London Protocol of 1830, imposed a Bavarian prince as king in 1832, and directed the foreign (and occasionally domestic) affairs of the kingdom through the end of the 19thC.

Culture: The clash between traditional "folk" culture and the Classical ideal imposed by Europeans and Western-educated elites runs through many aspects of modern Greece.

The *katharevousa,* an artificial dialect based on Classical Greek and incomprehensible to the uneducated, was devised shortly before independence to "raise" the cultural level of the Greeks, and remained in use as the official language of the state until 1976. On a similar level, most place names in the country were changed by fiat to conform with Classical precedent, while the popular names died hard among uneducated folk. A further factor was that a large segment of the population did not speak Greek as its native tongue: speakers of Albanian, Vlach, Turkish and various Slav languages formed perhaps a majority until the turn of this century.

The Neoclassical architecture of Greece was developed by Europeans, and European court architects built nearly every building of note in 19thC Athens. Similarly, the straight-line plan of the capital and scores of other rebuilt cities was the work of Westerners, and contrasted with the maze-like structure of traditional Greek towns.

The choice of Athens as capital was itself a European imposition, while the devoutly Christian Greeks themselves set their sights upon Constantinople at least until 1922. In this homeland of European civilization, and, since 1981, member of the European Community, the term "Europe" still refers in popular parlance to the lands west of the Adriatic.

Literature: Greece has produced several of the most brilliant poets of the 20thC. Two, George Seferis (1900-71) and Odysseus Elytis (1911-) were crowned with the Nobel prize; two others whom many would consider superior, Constantine Kavafis (1863-1933) and Yannis Ritsos (1909-90), were not. The internationally well-known novelist Nikos Kazantsakis (1885-1957) suffers from an excess of folksiness and mush.

Politics: Two great crises stand in the background of contemporary Greek politics: the prolonged quarrel *(dichasmos)* between the liberal-republican followers of Prime Minister Eleftherios Venizelos and conservatives supporting the king in 1915-35, and the bloody civil war against communist partisans in 1944-49. Conservatives were victorious in both instances.

In the 1970s, Andreas Papandreou rallied remnants of the old Venizelist guard under the new, "socialist" banner of PASOK. He reconciled many former communists by offering them a belated amnesty and access to jobs in the early years of his government (1981-89). PASOK's attempt to break the stranglehold of the conservatives on Greek politics enjoyed wide early support, but the party fell victim to the dangers of partisanship, nepotism and corruption inherent in that task.

In the 1980s, the conservatives themselves evolved toward a more liberal, pragmatic and pro-European image under the leadership of Mitsotakis. They alleged that Papandreou's policies had caused Greece to lag behind the rest of the world in the economic and technological evolution of the 1980s.

Greek mythology

Ancient Greek gods had local origins and were bound up with specific local myths. Some of these traditions can be traced with reasonable certainty to pre-Greek beliefs and rituals; others seem to hint at some half-remembered prehistoric events. Some of the more popular gods combine several distinct strands of legend. Thus Apollo has separate Cretan, Lycian and Phrygian antecedents, among others. Later attempts to weave such incompatible histories into a coherent biography often result in utter confusion. Thus, Apollo and Artemis are supposed to be twins, yet they have separate birthplaces, and several other places claim the honor of nurturing one or the other when they were small. Hence the sometimes elaborate myths to explain how they got from one place to another.

Each tribe, town and locality had its particular deity: Athens worshiped Athena, Argos was devoted to Hera, Ephesus was sacred to Artemis.... It never occurred to Greeks to suppose that their own gods were unique or that their neighbors worshiped false notions, so they simply took note of the multiplicity of gods, and occasionally imported some alien deity when he or she had proven his/her efficacy in some way. They also noted the similarities between the personalities of various gods, and assimilated them under a single name. Thus what appears to have been two distinct goddesses worshiped in Samos and Argos were *both* identified as Hera; or the Anatolian Mother Goddess, usually translated as Artemis, occasionally also got mixed up with Demeter or Leto. (St Paul, incidentally, was worshiped as Hermes when he showed up in Lycaonia to preach the gospel.) At times alien gods were adopted through family ties: Eros, a god of love worshiped only in the Boeotian town of Thespiae, was said to be a son of Aphrodite, the more common goddess of love.

In this way the Greek Pantheon was consolidated into a set of 12 major divinities, who (with the exception of Hades) were said to reside in the nebulous region of Mt. Olympus, presiding over innumerable godlets. There were some 30 mountains that claimed this name in Antiquity, and it seems possible that the word simply meant "mountain" in some pre-Greek language. The Olympian system, however, was shaken in the late Archaic period when the cult of a new god, Dionysus, arriving from Lydia in Asia Minor, spread through Greece like wildfire.

Inclusiveness, however, had its limits. The pre-Olympian generation or generations of gods (Uranos, Gaea, Cronos and the Titans) were said to have been defeated and overthrown by the current gods. These were almost certainly the divinities of the Early Bronze Age or Neolithic peoples of Greece. Yet a sanctuary of Gaea was scrupulously maintained at Delphi long after Apollo had usurped her reign there by murdering her son; and Cronos was still remembered at Olympia, although he had been knocked out in a wrestling match and banished by his son Zeus.

Originally each god was a full-blown personality with a life story, habits, character traits and anecdotes. Earlier yet, at least some of them were probably depicted as animals: Apollo was a dolphin or a wolf, or even a mouse; Artemis was a bear or a stag; Poseidon was a horse. Later on, when they were definitively humanized, their earlier attributes still clung to them in the form of their "sacred animals." Thus Artemis was always shown with a stag, while her priestesses adopted the name of she-bears; Athena often brandished a snake; and Poseidon rarely went anywhere without his horse. The association of the gods with abstract notions ("god of music," "goddess of love," etc.) appears to have been a late development. The Roman age went further still, reducing them to poetic allegories: Aphrodite now became a mere personification of Love; Apollo was said to be Light itself.

Apollo

The god of light, youth and music was also the god of mice, lizards, wolves and pestilence, and the bringer of sudden death. He was born on the island of Delos, yet his cult was imported to Greece from Minoan Crete. His mother Leto was the goddess of the Lycians in Asia Minor, and he himself acquired his musical education in Phrygia, also in Asia Minor. His twin sister Artemis was a predominantly Asiatic divinity.

Apollo was venerated by the Greeks above all as the god of soothsaying, and Delphi, one of his two holiest sanctuaries (the other was Delos), was honored as the home of the most respected oracle of the ancient world. He was also famous for ravishing lone nymphs and beautiful mortals in faraway places. Daphne saved herself from his pursuit by turning into a laurel tree (on a hillside near Athens, or perhaps near Antioch in Syria), so he cherished the laurel bough; his lover Hyacinth he killed in a sporting accident (at Amyclae near Sparta), so the flower bearing the youth's name was sacred to him. On Mts. Helicon and Parnassus he was seen playing the zither to the singing and dancing of the Muses; and in Phrygia he flayed the Satyr Marsyas alive after beating him in a flute-playing contest.

Artemis

Artemis, the virgin goddess of the wilderness, came into the Greek world from Ephesus in Asia Minor, where in earlier times she had been worshiped as the Phrygian-Lydian Kubaba (Cybele). (The original Cybele was in fact a meteorite that was idolized at Pessinus in Phrygia. She was later carried off to Rome.) The Cretans also had their Lady of the Wild Beasts, who was explicitly related to the Artemis cult at Brauron, in Attica.

Artemis spent most of her time hunting in the wilderness with her nymphs. She was ruthless toward men who dared approach her and toward those of her nymphs who showed a weakness for men. The hunter Orion was slain and hurled into the skies for approaching her; Actaeon was turned into a stag and devoured by dogs for seeing her bathe; Kallisto the nymph was made a she-bear for yielding to Zeus. The Ephesian Artemis was depicted with a necklace of severed testicles.

For all her relentless virginity, Artemis was also revered by Greeks as the goddess of childbirth. Her dual character may have influenced the Christian cult of the Virgin Mary, which also had its origins in Ephesus.

Athena

Athena was the patron goddess of the Athenians, whose favor she won by giving them the olive tree. She was born by parthenogenesis, fully grown and armed, from the head of Zeus, who had swallowed up her mother Metis. Her principal attributes were chastity, wisdom and prowess in war. Her wisdom was practical: she taught Danaos to build the first double-prowed ship; she invented the weaving-loom and the double flute. She led the Athenians in war, and was often depicted with helmet and shield (Athena Promachos). Her holiest sanctuary was the Parthenon on the Athenian Acropolis, where her cult had been established in time immemorial by the Phoenician snake-kings Cecrops and Erechtheus, and where her ancient sacred image in olive wood was kept.

Demeter

The eldest sister of Zeus was perhaps the only pre-Hellenic deity of Greece to survive into Greek religion. She rarely visited Olympus, preferring to wander instead on Earth, whose productiveness she ensured. The death and rebirth of her daughter Persephone was celebrated in the Mysteries of the Eleusinian cult (see ELEUSIS, page 79). The primitive Arcadian tribes worshiped an unnamed horse-goddess known as Despoina (Lady), a daughter who was born when Demeter was raped by a stallion. During her interminable wanderings the goddess cut a sorry barefoot figure in rags, reviled and banished by tyrannical kings. This may suggest a time when her cult was suppressed by ruling princes and perhaps carried on in secret.

Mythology

Dionysus

According to one account, the god of wine and orgies was a native of Lydia in Asia Minor, where he acquired the surname Bacchus. Others said he was the son of Zeus from Semele, a daughter of King Kadmos of Thebes, who was struck dead when the Father of the Gods revealed himself to her in his divine aspect. Zeus then implanted the unborn Dionysus in his thigh, and in due course gave birth to him. The baby Dionysus was spirited away by Hermes, and had to be kept hidden to save him from Hera's wrath.

The cult of Dionysus took Greece by storm in the 7th-6thC BC. His devotees, who were all female and took the name of Maenads, fell into trances and engaged in unspeakable acts during the Bacchic rites which they performed in the open countryside. Pentheus, who was once foolish enough to peek in, was ripped apart limb by limb by the demented revelers, who included his own mother.

Various kings who tried to ban the worship of Dionysus met particularly gruesome ends. The Athenian tyrant Peisistratus domesticated the phenomenon by instituting a milder form of the Dionysian rites in the city. Attic drama grew in the 5thC out of the wild performances of the Athenian Dionysia.

Hephaestus

The god of volcanoes and metalsmiths was lame and ugly, so much so that Hera hurled him in disgust down into the sea after she had given birth to him. The spot where he hit the Aegean was marked by the island of Lemnos, where a volcano was still active in Antiquity, and he was saved by the Sintians, an archaic Lemnian tribe. Later he returned to Olympus, and even married Aphrodite for a short period. According to some accounts he was the father of Erichthonius, one of the half-snake founding kings of Athens. His temple in Athens was built in the market district of the ironsmiths.

Hera

The wife of Zeus was the goddess of the Argives, the dominant tribe of the Mycenaean Greeks. One myth placed her birth at the Stymphalian Lake near Nemea in the Peloponnese, others at the islands of Euboea or Samos. Her legends almost exclusively concerned her tantrums over Zeus's various loves and her merciless vendettas against their offspring. She pestered Io with a horsefly so that she had to run as far as Egypt; she led Semele, the hapless mother of Dionysus, to her death by tricking her to ask Zeus to reveal his divine light (it fried her instantly). Leto was driven into destitution for bearing Apollo and Artemis, Zeus's children; Heracles, another illegitimate son of the Father of Gods, was cheated out of his kingdom at Tiryns and made to waste his life in senseless labors. Yet Hera was also the protectress of the Greeks in the Trojan War: it was at her temple near Argos that Agamemnon was chosen as the leader of that expedition.

Hermes

Hermes was born from the union of Zeus with a nymph in the mountains of Arcadia, and his most famous exploit involved stealing Apollo's cattle from the vicinity of the river Alpheios, an activity in which the wild pastoral nomads of Arcadia, too, often engaged. He was employed as the messenger of the gods; in a similar capacity, he guided the souls of the dead to the nether world (Hermes Psychopompos). In earliest times he appears to have been worshiped in the form of milestones set upon roadsides. Even in some later representations, he is shown as a stone stele with a human head and penis.

Zeus

The "Father of Gods" was in fact the brother of five (Demeter, Hades, Hera, Hestia, Poseidon) and father of six (Apollo, Ares, Artemis, Athena, Hephaestus, Hermes) Olympians. When his father Cronos took to gulping down his offspring, Zeus was saved by serving the wicked father a stone concealed in a crib. He was spirited away to Mt. Ida in Crete, where he was raised by nymphs, and returned to topple Cronos in a wrestling match, forcing him to regurgitate all his swallowed children.

Zeus was probably the chief deity of the Indo-European races that invaded Greece in the early 2nd millennium BC, although his association with Crete suggests a parallel Minoan origin. He was the god of heavens and thunderstorms, honored on the peaks of high mountains. Since most Greek cities claimed him as the ancestor of their founder, royal dynasty or local nymph, he had to be cast as an amazing womanizer; hence his scores of escapades, which were a source of permanent friction with his wife Hera. His chief sanctuary was at Olympia, venerated by all Greeks regardless of the rivalries of tribe or city.

Other gods

Poseidon, the god of the seas, and **Hades**, the god of the underworld, had nearly equal status with Zeus their brother, and there are indications that in an earlier mythology the three brothers formed the three constitutive elements of the universe. Hades was offered worship near mysterious holes and foul-smelling caves in the ground, while Poseidon was one of the most popular deities of the seagoing cities of Greece.

Aphrodite was born from the sea foam off the coast of Cyprus. She had a complex personality that involved not only her usual role as the goddess of love, but also an all-encompassing spirit that held the world together, and occasionally even a goddess of war, or of war-madness. Her priestesses served her by prostituting themselves.

Ares, the warrior god, was rather short on brains but astonishingly good-looking. He had temples in all parts of Greece, though none of great importance.

Hestia was a shadowy spirit who protected the hearth of each house, and each city had a perpetually burning flame that was devoted to her cult.

Athens *(Athína)*

Capital of the Greek Republic. Municipal area 414 sq.km (160 sq. miles). Population: over 4 million ☎ code: 01. Airport: Elinikon, 11km (7 miles) from city center.

Athens was the first great metropolis of the ancient world. Although its period of greatness lasted less than 150 years (c.480-338BC), the city was seen and emulated as a model of urban civilization for some 800 years afterwards until the downfall of pagan antiquity. The most important traditions of Western political democracy, philosophy and drama were born in this city.

During the long centuries of Byzantine, "Frankish" and Turkish rule, Athens declined to the status of an insignificant town. It was rebuilt virtually from the ground after 1834, when it was adopted as the capital of newly independent Greece. Present-day Athens is a modern city with a small 19th century core. The ruins of ancient monuments lie scattered in various parts of the town.

Legends

Athena, the goddess of wisdom, and **Poseidon**, the god of the sea, contended for the patronage of the city. Poseidon struck his trident and caused a spring to flow from the Acropolis; Athena made an olive tree grow, a source of peace and prosperity. The latter was deemed the more valuable gift, so Athena was adopted as the chief divinity of Athens. Her sacred symbols (the olive tree, the owl) were the symbols of the city.

The founder of the Athenian royal line was the Phoenician **Kekrops**, who was born of the earth and was half man and half snake. One of his descendants, **Erechtheus** (sometimes confused with Erichthonius, also a serpent-king), introduced the worship of Athena and founded the Panathenaea, the most important religious festival of the Athenians.

Many generations later, **Theseus** put an end to Cretan supremacy by killing the Minotaur, a fiery bull-man who was kept in the famous Labyrinth of the palace of King Minos. He married Ariadne, the daughter of the Cretan king, united the communities *(demes)* of Attica under Athenian leadership, and subjected the hitherto independent cities of Eleusis and Megara.

During the Dorian invasions of the Dark Age, a wave of Achaean-Ionian refugees from the Peloponnese flocked to Athens. Their leader, **Kodros**, married into the Athenian nobility, became king and defeated the Dorians. His sons established the Ionian colonies of western Asia Minor.

History

Recent research has found signs of Neolithic and early-Helladic ("Pelasgian") settlement on the Acropolis going back to c.5000BC. A Mycenaean royal palace existed on the Acropolis (c.1500-1200BC), although there is no indication that Athens was an important place in this period. It must have acquired some importance as a refugee stronghold around 1200-1000BC, during the Dark Age. It was only under the tyranny of Peisistratus (c.561-527BC), however, that it began to achieve a leadership position among Greek city-states.

The economic base of Athenian prosperity was originally the export of pottery, the marble of Mt. Pentelicon (Pendeli), the honey of Mt. Hymettus (Imitos) and olive oil. In the 5thC BC Athens became the leading naval and commercial power of the Eastern Mediterranean. In Hellenistic and Roman times it survived as an academic and intellectual center and meeting point of students from all over the ancient world. Its academic institutions were weakened by the advent of Christianity, and were destroyed by the Edict of Justinian in AD529.

Despite mild bouts of resurgence in the early 11thC, under Frankish feudalism (13th-14thC) and the early part of Turkish rule (16th-17thC), Athens was never more than a sleepy town until the beginning of the modern era. The decision to revive it, in 1834, was mostly sentimental, as several Greek towns such as Nafplio, Livadia, Halkida and the port of Syros were at the time better developed than Athens.

Between 1834 and the end of the 19thC a bevy of European architects planned, built and embellished a small, oligarchic Athens. Many public buildings were erected in the Neoclassical, or "Othonian" style (from King Otto, 1832-62), a mixture of idealized Greek motifs and Italian *palazzo* architecture.

In 1922, the population of the city more than doubled with the arrival of a huge wave of refugees from Turkey. The newcomers settled mostly in the southern suburbs and Piraeus, which quickly became engulfed within the city. They brought with them their own music, nightlife, food and culture, which were generally regarded as more sophisticated than those of the natives. To this day the two communities retain their separate identities, with the two major soccer teams of the capital, Panathinaikós and AEK, drawing upon the loyalties of "old" Athenians and Anatolians, respectively. Politically, "natives" have generally been associated with conservative parties, while "refugees" have formed the strongest base of support for liberal-republicans and the left.

Before the wounds of 1922 could fully be healed, the city was hit by a second wave of refugees fleeing the civil wars of 1944-49. The 1960s, in turn, saw the start of rapid industrialization, which drew in an average of 100,000 immigrants a year. The population of Greater Athens surpassed 1 million in the early 1960s, 3 million around 1980, and 4 million at the end of the 1980s. A majority of Athenians today keep strong ties with the village and region of their origin. Many have family ties and very often property "at home," take their vacations there, and tend to socialize in the capital with compatriots from the same region. The widespread habit of going home for census and elections suggests that the official figures may underestimate the city's real population.

Sudden growth, combined with the refusal of most inhabitants to identify strongly with the city, has created serious urban problems, which over-politicized governments have been inadequately equipped to solve. Construction has gone on in a haphazard manner, with minimal planning and little regard for public spaces. Car traffic is among the worst of any major European city, and air pollution frequently exceeds the limits set by international health agencies.

It must be mentioned, however, that Athens does not have any slums (either of the inner-city variety as in Anglo-Saxon countries, or suburban ones as in the Third World), and hardly any neighborhoods that display conspicuous poverty. A strong middle-class flavor pervades the city. It owes much to the traditional aptitude of the Greeks for small commerce, as well as to the continued existence of solid networks of family and community carried over from the countryside.

Organizing your time

Nearly all points of interest in Athens are concentrated in a compact central area that can easily be explored on foot.

The **Acropolis**, the **National Archeological Museum** and **Plaka**, the older part of town with its narrow streets and lively evening crowds, form the main highlights of a visit. Various ancient ruins are scattered in and near Plaka. **Lykavitos Hill** offers a splendid bird's-eye view of the whole city.

The **Benaki Museum**, the historic **First Cemetery**, the **flea market** at Monastiraki and the **Meat and Produce Markets** on Athinas St. are all sights that are worth including on an extended itinerary.

In the outskirts of the city, the Byzantine monasteries of **Daphni** and **Kesariani**, and the harbor of **Mikrolimano** in Piraeus, full of popular fish tavernas, justify an excursion.

A one-day sightseeing program might look like this:
• Start early in the morning with an overview of the city from the Lykavitos (1hr) • Walk to the Archeological Museum for a quick visit (1.5hrs) • Stroll through Omonia and Athinas St. markets to the Monastiraki flea market (2hrs) • Visit the Agora (45mins) or proceed directly to the Acropolis (2hrs) • Walk down to Plaka

via the district of Anafiotika, join the strolling evening crowds, and choose your favorite taverna for dinner.

Three special activities recommend themselves on **Sunday mornings**: Greek Orthodox mass at any church, notably at the Metrópolis (Athens' cathedral); changing of the *Evzones* guard at the Parliament (Syntagma Sq.); and the full-scale flea market at Monastiraki.

Ancient Athens

The city from about the time of Themistocles (early 5thC BC) to that of Hadrian (2ndC AD) formed an irregular elongated circle, with the Acropolis set at the middle, and edges that corresponded to the following current features: N at Eleftherias Sq., Sophokleous St. and Klafthmonos Sq., E at Filelinon St. and Amalias Ave., S along a line drawn from Philopappou to the beginning of Syngrou Ave., and E enclosing the Pnyx and Philopappos hill but excluding Keramikos. Hadrian extended the city to include today's Syntagma Sq. and National and Zapio Gardens. Most traces of ancient Athens lie within these boundaries.

The Classical monuments that remain relatively intact are the buildings of the **Acropolis**, the **temples of Hephaestus ("Theseum") and Olympian Zeus**, and the **Odeon of Herodes Atticus**. A visit to the **Agora** and the various minor edifices scattered through **Plaka** can be combined with a tour of PLAKA AND MONASTIRAKI (see pages 55-56).

ACROPOLIS *(Akrópolis)* ▥ ★ ◁€
Entrance on W end, accessible from Dionysiou Areopagitou or Plaka. Map 1E3 ▨ *800dr. Open Mon-Fri 8am-6.30pm, Sat-Sun 8.30am-3pm.*

The Acropolis ("high town") is a steep limestone hill rising 156m (502ft) above the Athenian plain. In prehistoric times it was the site of a fortified town and a Mycenaean royal palace. As late as the 6thC BC, Peisistratus ruled Athens from a stronghold on this summit. As urban life took a firm hold on the plain, however, the hill became a sacred enclosure containing only temples and other ceremonial buildings. These Archaic buildings were destroyed by the Persians during the Second Persian War (480BC).

In the mid-5thC BC, Pericles initiated a vast building program on the Acropolis expressly designed to embody the highest achievements of Greek art and to confirm the pre-eminence of Athens among Greek cities. All the major monuments preserved or restored today (the **Parthenon**, the **Erechtheum**, the **Propylaea** and the **Temple of Athena Nike**) date from that grandiose effort. The Erechtheum, the last to be finished, was completed in 395BC.

In medieval and Turkish times the Acropolis reverted to its earlier role as a military stronghold. Under the Turks it housed a garrison and a Turkish residential quarter. The garrison, curiously, held on for 4yrs after the independence of Greece, surrendering to Bavarian troops after Athens had been inaugurated as the Greek capital. All post-Classical buildings on the hill were cleared by archeologists in the following century (in part at Schliemann's private initiative and expense), and an effort was made to restore the site to its Periclean appearance.

The Acropolis monuments were constructed in Pentelic marble, which takes on a rich yellowish hue over the course of the

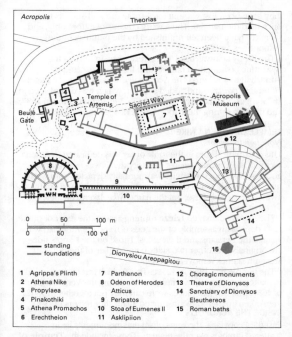

Acropolis
Theorias
N

1 Agrippa's Plinth
2 Athena Nike
3 Propylaea
4 Pinakothiki
5 Athena Promachos
6 Erechtheion
7 Parthenon
8 Odeon of Herodes Atticus
9 Peripatos
10 Stoa of Eumenes II
11 Asklipiion
12 Choragic monuments
13 Theatre of Dionysos
14 Sanctuary of Dionysos Eleuthereos
15 Roman baths

standing
foundations

0   50   100 m
0   50   100 yd

Dionysiou Areopagitou

centuries. In recent years air pollution and acid rain have caused an alarming deterioration of the marble surfaces. Various projects are now under way to protect the monuments against further damage, and certain limitations apply to the movement of visitors (4.5 million each year) within the precincts.

BEULÉ GATE

The present entrance to the Acropolis is through a monumental Roman gate (3rdC AD) named after French archeologist Charles-Ernest Beulé who discovered it embedded in a Turkish wall in 1853. The core of the supporting wall of the **Temple of Athena Nike**, on the right, is from the Mycenaean period (13thC BC).

A massive pedestal on the left, the so-called **Agrippa's Plinth**, bore various statues at different points of its career, including one of Antony and Cleopatra during the brief period in which the couple held sway in the East (36-31BC). It was eventually occupied by a monument of Vipsanius Agrippa, son-in-law and commander of Augustus (30BC-AD14).

PROPYLAEA

This magnificent gateway to the sacred precinct, which Pericles intended should "crown the citadel of the gods with a radiant diadem," was executed by the architect Mnesicles in 437-432BC. It consists of three wings. The **central hall** has two porticoes on its front and back sides, each supported by six massive Doric columns, with a vestibule between them lined with more slender Ionic columns. Neither the gilded marble ceiling nor the five monumental gates has survived. The **N wing**, dubbed the **Pinakotheke**, was decorated by a series of paintings by Polygnotus, which were counted among the greatest masterpieces of ancient art; like all of Classical Greek painting,

43

they have been lost without trace (note the wall-sockets that once held the panels). The **s wing** consists of a front only, and seems to have been left unfinished by the outbreak of the Peloponnesian War.

The Propylaea was used as the residence, in turn, of the Byzantine bishop, the Frankish and Italian dukes, and the Turkish aga of Athens. The Acciaiuoli dukes expanded it into a Florentine *palazzo* and added a tower, which was demolished in 1875. An accidental explosion in 1476, Venetian shelling in 1687, and fighting during the Turkish siege of 1827 caused much damage.

TEMPLE OF ATHENA NIKE
Not open to visitors.

This charming shrine in the Ionic order was dedicated to Athena Victorious. Pausanias relates the story that it was built for the goddess Nike (Victory), who was normally depicted with wings, but that the Athenians clipped her wings so she would not fly away. The story is false, but the name *Nike Apteros* (Wingless Victory) has stuck.

The heavily damaged **frieze** running around the exterior of the cella depicts an assembly of the gods (E), and the Athenian wars against the Persians and their allies. Those on the E and s sides are originals, the other two sides being copies of the British Museum statues removed by Elgin.

The temple was built in 425BC. The Turkish forces dismantled it to make place for a gun emplacement during the Venetian siege of 1687. The original pieces were carefully put together in 1842, then taken apart and reconstructed again after repairs in 1940.

INSIDE THE ACROPOLIS
Past the Propylaea, the ruins of several monuments lie in scattered jumbles over the plateau. These include the **Temple of Artemis Brauronia**, the bear-goddess who was served by little girls; the foundations of the Archaic **Temple of Athena**, built in 529BC and destroyed by the Persians, and the fragments of a **Shrine of Augustus and Roma**.

Pausanias describes over 40 of the statues he saw within the enclosure of the Acropolis. The most prominent of these was the bronze **Athena Promachos** (Combatant), a masterpiece of Phidias. The statue measured 9m (30ft) and stood facing the Propylaea; meager remains of its base are still in place. The statue was carried off to Constantinople at some late point and perished in riots during the 4th Crusade.

PARTHENON
The Temple of the Parthenos (Virgin Athena) is generally considered the greatest masterpiece of ancient architecture. It is a peripteral temple in the Doric Order measuring 69.5 x 30.8m (228 x 101ft) at the base, with a peristyle of 8 x 17 columns each 10.4m (34ft) high. The architects were Ictinus and Callicrates, who started work in 447; the temple was dedicated in 438 and the sculpture finished in 432. Phidias created the majestic gold-and-ivory cult statue of the goddess, and directed the execution of the matchless friezes of the pediments, the metopes and the outer wall of the cella.

The Parthenon was converted into the church of Agia Sophia in the reign of Justinian; a belfry was added and the interior was painted with frescoes. The Latins took it over in 1204 as the Roman Catholic cathedral of St Mary of Athens. The Turks then converted it into a mosque, replacing the belfry with a minaret.

During the Venetian siege of 1687 the mosque was used as an ammunition depot. On September 26, a shell fired by the

Venetians hit it, causing a huge explosion that blew apart the naos and demolished 14 of the columns. During the 6mth Venetian occupation that followed, Captain General Francesco Morosini (who was later to become Doge of Venice, 1688-94) made a clumsy attempt to remove the sculptures of the w pediment, destroying them in the process.

In 1801 Lord Thomas Elgin, the British ambassador at Constantinople, secured official permission to remove the remaining friezes. He acquired a 75m section of the Panathenaic frieze (see below), the surviving pieces of the E pediment, and 15 of the best-preserved metopes (out of the original 92, of which 57 remained in existence). No less than 37 ships and 500 workmen were employed for the task; the expense eventually bankrupted Elgin and forced him to sell his loot (the **Elgin Marbles)** to the British Museum. It may be noted in passing that admiration for the marbles was not universal: Byron railed at Elgin & co. —

"Waste useless thousands on their Phidian freaks,
    Misshapen monuments and maimed antiques."

Architecture: The Parthenon represents the culmination of the more than 100-year development of the Doric temple, where increasingly more refined solutions were sought for problems of proportion and spatial harmony. The size, form and spacing of the columns, their relationship with the superstructure, and the dimensions of the cella were subject to intense study and experimentation. Nearly every one of the apparently simple lines of the temple hides geometric complexities. Thus each of the columns has a slight curvature; the distance between columns decreases on each side toward the edges; corner columns are thicker than the rest; the pavement of the interior rises imperceptibly toward the center. Each of these refinements is designed to enhance the majesty of the overall effect.

The structure of the naos is unique in that it contains two halls instead of the customary one, squeezing the front and back vestibules into narrow porticoes. The larger hall (cella) housed the goddess; the smaller one was the *parthenon* (virgin's apartment) proper, and contained the state treasury of Athens. At the beginning of the Peloponnesian Wars, Athens shocked the civilized world by transferring here the allied treasury of the League of Delos. Traces of a Turkish minaret are visible at the corner of the *opisthodomos* (w vestibule).

Sculpture: The outer face of the naos was decorated on all four sides with a continuous **frieze** of a total length of 160m (525ft), which depicted the Panathenaic procession, the dazzling festival that took place in Athens every 4yrs on the feast of Athena. The frieze contained no less than 400 human and 200 animal figures. Of this, the w section remains more or less intact; a few slabs are in the ACROPOLIS MUSEUM, and much of the rest is in the British Museum.

The 41 **metopes** that remain in place are mostly disfigured beyond recognition. They picture, in serial form, the Trojan War (N), the battle of the gods and giants (E), the battle of the Centaurs and Lapiths (S), and the battle of the Athenians against the Amazons (W).

The **E pediment** represented the birth of Athena, in full armor, from the head of Zeus: what remains of it is in London, while existing fragments of the **w pediment**, depicting the contest of Athena and Poseidon over the city of Athens, are displayed in the Acropolis Museum.

Phidias' great chryselephantine statue of **Athena Parthenos**, 12m (39ft) high and renowned for the extraordinarily intricate detailing of her dress and shield, has disappeared without trace. An antique copy of poor quality can be seen at the NATIONAL ARCHEOLOGICAL MUSEUM (Hall 20).

ERECHTHEUM

The unusual shape of this Ionic temple resulted from the need to incorporate several of the holiest shrines of prehistoric Athens. The Periclean plan to build an entirely new temple was thwarted and delayed until 406 or 395, when it ran into opposition from the priests and the people.

It was on this spot that the contest between Athena and Poseidon was believed to have taken place (see page 40): the "marks" left by Poseidon's trident are still shown, and an olive tree has been planted where Athena's sacred tree used to grow in Antiquity. Also here were the tomb of Kekrops and the shrine of Erechtheus, the serpent-kings of the founding myths. Finally, the Erechtheum also housed the olive-wood statue of Athena Polias, the oldest and holiest icon of ancient Athens, which had dropped from the sky in the reign of Kekrops. Every 4yrs this was decked up in new linen garments and displayed to the populace at the conclusion of the Panathenaic procession.

In the famous s portico of the Erechtheum, six **Caryatids** replace the usual Ionic columns. Of the originals of these statues of young women, one was removed to London by Elgin, and five have been taken to the ACROPOLIS MUSEUM to prevent further deterioration due to exposure. The ones seen in place are copies.

ACROPOLIS MUSEUM

☎ 32.10.219. Open Mon 12.30-6.30pm, Tues-Fri 8am-2.30pm, Sat-Sun 8.30am-2.30pm.

The museum contains statues and fragments discovered on the Acropolis. Individually memorable pieces are few, but the collection as a whole is unique in presenting a comprehensive picture of Athenian sculpture from its Archaic origins through mature Classicism.

A large part of the exhibit consists of frieze fragments from earlier temples on the Acropolis and a series of *korai* (Archaic statues of young women with a characteristic smile), which were presented as votive gifts to Athena. Destroyed by Persians, these were carefully buried after 480BC and were discovered during excavations in the 1880s. Many carry traces of paint, recalling the fact that like all ancient sculpture they originally stood in vivid color. A colossal fragment of a *Bull Attacked by Lions,* apparently from the pediment of the Peisistratid Temple of Athena, is particularly impressive.

The admirable band of the **Parthenon frieze** displayed here *(Hall 8)* was blown off and buried in debris in the 1687 explosion, thus escaping Elgin.

ACROPOLIS, THE SOUTH SLOPE 🏛 ☆

Map 1E2-3.

The imposing **walls** that girdle the Acropolis were erected in the years following the Persian Wars under the guidance of Cimon. Sections of the prehistoric "Pelasgian" wall can be seen behind the s wing of the Propylaea and along the s platform of the Parthenon.

At the foot of the s slope of the Acropolis are the **Theater of Dionysus** and the **Odeon of Herodes Atticus**, separated by the scant ruins of the **Asclepeion** and the **Stoa of Eumenes**. The Asclepeion was a medical center and shrine dedicated to Asclepius, the god of medicine (compare EPIDAUROS, page 112). The Stoa was erected for the convenience of the theater-goers as a gift of Eumenes II, the king of Pergamum (197-158BC), who, like his son Attalos, was a prolific benefactor of Greek cities (see under AGORA, page 48).

THEATER OF DIONYSUS

☎ *32.24.625. Open Mon-Fri 9am-1pm. Closed Sat, Sun.*

The Dionysus theater, now in ruined condition except for some 15 of its bottom rows, was the principal public stage of ancient Athens; here the plays of Aeschylus, Sophocles, Euripides and Aristophanes had their first performance. In the Classical era the theater consisted of wooden seats and a makeshift stage. A stone structure was first constructed towards the end of the period in 342-326BC, and remained in use for about 750yrs. On the first row, 67 thrones (many still in place) were reserved for the priests of Dionysus and other dignitaries; on the stage stood an altar of Dionysus (now disappeared), where libations were made before each performance.

‡ *The cult of Dionysus, a relatively late development in Greek religion, was brought to Athens by Peisistratus as a populist alternative to the aristocratic/conservative cults of Athena and Apollo. The annual festival of the Great Dionysia was celebrated with competing choruses and masked satyrs performing* tragoedia *(goat songs) and* comoedia *(ribald songs). Aeschylus was first to develop these primitive shows into a refined art form after 480BC. During the 5thC, the state commissioned a cycle of three tragedies and one comedy for performance each year at the Dionysia.*

In addition to drama, the theater was used for annual cockfights, meetings of the assembly (after the 4thC), the presentation of foreign ambassadors and various parades. In Roman times, gladiator fights and wild animal shows became equally popular. The Romans sealed the bottom part of the theater, which was then filled with water for mock naval battles (*naumachia*).

At the top edge of the theater is the marble **Monument of Thrasyllus**, commemorating a chorus-master of 319BC. The E edge of the theater abuts a platform with the scant foundations of the **Odeon of Pericles**, which was built entirely from the masts of Persian ships captured at the Battle of Salamis.

ODEON OF HERODES ATTICUS

Closed to the public except during performances.

The best-preserved Roman-period structure in Athens was funded privately by the wealthy patrician Herodes Atticus in the year AD160. The semicircular shape and heavy facade with arched portals are typically Roman. The auditorium, seating 5,000, has been restored and is used for performances during the Athens Festival.

‡ *Herodes Atticus is the subject of a brilliant passage in Gibbon. "The family of Herod, at least after it had been favored by fortune, was lineally descended from Cimon and Miltiades, Theseus and Cecrops, Aeacus and Jupiter. But the posterity of so many gods and heroes was fallen into the most abject state. His grandfather had suffered by the hands of justice, and Julius Atticus, his father, must have ended his life in poverty and contempt, had he not discovered an immense treasure buried under an old house.... Herod became a celebrated orator according to the useless rhetoric of that age; his life was spent in a philosophic retirement at Athens, perpetually surrounded by sophists, who acknowledged, without reluctance, the superiority of a rich and generous rival ... The most splendid ornaments bestowed on the Temple of Neptune in the Isthmus, a theater at*

47

Corinth, a stadium at Delphi, a bath at Thermopylae, and an aqueduct at Canusium in Italy, were insufficient to exhaust his treasures, and many inscriptions of the cities of Greece and Asia gratefully style Herodes Atticus their patron and benefactor."

AGORA 🏛

☎ 32.10.185. Map 1D2 🚌 400dr. Open Tues-Sun 8.30am-3pm. Closed Mon.

The Agora was the center of public life in ancient Athens. In this broad open space, built upon irregularly with temples, colonnades and public edifices, marketers sold their wares, public councils did business, sophists and politicians held forth, and citizens received the latest news. The area has been excavated since 1931 by American archeologists, who removed about a third of the old town of Athens (more than 350 houses) to reveal a vast field of broken rubbish. Of the three standing edifices within the precincts, one is a late Byzantine church (AGII APOSTOLI, described on page 52), one, the Stoa of Attalos, is a recent reconstruction, and the third, the "THESEUM" (see separate entry), is not strictly speaking a part of the Agora.

The **Stoa of Attalos** was one of several sumptuous colonnaded galleries *(stoae)* that framed the Agora on all sides and were used for promenades and for the retail trade. It was named for Attalos II, Hellenistic king of Pergamum (159-138BC), who pursued his family's long-standing policy of buying the allegiance of Greek cities by lavish gifts. A copy of the original stoa was rebuilt in 1953-56, in part through a generous donation of the Rockefeller family, and is now used as a **museum** to exhibit finds made during the excavations. The most memorable items on display are the potteries, among others a splendid **calyx** (wide-brimmed urn) by Exekias, the greatest master of the "black figure" style (c.530BC). Also notable are some of the 1,200 **pot shards** *(ostraka)* that archeologists discovered at the SW corner of the Agora, inscribed in clumsy hand with such names as Themistocles, Cimon, Pericles, Alcibiades and Demosthenes.
‡ *The practice of* ostracism *was one of the more intriguing features of Athenian democracy. Each year in winter the Assembly was asked to submit the names of citizens it wanted to see banished from Athens. Votes were dropped in on shards of broken pottery, and anyone who received 6,000 of these had to go into exile for ten years under pain of death in case of noncompliance. The practice was instituted by Cleisthenes after the fall of the Peisistratids to bar "for ever" the emergence of another tyrant. Ironically, Cleisthenes himself was one of the first to be ostracized.*

In the field of excavations can be discerned vague traces of the **Tholos**, a circular structure where the 50 permanent councilors selected from the Council of 500 met and dined at public expense; the **Metroon**, a temple of the mother of gods; the sanctuary of **Apollo Patroos**; and two other **stoae**. The starting point for measuring all distances from Athens, the **Altar of the Twelve Gods**, is reduced to a few dusty stones, although the great *Ara Pacis Augustae* of Rome is said to have been a copy.

The excavations have now been extended to the N side of the railroad, where the strip between Adrianou and Ermou is slated for demolition. Here archeologists discovered in 1980 the foundations of the famous **Painted Stoa** *(Stoa Poikile),* where the philosopher Zeno used to hold court and from which his disciples took the name of Stoics. Pausanias describes the paintings of the stoa in great detail.

AGORA, ROMAN   See PLAKA, ANCIENT MONUMENTS.

AREOPAGUS, PNYX AND PHILOPAPPOS 🏛 《€
Map 1E2-3.

The three hills w of the Acropolis are rich in Classical associations but hold little interest in terms of actual sights.

The **Areopagus** (Hill of Ares) gave its name to a council of nobles that was instituted probably by Draco (7thC BC) as a high tribunal to judge murder cases. In later times it acted as a sort of senate.

‡ *St Paul preached upon the Areopagus without much success (Acts 17.16-34). St Dionysus the Areopagite, perhaps a member of the council, was converted and became the first Bishop of Athens. An immensely influential treatise concerning the celestial hierarchies that appeared in Syria in the 6thC was fraudulently attributed to him. In the 9thC the legend grew that the saint (known in French as St Denis) had traveled to France and founded the Parisian church.*

The peak of the **Lófos Nimfón** (Hill of the Nymphs) is occupied by an **Observatory** built in 1846 from the funds of the Austrian Greek banker Baron Sina. A short way below this is the **Pnyx**, a large semicircular platform that was the meeting place of the popular assembly in the heyday of Athenian democracy. It is now used as an auditorium for the Acropolis light-and-sound show.

‡ *Athenian democracy in its extreme form flourished from Cleisthenes' reforms (c.508BC) to the coup of the 30 Tyrants (404BC). Nearly all political decisions in this period were referred to the assembly (ecclesia) of all adult Athenian citizens, which also elected all public officials and military and naval officers for one-year terms. The quorum for meetings was 5,000, and since people were paid for attending, the assembly became dominated by the poorest class of citizens. The system had many critics in Athens, including Socrates, and was generally loathed elsewhere in Greece.*

The Philopappos Hill, which was known in Antiquity as the Hill of the Muses, is crowned by the **Philopappos Monument** (《€), the tomb and memorial (built AD114-116) of a Syrian prince from the royal family of Commagene who lived in exile at Athens. The NW face of the hill is pockmarked with caves, which appear to have been used as dwellings and tombs in different periods. One of them is said, without much evidence, to be the **"Prison of Socrates"** where the philosopher drank his cup of hemlock.

‡ *Execution for political crimes was extremely rare in ancient Athens. The condemnation of Socrates in 399BC came shortly after the fall of the terror regime of the "30 Tyrants" in which several of the philosopher's closest associates had played leading roles, although he himself had stayed aloof. Socrates refused to defend himself at the trial or to make the routine plea for the commutation of his sentence to 10yrs' exile.*

KERAMIKOS 🏛
☎ 34.63.552. *Map 1D2* 🎫 *200dr. Open Tues-Sun 8.30am-3pm. Closed Mon.*

The Keramikos excavation, situated in an unattractive area of railroad tracks and dilapidated workshops, has laid bare parts of the cemetery of ancient Athens. The cemetery lay immediately outside the city walls, near the principal gate (Dipylon) where the ceremonial road (Hiera Odos) to Eleusis and the highways to Corinth and Delphi entered the city. A large number of funeral stelae (tombstones), sarcophagi (stone caskets) and *naiskoi* (miniature temples) lie scattered along the **Street of Tombs**, although the most important pieces have been removed to the NATIONAL ARCHEOLOGICAL MUSEUM and replaced with copies. A small **museum** exists in the excavation area.

About 1km ($\frac{1}{2}$ mile) NW of Keramikos, at Platonos and Palamidiou *(map 1 B1)*, another excavation has revealed the site of Plato's **Academy**. The road between Keramikos and the Academy was dotted with the tombs and the memorials of all the greatest Athenians; now they are replaced by repair shops and run-down apartments. Farther N, behind the train station, is the hill of **Kolonos** immortalized as the setting of Sophocles' *Oedipus at Colonus*.

‡ *The Academy was a sacred olive grove in the outskirts of Athens. Plato taught at the gymnasium here, unlike his mentor Socrates who had preferred the bustle of the Agora, and was buried nearby. His successors maintained the Platonic School at the Academy for over 900yrs.*

LYSIKRATES MONUMENT   See PLAKA, ANCIENT MONUMENTS.

PLAKA, ANCIENT MONUMENTS 🏛
Map 1D-E3. See also PLAKA AND MONASTIRAKI, pages 55-56.
Several minor but relatively well-preserved Classical monuments stand in various parts of Plaka and blend nicely with the surrounding old-town architecture.

The **Library of Hadrian** was described by Pausanias as a building with a "hundred columns of Phrygian marble, and pavilions with gilded roof-work and alabaster, decorated with statues and paintings." The inner courtyard measured 90 x 30m (295 x 98ft) and had a large water basin at its center. An imposing facade crowned with Corinthian capitals survives along Areos St., s of Monastiraki Sq.

Behind the library lies the large excavated area of the **Roman Agora** (🕿 *32.45.220* 🖭 *200dr, open Tues-Sun 8.30am-3pm, closed Mon*). Unlike the Greek original, this was a single architectural complex consisting of a vast rectangular court surrounded by colonnades. It was founded as a gift of Julius Caesar and Augustus, although construction was only completed under Trajan (AD98-117).

Adjoining the Roman market is the **Tower of the Winds (Aerides)**, an octagonal structure of white marble that was built in the early Roman period as a public water-clock, compass and weather-vane. Each of its sides faces one of the cardinal or half points of the compass, and is decorated with symbols of the respective winds. The inside used to be a reservoir that filled with water at a precise rate and thus allowed people to measure time. Under the Ottomans the tower was used as a *tekke*, a house of meditation of the Bektashi dervishes. Across the street are the ornamental gate of a destroyed Turkish *medrese* (religious school), dated 1720/21, and the derelict **Fethiye Mosque** (Conqueror's Mosque), a work of the 15thC.

The **Choregic Monument of Lysikrates**, a circular structure supported by Corinthian columns, graces a pleasant little square near the other end of Plaka. This was one of the countless similar memorials erected along the Street of the Tripods (Tripodon) in honor of winners of the choral competitions at the Great Dionysia, and commemorates the winner of 334BC, a man otherwise unknown. A Capuchin convent that existed here from

1669 to 1827 once incorporated the monument, which was put to use as a little library. Byron, who stayed at the convent during his first visit to Athens in 1809-10, is said to have composed parts of *Childe Harold's Pilgrimage* in it.

TEMPLE OF OLYMPIAN ZEUS AND HADRIAN'S ARCH 🏛

☎ *92.26.330. Map 1E3* 🚇*200dr. Open Tues-Sun 8.30am-3pm. Closed Mon.*

A group of tall Corinthian pillars survive from this vast temple, which was started in Hellenistic times (2ndC BC) but completed by Hadrian some 300yrs later. The statue of the god, dedicated by Hadrian, was according to Pausanias larger than any in the world except the Rhodian and Roman colossi; in addition, the Athenians erected a grandiose statue of the emperor himself beside the temple. In the Middle Ages a stylite hermit lived on top of the pillars; his shack remained in place until after independence.

The **Arch of Hadrian** is located a short distance from the temple. It separated the ancient city of Athens from the additional district that was walled in by Hadrian, covering roughly today's Syntagma Sq. and the parks. On either side of the gate one reads the inscriptions, "This is Athens, the old city of Theseus," and, "This is Athens, the city of Hadrian and not of Theseus."

‡ *Hadrian was one of the most brilliant and active of Roman emperors (reigned AD117-135). He studied in his youth at Athens, developing an enthusiasm for things Greek that earned him the nickname "Graeculus." He came back twice during his reign, once (AD125) to take part in the Eleusinian Mysteries, and a second time (AD128-9) to inaugurate the various monuments built in his name. His excessive sexual appetite for men was commented upon. His beloved Antinous, an Anatolian youth, was deified after his death, with statues, temples, cities and a constellation named after him.*

THESEUM (*Thísio*) 🏛 ☆
Access from the Agora (see page 48). Map 1D2.

The Doric **Temple of Hephaestus**, misnamed Theseum since the Middle Ages because of a series of friezes on the E facade depicting the exploits of Theseus, is the best-preserved temple of the ancient Greek world and deserves a visit on that account. Built in the Periclean era, it was dedicated to the god of volcanoes and metalsmiths and apparently stood near a market district populated by iron, copper and brass shops, perhaps like the present Iféstou (Hephaestus) St.

The temple was converted into a church of Agios Georgios in early Byzantine times and remained in Christian religious use until 1834. The interior has been allowed to keep some of its Byzantine additions, which gives it a less sterile appearance than most other ancient temples. Buried under the marble floor are tombs dating from the 9th through the 19thC, including those of several Englishmen.

‡ *Theseus was born of the royal family of Troezen. After defeating the bully Periphetes of the bronze club, the robber "Pine-Bender" Sinis, the wild sow of Crommyon, the man-eating sea turtle of the Isthmus and the wrestler-king of Eleusis, he came to Athens and obtained the kingship against the machinations of the witch Medea. He freed Athens from the Cretan yoke by killing the bull-man Minotaur in the Labyrinth of the palace of King Minos with the help of Ariadne, the king's daughter,*

51

although he later abandoned her on the island of Naxos. After subjugating all of Attica, he took part in the wars against the Centaurs in Thessaly and the Amazons on the Black Sea coast. His last wife Phaedra fell in love with Hippolytus, a son of his from an Amazon concubine, and committed suicide when he rejected her advances.

TOWER OF THE WINDS See PLAKA, ANCIENT MONUMENTS.

Byzantine churches

Almost all of Athens' one-dozen Byzantine churches date from the early 11thC and owe their origins to the Christian restoration that followed the campaigns of Emperor Basil II "the Bulgar-slayer" in the Balkans. Only the **"Old Metrópolis,"** arguably the most graceful of all, belongs in its present form to the late 12thC. The churches are of minuscule proportions and do not claim any great architectural distinction. Although they have been more or less in continuous use as churches, none has retained frescoes or other interior ornamentation of historic value. Nevertheless they form quaint oases of peace that many visitors will cherish amid the frantic rush of modern Athens.

(See under OUTSKIRTS OF ATHENS for the DAPHNI and KESARIANI Monasteries, on pages 78 and 80 respectively.)

AGII APOSTÓLI *(Holy Apostles)* ♠
Agion Apostolon. Map 1D2.
Located within the excavation area of the AGORA, the church was spared when this part of the old town was razed by the American archeologists. In the 1950s it was stripped of later accretions and restored to its original form of c.1020; the four incorporated Classical columns were replaced by copies, and a number of post-Byzantine frescoes from the demolished church of Ag. Spiridon were transferred here at that time.

AGIOS NIKODÍMOS ♠
Filelinon. Map 2E4.
The largest medieval structure in Athens was founded in 1031 as part of a monastery that survived until 1701. The building was restored with the addition of a belfry by Czar Alexander II in the 1850s, and is now used as the Russian Orthodox church of Athens.

AGII THEODÓRI ♠
Klafthmonos Sq. Map 1D3.
Founded in 1049 but completely rebuilt in alternating courses of stone and brick in the following century. The belfry and the interior decoration date from the 19thC.

KAPNIKARÉA ♠
Ermou. Map 1D3.
Despite its doubtful attribution to Empress Irene, the Athenian lady who married Leo IV and reigned alone in 797-803, the church is almost certainly an 11thC work. The porch and N chapel were added in the 13thC. The contrast between the graceful ensemble and the surrounding business district is striking.

OLD METRÓPOLIS ⛪

Mitropoleos Sq. Map 1D3.

Properly Panagía Gorgoépikoos or Agios Elefthérios, this charming little church is entirely constructed of architectural fragments of Classical and early medieval origin. It was used as the Orthodox episcopal seat of Athens when the bishops were ousted from the Parthenon, first by the Franks, then by the Turks.

The adjoining "new" **Metropolis** (cathedral), a work of large-scale kitsch, was built in 1840-55 as the archiepiscopal church of Athens. A rather impressive **Orthodox mass** (✭) is celebrated here on Sundays with the participation of the archbishop and a substantial crowd of priests and acolytes.

‡ *The Metropolitan Archbishop of Athens is the head of the autocephalous Greek church, which formally severed its ties with the Oecumenical Patriarch of Constantinople in 1864. A number of Greek prelates, however, are still subject to the Patriarch, although his authority in their case is "temporarily" relegated to the Archbishop of Athens. The Archbishop of Crete and the monasteries of Mt. Athos have independent status.*

OTHER BYZANTINE CHURCHES IN ATHENS

These include **Ag. Nikoláos Rangavás**, **Ag. Ioánnis Theólogos**, **Ag. Anargyri** and **Metamórphosis (Sotiráki)** in Plaka; the **Theotokos (Pantánassa)**, which gives its name to **Monastiraki** ("little monastery") square; the nearby **Ag. Ioánnis stin Kolóna**, built around a Roman column believed to have the power of curing fevers; **Ag. Asomaton** at Keramikos; and the chapel of **Panagía Chrysospiliótissa** above the Dionysus theater, the only one still bearing traces of Byzantine wall painting.

There are also several small churches dating from the Turkish period, some replacing or reproducing earlier Byzantine edifices. Notable among these is the church of **Ag. Simeon** in the Anafiotika district, renowned for its miracle-working icon of *Our Lady of the Reeds.*

Modern Athens

Plaka is the heart of tourist Athens, Syntagma the center of government and business, Omonia the lower-class underbelly and Kolonaki the upper-class diadem. A vast city of residential and industrial suburbs spreads around them for miles in every direction, unknown and unvisited by foreigners.

FIRST CEMETERY (*Próto Nekrotáfio*) ✭

Map 2F4.

This cemetery, containing the tombs of nearly every prominent Greek in the 19th and early 20th centuries, is of greatest interest both from a historic and artistic point of view. A visit may constitute one of the more satisfying surprises of a tour of Athens.

Many of the tombs are built in the shape either of elaborate Greek temples or Byzantine churches. All are of Pentelic marble, which looks dazzling against the profusion of palm trees and dark cypresses; they lie thickly together on the irregular terrain, creating a spectacle of monumental pomp. Many contain statues of excellent quality, presenting a full parade of bearded statesmen, operetta generals, dreamy-eyed poets, stern matrons and innocent damsels in the flower of youth.

Prominent monuments commemorate prime ministers (Chalcocondylis, Deligiorgis, Koumoundouros, two each of Trikoupis, Voulgaris and Zaimis), founding fathers (Kolokotronis, Mavromichalis), dictators (Metaxas), politicians (Rallis) and plutocrats (Averoff, Benaki, Pesmazoglou, Siniosoglou, Syngros, Tositsa, Zarifi). One of the finest tombs, shaped as the portico of a Doric temple (high on the left near the entrance), belongs to Heinrich Schliemann (1822-90).

‡ *Born in Mecklenburg, Schliemann joined the California gold rush, made a fortune as a St Petersburg merchant during the Crimean War, and devoted the rest of his life to Homeric archeology. In 1873-74 he discovered Troy, confounding 2,000yrs of skepticism by proving the reality of the Trojan legend. In 1874-76, he unearthed at Mycenae the first tangible artifacts of the Bronze Age ("Mycenaean") civilization of Greece. He was married to a very young Greek woman, and lived in grand style at the Iliou Melathron, "the Palace of Ilium," on Stadiou St.*

KOLONÁKI AND MOUNT LYKAVITÓS
Map 2D4-5.

The district of Kolonaki, ascending from **Kolonaki Sq.** to the western and southern flanks of Mt. Lykavitos, is the most fashionable residential quarter of central Athens. Many of the city's better restaurants, designer boutiques, art galleries and fine furniture stores are to be found in this part of town. Also located here are the British and French Schools of Archeology, the German Archeological Institute and the American School of Classical Studies, prestigious institutions that played such a crucial role in shaping the cultural identity of Greece in the past century and a half.

‡ *The institutes are supported by the governments and academic institutions of their respective countries. Major archeological achievements include Knossos and Mycenae for the British, Delphi for the French, Olympia for the Germans, and the Athenian Agora and Corinth for the Americans. Apart from their narrowly academic significance, the activities of the schools were instrumental in transforming the image of Greece from a backward Oriental country into a reincarnation of ancient Greece.*

Stepped streets lead up to the higher reaches of Kolonaki, above the cloud of polluted air that often envelops the city; the area at the foot of the **Lykavitos funicular** has a rarefied atmosphere and some of the most exclusive residential streets of Athens.

The peak of the **Lykavitos** (★ ◁€) (ancient Mt. Lycabettus, 277m/909ft), reached either by funicular or footpath, offers a magnificent panorama covering all of Greater Athens, surrounded by the theater of Mts. Parnitha (N), Penteli (NE) and Imitos (E). The Acropolis is seen against the background of the sea, and on clear days the view extends beyond the craggy masses of Salamis and Aegina to the Peloponnesian mountains. A taverna and a pleasant 19thC church exist at the top.

OMÓNIA AND VICINITY
Around map 1C3.

Omonia Sq. *(Homonoia = Concord)* is the center of commercial Athens, with a vast and chaotic mass of shops, offices, discount stores, travel agencies and *souvlaki* stands spreading along each of the eight thoroughfares that intersect here. At night the area tends to be livelier than Syntagma, particularly around the various questionable bars and all-night restaurants that dot the back streets in the vicinity. For many decades Omonia has attracted visitors from the Greek countryside just as the Acropolis and Plaka draw foreign tourists — a role that is bound to erode as increasing prosperity minimizes the economic and cultural differences between Athens and the provinces.

MUSEUM AND EXARHÍA

Walking N of Omonia one passes Kaningos Sq., lying in close proximity to Gladstonos and Tsorts Sts.

‡ *British Prime Ministers George Canning, William Ewart Gladstone and David Lloyd George played crucial roles in the creation of modern Greece. Canning was instrumental in rallying English support for the War of Independence, Gladstone elevated philhellenism to the level of a moral crusade, and Lloyd George coaxed the Greeks into the ill-fated Anatolian adventure. Philbellenism was one of the cornerstones of the foreign policy of the Liberal Party in the 19thC, and the last Liberal-led government of Britain, that of Lloyd George, was brought to an end by the Greek debacle in 1922.*

Farther on is the **Athens Polytechnic**, remembered above all for the student uprising of 1973 that brought down the colonels' junta. The NATIONAL ARCHEOLOGICAL MUSEUM (see page 60) is located next door. Student disturbances at the polytechnic developed into a city-wide revolt on Nov 13, 1973. Tanks were deployed against the demonstrators, and at least 13 students were killed on the cast-iron gates facing the avenue. On Nov 25, Colonel Papadopoulos was ousted by a hard-line military faction, which, however, survived but for a little over 8mths.

NE of Omonia lies the district of **Exarhía** *(map 2 C4)*, the center of Athenian student life and a hub of "alternative" political and cultural activities. Some of the best cafés in town, as well as the best venues to hear the less cliché-ridden forms of Greek music, are located here.

THE MARKET DISTRICT

Running S of Omonia toward Monastiraki, the market street of **Athinas** presents Athens at its most "Oriental." **Kotsiá Sq.** (now Ethnikis Andistaseos) has only the facades of elegant old buildings to remind one that this was the center of Athenian high life in the 19thC. The area is now devoted mainly to the food and grocery trade, though there are also specific parts and side streets specializing in cheap clothes, kitchen utensils, garden implements, gold jewelry, and spices. Old-style grocery stores carry fabulous quantities of cheese, dried codfish, olives, coffee, spiced meats, wild herbs and dried fruit in sacks and barrels; they emit the satisfying smell of a well-stocked cellar.

Of greatest interest to the stout-of-heart is the **Fish and Meat Market** (✿), a giant cast-iron structure housing several hundred butchers' and fishermen's stalls in separate sections. The stench is strong, sheep's heads roll around freely, but the lively commotion and the sheer scope of the market are worth experiencing. Noticeable among marketers is a considerable proportion of Gypsies. Like other Balkan countries, Greece has a substantial Gypsy population. Many speak the Gypsy language (Romany), and lead a seminomadic life as artisans, tradesmen and entertainers.

PLÁKA AND MONASTIRÁKI 🏛 🏛 ♠ ★
Map 1D-E3. See also page 50 for PLAKA, ANCIENT MONUMENTS.
These districts together with the now bulldozed area of the ancient Agora formed the town of Athens as it existed at the time

of independence. The narrow, irregular street pattern goes back to pre-independence days; most of the buildings are pleasant, relatively modest 19thC houses or their modern successors.

Thanks exclusively to tourism, Plaka, which had declined into a poor and derelict quarter by the mid-20thC, was revived in recent decades and now bustles with lively shops and outdoor tavernas catering to more than 5 million visitors a year. Most streets have been closed to vehicle traffic, creating a good setting for strolling at leisure in a small-town atmosphere dotted with traces of Classical, medieval, Turkish and Neoclassical architecture.

‡ *The word* Plaka *appears to derive from* pliaka, *the Albanian for "old." The Christian population of Athens and Attica at the time of independence consisted mainly of Albanians, a fact that modern Greek nationalism still finds uncomfortable to deal with. Albanian was spoken widely until late last century.*

Adrianou, lined with souvenir stores, and **Kidathineon**, densely populated with outdoor tavernas, form the principal axes of Plaka. Charming little squares are found around the TOWER OF THE WINDS, the church of Metamorphosis and the LYSIKRATES MONUMENT. Surprisingly peaceful streets abound in the upper reaches of Plaka at the edge of the Acropolis, called **Rizokastro**, or "Castle's Foot." A walking tour should by no means miss the district of **Anafiotika** (✪ 🏛 ◀€), settled by immigrants from the island of Anafi, who created a veritable corner of the Cyclades in the heart of the city with its whitewashed houses, corridor-like streets and tiny gardens.

Monastiraki Sq. derives its name from the "little monastery" of Pantánassa that formerly existed here, of which only an ungainly church of (dubious) Byzantine origin survives. The square was the hub of the bazaar district of Turkish Athens, and is dominated by the **Bazaar Mosque** (also known as Mustafa Aga Mosque or Sidriváni); dedicated in 1759/60, the mosque, minus its minaret, was used from independence until 1918 as a precinct jail, and now remains locked up. The spirit of the bazaar survives on **Pandrossou**, and especially on **Ifestou St**., where a lively flea market is held on Sundays and most other days.

A covered bazaar indeed existed at the site of Hadrian's Library, taking in the now excavated area bound by Areos, Pandrossou and Eolou. The middle part of Adrianou (now excavated) ran through it. When the bazaar burned down in 1885, archeologists prevailed upon the government to clear the site so they could dig for the foundations of Hadrian's Library.

SYNTAGMA AND VICINITY
Around map 2D4.

Syntagma (Constitution) Square is the heart of modern Athens. The **Parliament** dominates the square from a height in the E. Several of Athens' principal hotels, airline companies and the head offices of Greece's major banks occupy the other three sides. The ministries of finance, economy, foreign affairs and the interior are located in the immediate vicinity. The top commercial establishments of Athens fan out from the W and N. The embassies of the 19thC Great Powers and the residences of many of the people who command the destinies of the country are lined along **Vassilissis Sofias Ave**., while the **Presidential Palace** and the **Prime Ministry** are located on the opposite edge of the park on Irodotou Attikou St.

Political demonstrations and marches are traditionally held on Syntagma Square. The custom goes back to 1843 when a riot here compelled King Otto to grant the country's first constitution.

The area extending s of the square part of the way into the park was occupied in Antiquity by the grounds of the **Lyceum** ("Wolf's Field"), a sacred grove of Apollo lying outside city walls. Aristotle used the Lyceum to teach his philosophy. His successor Theophrastus acquired the so-called **Museum**, or Garden of the Muses, corresponding almost exactly to the present Syntagma Sq., which remained the precincts of the Aristotelian school for over 800yrs. The area was included within city boundaries during Hadrian's extension of the walls.

Along with Omonia, Syntagma Sq. formed one of the nodal points of the new Athens that was drawn by Schaubart in 1834, but realized on a more modest scale by Leo von Klenze when the former's grandiose concepts failed to mesh with Greek realities.

The principal architectural landmark of the square is the **Parliament** *(Voulí)*, formerly the Royal Palace, built by Friedrich Gaertner for King Otto in 1836-42 and used as the residence of the kings of Greece until 1924. The constitution of 1843 was promulgated by Otto from a balcony of this palace. The parliament, which was formerly housed at Stadiou 13 (now the NATIONAL HISTORICAL MUSEUM), moved here in 1935 when the monarchy was restored after an 11yr republican interregnum. Visits to the building are possible by invitation only.

Two republican guards *(évzones)* stand in front of the parliament in ceremonial uniforms of white pleated skirt *(foustanélla)*, pompom slippers *(tsaroúhia)* and tasseled caps. The costume was inspired by the attire of Albanian *klephts* (bandits) who fought heroically in the Greek war of independence, and was adopted by King Otto. Other *evzones* are posted in front of the Presidential Palace (see page 58). A **parade** (★) of *evzones* accompanied by a military band takes place on Syntagma Sq. every Sun at 11am.

Located a block away on the N side of the square, the stately **Hotel Grande Bretagne** was built in the 1840s by the Danish architect Theophil von Hansen as a private mansion that doubled up as a royal guest house. It was used for a time by the French school of archeology, before being converted into a hotel in 1874.

Famous guests of the Grande Bretagne included Gabriele d'Annunzio, Saint-Saëns, Richard Strauss, and the Prince and Princess of Monaco. During World War II it served as the headquarters of German, then of British occupying forces. An attempt to blow it up from the sewers on Christmas Eve 1944, when Churchill was staying here, was foiled at the last moment. Constantine Karamanlis directed the restoration of Greek democracy in 1974 from temporary government headquarters on the 5th floor.

STADIOU AND PANEPISTIMIOU AVENUES

Stately 19thC buildings alternate with elegant and not-so-elegant stores along the two principal thoroughfares of central Athens. The main landmarks along Panepistimiou (officially called **Venizelou**, after Eleftherios Venizelos, the leading political figure of the early 20thC) are the **Iliou Melathron** (Palace of Ilium), once the home of Heinrich Schliemann (see page 54), now the Supreme Court of Appeals; the Catholic cathedral of **St Denis**; the majestic pseudo-Classical monuments of the **Hellenic Academy** (built by Th. von Hansen in 1859-85), the **National Library** (1887-91) and the now ceremonial main hall of the **University** (Christian Hansen, 1837-42).

Klafthmonos Sq., on Stadiou, is dominated by a statue of **Kolokotronis**, the heroic bandit-leader of the War of Independence (1770-1843) who was twice condemned to death by different Greek governments. Nearby is the **Old Parliament**, now housing the NATIONAL HISTORICAL MUSEUM.

THE PARKS

The National Garden *(ethnikós kipós)* and the adjoining Zapio Park extend behind the Parliament like a green oasis in the heart of the city. The **National Garden** (✶ *open dawn to dusk)* was created by Court Gardener Friedrich Schmitt as a private garden for Amalia, Otto's queen, who raised eyebrows by dispatching the navy's one battleship on missions to bring exotic plants from all parts of the globe. The garden retains something of a German and royal character with its luxuriant vegetation, well-tended paths and strutting peacocks. Within it are a Botanical Museum and a tiny Zoo. The **Zapio Park** *(Zappeion)* was donated to the state by the Zappas family in the 1870s. At its center stands a grand **Exhibition Hall** designed by Th. Hansen in the 1870s, with a popular outdoor movie theater and café where concerts are given on summer evenings.

On the E side of the park, across a sidewalk occupied by a colorful row of florists, is the **Presidential Palace** *(Anáktora)*. Built by Ernst Ziller, this was used as the royal residence from 1935-67 and has been the official home of the president of the republic since the establishment of that largely ceremonial office in 1975. Next door at #19 is the **Prime Ministry**, the real seat of political power.

A short walk S of the palace leads to the **Stadium** *(Stádio)*, a vast expanse of gleaming Pentelic marble flanked by the pine-covered hill of Arditos. The present structure was built in 1896, as a gift of the Alexandrian plutocrat George Averoff, to host the first of the modern Olympic Games, which took place in Athens. It occupies, however, the precise location of the ancient Panathenaic stadium, and its form is a faithful copy of the original as described by Pausanias.

The ancient stadium was built in 330BC as a venue for the quadrennial Panathenaic Games. Its length, as now, was one *stade* or 204m (223yds), the standard measure of the Olympic foot race. Hadrian held the presidency of the games during his first imperial visit to Athens, and 1,000 wild beasts were set loose on the field on this occasion.

METS

The small rectangular area circumscribed by Arditos Hill, the TEMPLE OF ZEUS and FIRST CEMETERY is known as **Mets** (from the French city of Metz, the name of a pro-Entente café that flourished here during World War I), a quiet district of many old garden houses and a village-like character. It has recently become a favorite residence of the Athenian literati and younger professionals, and consequently possesses a number of good bars, interesting boutiques and art stores concentrated along Markou Mousourou, the main street.

Museums of Athens

The **National Archeological Museum**, containing one of the world's most important collections of Classical Greek art, is among the highlights of Athens and should not be missed under any circumstance. The **Benaki Museum** complements it nicely, devoted as it is to the opposite (Christian, Byzantine, Oriental) pole of the Greek cultural heritage. The **Cycladic Art Museum** deserves a visit if only for the admirably clear and enlightening displays. The others are of secondary interest.

The **Acropolis and Agora museums** have been described, above, in connection with the archeological sites. Unless otherwise noted, all museums open 8.30am-3pm except Mon and charge 200dr.

BENAKI MUSEUM ☆
Vassilissis Sofias 17 ☎ 36.11.617. Map 2D4. Open Mon-Sat 8.30am-2pm. Closed Sun.

The Museum is a fantastic, colorful treasure-trove of Byzantine, late-Greek and Muslim antiquities from all over the Near East.
‡ *Emmanuel Benakis (1843-1929) was a Greek who made his fortune in the cotton trade in Egypt. His son Antonis (1873-1954) devoted his life to collecting antiquities, which he donated to the public in 1931 together with his Neoclassical mansion.*

The large collection of **Byzantine icons** includes some excellent examples of the 15thC Cretan school, including two early El Grecos. These clearly demonstrate the cross-fertilization of Greek and Italian art in the early Renaissance, while the following centuries show a precipitous return to rigid conservatism in church art.

Other gems include several Roman-period **portraits** from Faiyoum (Egypt), fine specimens of **Iznik ceramics** and **Bursa textiles** (Turkey), and fabulous **silver filigree** and **carved wood work** from Asia Minor. A 17thC marble-inlaid Egyptian **fountain hall** has been reconstructed in its entirety. Many of these items represent cultural traditions in which Greek artisans were active, or which were influenced by, and in turn enriched, Byzantine/Greek art.

The upper floor, containing the Far Eastern collection as well as old paintings, drawings and engravings of Athens, is currently closed to visitors. A wonderful collection of Greek **folk costumes** is exhibited in the basement. The **library**, one of the world's richest repositories of Byzantine and post-Byzantine manuscripts and archival material relating to modern Greek history, is open by permission only.

BYZANTINE MUSEUM
Vassilissis Sofias 22 ☎ 72.11.027. Map 2D5 🖾 400dr.

The neo-Renaissance building now housing the Byzantine Museum was erected in 1840 as a residence for the Duchesse de Plaisance, one of the most eccentric figures of 19thC Athens. The museum possesses a great wealth of Byzantine **icons**. There are also reconstructions of several church interiors from various periods of Byzantine architecture, and ecclesiastical objects and embroideries of obsessive workmanship.
‡ *Née Sophie de Marbois (1785-1854), the Duchesse de Plaisance married Lebrun, one of Napoleon's generals, helped finance the Greek war of independence from her personal fortune, and took up residence in Athens in 1837. She always traveled with a crystal casket containing the embalmed body of her daughter, and a pack of wild dogs which terrorized Athens. She devised a private religion that she evangelized enthusiastically, was reputed to yield willingly to brigands in mountain paths, and died reciting some verses of Lamartine.*

CYCLADIC ART MUSEUM
Neofitou Douka 4 ☎ 72.49.706. Map 2D5. Open Mon, Wed-Sat 8.30am-3pm. Closed Tues; Sun.

Managed privately by the Nicholas Goulandris Foundation, this deserves to be called the only modern museum in Athens. The presentation is lucid, with expert and detailed documentation, well-designed charts and illustrations. The collection comprises a large number of artifacts from the early Cycladic cultures of 3300-2000BC, including several well-preserved marble **figurines**. The astonishing "modernity" of these idols juxtaposes interestingly with the modern artists exhibited on the upper floor.

The museum has a good, if expensive, shop selling replicas of exhibited items.

FOLK ART MUSEUM
Kidathineon 17, in Plaka ☎ 32.13.018. Map 1E3.
An attractive museum housing a remarkable collection of embroidery ranging from the 2ndC AD to the present, domestic articles from the 18th and 19thC, and native costumes from various parts of Greece. The presentation is modern and pleasantly designed. The upper floor has the reconstruction of the interior of a village house, with wood panels painted by the naive painter Theophilos of Lesbos (1878-1934).

JEWISH MUSEUM
Amalias 36 ☎ 32.31.577. Map 2E4. Free entrance. Open Sun-Fri 9am-1pm. Closed Sat.
This has a small collection of memorabilia relating to the Jewish community of Athens.

The origins of Jewish presence in Greece go back to the 3rdC BC, although the modern community has its roots in the mass emigration of Sephardic (Spanish) Jews to the Ottoman domains in 1492. Under Turkish rule most Greek towns had substantial Jewish populations, and Thessaloniki in particular was an important Jewish center. These communities shrank after independence, mostly by emigration to Turkey and America, and were almost wiped out by the Nazis during World War II. Greek Jews now number less than 5,000, most of them in Thessaloniki.

KANELLOPOULOS MUSEUM
Theorias and Panos, in Plaka ☎ 32.12.313. Map 1E3.
An eclectic family collection somewhat similar in scope, though not in wealth, to the Benaki Museum. In addition to icons and folkloric items, the museum holds a vast quantity of Archaic and Classical small objects, vases and jewelry.

NATIONAL ARCHEOLOGICAL MUSEUM ★
28 Oktovriou (Patission) 44 ☎ 82.17.717. Map 2B4
▨ 600dr. Open Mon 12.30-7pm; Tues-Fri 8.30am-7pm;
Sat-Sun 8.30am-3pm.
The museum was erected in 1866-89 (extended 1925-39) to house finds from the excavations of the British, French, German and American Archeological schools and the Greek Archeological Society.
‡ *The earliest core of the collection were the Aegina friezes, which were recovered by the Germans in 1833 and displayed at the Theseum. The collection was enriched substantially by the discoveries of Schliemann at Mycenae in 1874-76, important bronze statues salvaged from the sea off Kythera in 1900 and off Euboea in 1928, and most recently by Minoan frescoes unearthed by Professor Sp. Marinatos at Akrotiri on the island of Santorini in 1967-74.*

The **Mycenaean collection** (hall 4) is the world's richest, and includes the golden **death masks** whose discovery prompted Schliemann to send the famous telegram, "Today, I gazed upon

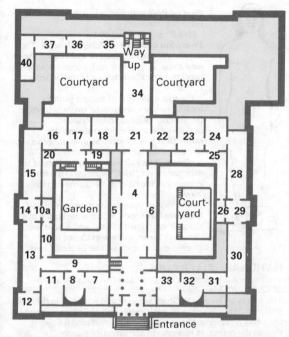

Agamemnon's face." The **Linear-B tablets** are among the very few that survived thanks to a fire at the palace of Pylos that baked the soft clay. The **bronze weapons** and **gold and bronze cups** are reminiscent of Homeric passages.

A small number of excellent **Cycladic figurines** are found in hall 5. The Minoan collection is weak, as most Minoan artifacts are kept at the Iraklion Museum in Crete.

A splendid **geometric amphora** from c.760BC is displayed in hall 7. Of the great variety of Archaic kouroi (halls 8-13), the finest is probably the *Anavysos kouros*, found in 1936 (hall 9 — see illustration on page 62); it dates from c.520BC and bears the inscription, "Stop and lament over the tomb of dead Kroiros whom furious Ares destroyed as he fought in the front rank."

Halls 14-18 and 23-24 contain **funeral stelae**, mainly from KERAMIKOS. The eloquent, subdued beauty of these sculptures was perhaps best captured by Rilke in the *Duino Elegies:*

"On Attic stelae, did not the circumspection
    of human gesture amaze you? Were not love and farewell
so lightly laid upon the shoulders, they seemed to be made
    of other stuff than with us? Think of the hands,
how they rest without pressure...."

Four magnificent bronzes deserve special notice among the many Classical and Hellenistic statues on display. The early Classical *Poseidon* in hall 14 (c.460BC) and the Hellenistic *Horse with Child Rider* in hall 21 (2ndC BC), though widely separated in time, were found in the same shipwreck off Euboea. The *Youth of Anakythera* (hall 28), a Peloponnesian work of c.340BC, has a masterfully expressive face and body, while the

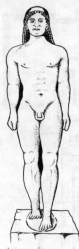

Bust of Philosopher in hall 30 is a tour de force of portraiture.

Hall 30 is dominated by the colossal *Poseidon of Melos*, a Hellenistic work. The translucent marble group of *Aphrodite, Pan and Eros*, in the same hall, exemplifies the precious style characteristic of the Hellenistic epoch.

The vast collection of ancient **pottery**, located upstairs, tends to be overwhelming in the absence of lucid and systematic documentation. The rich **numismatic collection** is an object-lesson in the general decline of the quality of coins over the centuries. It includes several specimens of the Athenian silver **"owl,"** which was the leading currency of the Eastern Mediterranean for 200yrs.

Also located upstairs are the splendid **Santorini frescoes**, which were buried in a volcanic eruption c.1500BC, and whose recent discovery furnished new evidence of the extension of Minoan culture beyond Crete.

Anavysos kouros

NATIONAL GALLERY *(Pinakothíki)*
Vassileos Konstantinou 50 (opposite the Hilton)
☎ *72.11.010. Map 2D6.*
The gallery is devoted to Greek painting and sculpture in the 19th and 20thC. With the possible exception of Ghikas, none of the artists represented has a significant international following, though the collection of works by the primitive painter Theophilos holds some interest. There are also three paintings ascribed, doubtfully, to El Greco, as well as minor pieces by Delacroix, Picasso, Magritte, Utrillo and Picabia.

NATIONAL HISTORICAL MUSEUM
Stadiou 13 ☎ *32.37.617. Map 1-2D3-4* 🖾 *100dr. Open Tues-Fri 9am-2pm; Sat-Sun 9am-1pm. Closed Mon.*
The collection holds various relics of modern Greek history, particularly of the war of independence. Among objects displayed are the personal effects of Patriarch Gregorios, who was hung in Constantinople in 1821, the ashes of a nephew of Napoleon Bonaparte, an urn containing the heart of revolutionary war hero Admiral Kanaris, the death mask of the bandit-hero Kolokotronis, and a helmet and sword said to have been worn by Byron when he commanded the garrison of Missolonghi as an officer of the Greek liberation army.
‡ *The building, designed by Florimond Boulanger in 1858 to house the Greek parliament, was used as such until the 1930s. On its steps Prime Minister Deligiannis was assassinated in 1905.*

OTHER MUSEUMS IN ATHENS
Look out for the **Center for Popular Arts and Traditions** *(Hadzimihali 6, map 1 E3)*, a fine old Plaka mansion devoted to the vanishing heritage of Greek village life; the **Museum of the City of Athens** *(Paparigopoulou 7, Klafthmonos Sq., map 1 D3)*, housed in a stately mansion that was the first residence of King Otto and Queen Amalia in 1834-42; and the **War Museum** *(Vassilissis Sofias and Rizari, map 2 D5)*, containing mementoes of Greece's various wars since 1821.

Where to stay in Athens

See ACCOMMODATIONS, page 18, for a general introduction.

Most hotels favored by tourists in Athens are found in the area around **Syntagma** and s toward **Dion. Areopagitou** and **Syngrou**. Some are scattered along **Stadiou**, **Panepistimiou** and **28 Oktovriou** in the noisy and traffic-infested area N and SE of **Omonia**. A number of hotels are located in the area near the **US Embassy** and the **Hilton**, elegant, less crowded, but a rather long walk from the main sights and shops.

Plaka and **Monastiraki** have a limited number of inexpensive and rather run-down hotels catering primarily to younger travelers. A variety of down-and-out hotels, geared mainly to visitors from the provinces rather than foreign tourists, are located in the market area SW of Omonia and in the vicinity of the railroad stations. Be aware that some of those near Omonia rent rooms by the hour.

Travel and accommodation agencies around Syntagma Sq. can help locate pensions or furnished efficiency (self-catering) flats. However, private pensions in Athens are few and mostly unattractive.

Most hotels in Athens suffer from a high level of noise from street traffic, and it is usually advisable to ask for a room that does not face street-side. Another very prudent precaution is to have some form of protection against mosquitoes. The most effective means of combat are the plug-in devices that use odorless tablets; they are available in every pharmacy and supermarket.

Visitors who prefer to stay near the sea and can put up with the inconvenient public transportation and the noise of airplane traffic might choose from the large number of hotels located between **Paléo Faliró** (6km/4 miles from downtown Athens) and **Vouliagméni** (18km/11 miles) on the Attic coast. The northern suburb of **Kifissiá** (15km/9 miles) is quiet, cool, and offers a variety of fine hotels. For details of accommodations in these areas, see OUTSKIRTS OF ATHENS, pages 77 and 81. **Piraeus** cannot be generally recommended, but if Athens is too full, or you have a boat to catch next morning, we suggest three hotels on page 83.

Luxury hotels

All hotels in this category accept major charge and credit cards and have air conditioning in all rooms. Prices quoted — for double room with breakfast — were valid in the summer of 1990, and are included to give a general idea only.

ATHENS HILTON
Vassilissis Sofias 46
☎ 72.20.201. Map 2D6. 480 rms
◀€ ☰ 🕭 ⋔ ☐ ₲.
The oldest and most expensive of international chains represented in Athens, a hub of the capital's diplomatic and business life. Large and popular swimming pool. Galaxy roof garden with splendid view over the Acropolis and the sea. A choice of restaurants, including **Ta Nissia**, "where Athens meets for dinner!" — 36,000dr.

GRANDE BRETAGNE
Syntagma Sq. ☎ 32.30.251/9
⊕ 32.28.034. *In US, toll-free* ☎ (800) 223.6800 or (800) 838.3110. *London offices* ☎ (071)

583.4211. Map 2D4. 400 rms, 25 suites ◀€ ☰ ☐ ₲.
Oldest and grandest of Athens' hotels, completely renovated and modernized in 1956. Two bars, three restaurants. Prices range from 27,000-40,000dr.

LEDRA MARRIOTT
Syngrou 115 ☎ 93.47.711. 265 rms ☰ 🕭 ⋔ ☐ ₲.
Located somewhat off-center, but the newest and arguably the best of the US chain representatives. The **Kona Kai Polynesian** restaurant, the **Bali Lounge** and the **Sun** buffet-brunch in the **Zephyros Café** are all noteworthy. Rooms have video with a selection of movies. 28,000-32,000dr.

63

Other L-class hotels in Athens are:

Acropole Palace   28 Oktovriou 51 ☎52.21.521. Map **1**B ⊟ ⇌

Astir Palace   Syntagma Sq. ☎36.43.112. Map **2**D4.

Athenaeum Intercontinental   Syngrou 89 ☎92.20.007. Greek, French and Mongolian ⇌ 🐾 🜊 ▢ ⅄ Roof-garden. Shopping arcade.

Athens Chandris   Syngrou 385 ☎94.14.824 ⇌ 🐾

Caravel   Vass. Alexandrou 2 (near the Hilton) ☎72.90.721/60. Map **2**D6. A favorite of Arab visitors, with an in-house mosque. Italian ⇌ Piano bar, and rooftop 🐾

Divani Palace Acropolis   Parthenonos 19-25 ☎92.22.945. Map **1**E3 🐾

Holiday Inn Mihalakopoulou 50   Behind the Hilton ☎72.48.322. Map **2**D6 ⇌ 🐾 🜊

Meridien Athens   Syntagma Sq. ☎32.55.301. Map **2**D4. Superb French ⇌

Park Hotel   Leof. Alexandras 10 ☎88.32.711. Map **2**B4 ⇌ 🜊

Royal Olympic   Diakou 28-32 ☎92.26.411. Map **1**E3. At 17,000dr the least expensive of luxury-class hotels ⇌ ▢

St George Lycabettus   Kleomenous 2 ☎72.90.711. Map **2**D5. Lovely position overlooking all Athens on the most exclusive street in Kolonaki. Rooftop ⇌ "Grand Balcon" has spectacular view.

Expensive hotels (9,000-18,000dr)

Class-A hotels, all with restaurant, air conditioning, major charge and credit cards, include:

ASTOR
Karageorgi Servias 16
☎ *32.55.555. Map **2**D4. 117 rms*
⇌
Located just off Syntagma Sq., Astor has an impressive marble lobby and comfortable rooms. Some rooms have terraces overlooking the Acropolis. Good value at 9,000dr.

ATHENS GATE
Syngrou 10 ☎*92.38.302/8*

ⓢ*92.37.493. Map **1**E3. 100 rms*
《 ⇌
Modern hotel facing the Temple of Olympian Zeus, with a roof garden restaurant offering splendid views.

NOVOTEL MIRAYIA ATHENS
Mihail Voda 4-6 ☎*86.27.133.*
*Map **1**B3. 180 rms* ⇌ 🐾 ▢
Roof garden with swimming pool is an asset. Minibar and satellite TV in rooms.

Other centrally located hotels of the A class: **Divani Zafolia** *(Leof. Alexandras 87-89* ☎ *64.49.012, map **2**B5)*; **Electra Palace** *(Ermou 5, off Syntagma Sq.* ☎ *32.23.223, map **2**D4 🐾)*; **Esperia Palace** *(Stadiou 22* ☎*32.38.001, map **1**D3)*; **Olympic Palace** *(Filelinon 16* ☎ *32.37.611, map **2**D4)*.

Moderately priced hotels (3,500-9,000dr)

More than 200 class-B and C hotels exist in Athens. Most accept charge and credit cards, but only some offer air conditioning.

ACROPOLIS HOUSE (B)
Kodrou 6-8, Plaka ☎*32.22.344.*
*Map **1**E3. 20 rms.*
One of the few good hotels in Plaka, housed in an old family mansion. A favorite of academics and journalists. Rooms of widely varying standards.

ADONIS (B)
Kodrou 3, Plaka ☎*32.49.737.*

*Map **1**E3. 25 rms.*
Attractive roof garden overlooking the Acropolis, for breakfast and drinks.

APHRODITE (C)
Apollonos 21, between Syntagma Sq. and Plaka
☎*32.34.357. Map **1**D3. 84 rms*
〔AE〕 ⊙ 〔●〕 〔VISA〕 ▦
Excellent value, offering good

location and modern, efficient service. Top floors have good views.

ARIANE HOTEL APARTMENTS (A)
Timoleontos Vassou 22
☎ *64.66.361. Off map 2C6. 26 rms* AE ⊙ CB VISA ▤
In a quiet residential area near the US Embassy, one of the best of furnished apartment accommodations. Breakfast served.

AVA (A)
Lisikratous 9, between Plaka and Syngrou ☎ *32.36.618. Map 1E3. 25 rms* AE ⊙ CB VISA ▤ *in some rooms.*

Modern hotel, at 7,000dr one of the least expensive in class A.

OMIROS (B)
Apollonos 15, at the edge of Plaka ☎ *32.25.486. Map 1D3. 37 rms* AE ⊙ CB VISA
Handy location, acceptable standards, roof garden.

PALLADION (B)
Panepistimiou 54 ☎ *36.23.291/5. Map 1C3. 50 rms.*
Mildewed grandeur with marble staircases, 5m (16ft) ceilings, echoing hallways and falling plaster.

Inexpensive hotels (less than 4,000dr)

These do not have restaurants or air conditioning, nor do they accept charge and credit cards unless otherwise noted. As a rule, rooms do not have private bath.

ART GALLERY PENSION
Erechtheou 3 ☎ *92.31.933. Map 1E3.*
Pleasantly furnished and friendly place in the heart of Plaka.

ATHENS CONNECTION
Ioulianou 20 ☎ *82.13.940. Map 1B3.*
Between the Athens Station and the National Archeological Museum. One of the best among the many very cheap hostels in this area.

IDEAL
Voreas 2 (corner of Eolou). Map 1D3.
Nice old building, friendly service, few tourists.

JOSEPH'S PENSION
M. Mousourou 13 ☎ *92.31.204. Map 2E4.*
Fine Neoclassical mansion run by

young foreigners. Informal atmosphere in a part of town little visited by tourists.

OMONIA (C)
Omonia Sq. ☎ *52.37.210/20. Map 1C3* AE
Vast hotel, cheap rates, on the city's noisiest square.

PELLA INN (C)
Ermou 104, Monastiraki ☎ *32.12.229. Map 1D3.*
Mostly student clientele. Telephone in every room, balcony views of the Acropolis.

PHEDRE
Herefontos 16 ☎ *32.38.461. Map 1E3.*
A somewhat run-down hotel, but in one of the most pleasant and quiet corners of Plaka, near the Lysikrates monument.

Youth hostels

A member's card is required to stay in any of the Greek Youth Hostels, obtainable for a small fee at the **Greek Youth Hostels Association** (*Dragatsianou 4, off Stadiou* ☎ *32.34.107, map 1 D3*). An overnight stay costs from 500-1,000dr.
Youth Hostel Peoniou 57 (near Athens Station, map **1**B2) ☎ 88.32.878
Youth Hostel Damareos 75 (Pangrati, off map **2**E6) ☎ 75.19.530
YMCA Omirou 28 (map **2**D4) ☎ 36.26.970
YWCA Amerikis 11 (map **2**D4) ☎ 36.24.291

Camping

The best and nearest campsite in the Athens area is the **GNTO Camping** in the suburb of **Voula** (*16km/10 miles from* *downtown* ☎ *89.51.646 or 89.53.248).* Private campsites exist in Rafina, Kifissia, Daphni, Marathon, Sounion, Nea Makri and Varkiza. Camping in the open is not permitted.

Where to eat in Athens

See FOOD AND DRINK, page 19, for a general introduction to Greek food and restaurant culture.

The most popular tavernas of Athens are collected in Plaka. **Kidathineon St**. forms the main axis. Expect here neither culinary excellence nor a spotless standard of service. But you will find Plaka a delightfully pleasant place to enjoy an evening meal (except in Aug, when it may get too crowded, and in mid-winter, when it is too cold to sit outside), with a cheerful atmosphere and many quietly beautiful corners that more than compensate for the distinctly average food and pedestrian wine. Although Athens has some good restaurants, none really merits a gastronomic pilgrimage, and most short-stay visitors will be perfectly satisfied by sampling the great multiplicity of Plaka tavernas, trying to discover the most charming nook or the most quaintly outrageous waiter.

Plaka

We do not single out tavernas in Plaka to mention by name, as the food is pretty much identical in most places, menus are prominently displayed, and part of the fun of eating out in Plaka lies in the strolling and choosing. Some tavernas offer live Greek music and dancing in the later hours. Many of these are to be found on and around **Mnisikleous** and at the edge of the **Acropolis**. Their bills run up about double the regular fare, or 2,000-3,000dr per person.

For those who seek some variety, the only two eating establishments in Plaka that are not regular tavernas are **Eden**, a vegetarian restaurant at Flessa 3, and **Michiko**, a Japanese restaurant on Kidathineon. **Zafiris**, on Thespidos, is noted for its wild game — a rarity in Athens.

Alternatives

Going to Piraeus for seafood and jollity is a well-established Athenian custom, and the fish tavernas at **Mikrolimano** harbor form the Piraean counterpart to Plaka. The change of setting and the cool sea breeze are welcome differences, but prices at harbor tavernas tend to be high, rarely falling under 2,500dr.

A cluster of good tavernas catering mainly to the local student and young professional clientele is to be found in the district of **Exarhia**, NE of Omonia. The fine restaurants of Athens are to be found mostly in the fashionable neighborhoods of **Kolonaki**, **Mets** and **Pangrati**. A selection of favorites is listed below.

For truly "local" color, try the various working-man's eateries located s and w of **Omonia**. One type of establishment specializes only in *patsá* (see page 21). The famous **Monastiri taverna** within the meat market on Athinas stays open 24hrs to dish out the best *patsá* in town to late revelers.

Restaurants (Greek specialties)

APOTSOS
Panepistimiou 10 ☎ *36.37.046.*
Map 2D4 🏷
Traditional *ouzerí* with an excellent

selection of *mezedes* located in an arcade just off Syntagma. A favorite spot for politicians, businessmen and resident Englishmen.

BAJAZZO
Ploutarhou 35, Kolonaki (below the Lykavitos funicular)
☎ *72.91.420. Map 2D5* IIII AE ▣ ◫ ▦
Original and at times whimsical menu includes unique treats like *calamares* stuffed with pine nuts and rice, grape leaves filled with sea bass mousse, eggplants with ouzo-flavored mincemeat. In a converted Kolonaki mansion.

CORFU
Kriezotou 6 ☎ *36.13.011. Map 2D4* IIII AE ▣ ◫ ▦
Just off Syntagma Sq., a favorite for business lunches. Efficient and polite service, but the menu is uninspired, with only a nominal touch of Corfiote specialties.

DIONYSOS (ACROPOLIS)
Robertou Galli 43 ☎ *92.33.182. Map 1E3* IIII ♫ AE ▣ ◫ ▦
Good view of the Acropolis, a rich selection of traditional Greek fare and atmospheric music show: a favorite of package tourists. Like **Dionysos** on the summit of Lykavitos (☎ *72.26.374, map 2C5* IIII) and **Zonar's** pastry store *(Panepistimiou 9* ☎ *32.30.336, map 2D4* IIII *)*, it belongs to the Zonar chain, famous for its pastries.

GEROFINIKAS
Pindarou 10, Kolonaki
☎ *98.39.093. Map 2D4* IIII ▣ ▦
A grand old restaurant, offering the very best of Constantinopolitan/Greek cuisine. Old-fashioned looks; solid and honest food.

IDEAL
Panepistimiou 46 ☎ *36.14.001. Map 1C3.*
One of Athens' oldest and much-loved culinary institutions, Ideal was destroyed by fire in 1990, but is expected to reopen after repairs.

KENTRIKO
Kolokotronis 3 ☎ *32.32.482. Map 1D3* ▯
Varied and tasty taverna fare. A favorite place for business lunches.

KOSTOYIANNIS
Zaimis 37, Exarhia ☎ *82.12.496. Map 2B4* IIII AE ▣ ◫ ▦
Famous taverna with a vast selection, including game dishes and excellent desserts. Closed Sun.

MANESIS
Markou Mousourou 3
☎ *92.27.684. Map 2E4* IIII ▯
One of several interesting taverna/restaurants along this street patronized by the literati and yuppies (other good ones are **Arditos Hill** and **Taverna Pergoulia)**. Specialties from the Ionian islands. Open for dinner only.

TA NISSIA
In Hilton hotel ☎ *72.20.201. Map 2D6* IIII AE ▣ ◫ ▦
Traditional Greek and international cuisine with a Lucullan buffet board.

SOCRATES' PRISON
Mitseon 20 and Makrigianni
☎ *92.23.434. Map 1E3* IIII AE ▣ ◫ ▦
Amazing variety of *mezedes*. A favorite of package tours.

O VRAHOS
Likavitou 8, Kolonaki. Map 2D4 ▯
Charming taverna run by equally charming old couple.

Restaurants (international)
What are known as "French" restaurants in Athens tend to be remote echoes of the real article serving mainly culinary clichés. The two included below are among the exceptions to the rule. Athens' clutch of Chinese restaurants is generally adequate. A number of Arabic, Indian and other Asian restaurants have recently appeared in the area around the airport and Faliro.

L'Abreuvoir
Xenokratous 51, Kolonaki
☎ *72.29.061. Map 2D5* IIII AE ▣ ◫ ▦
The menu may be unadventurous, but this is one of the most highly regarded of Athens' French restaurants, with a commendable selection of wines.

Balthazar
Tsoha 27, Kolonaki ☎ *64.41.215. Off map 2C6* IIII AE ▣ ◫ ▦
Very fashionable place featuring famous bar frequented by prominent personalities and beautiful people. Located in a renovated mansion. International menu: Italian dishes and curries.

Brasserie des Arts
In Hotel Meridien, Syntagma Sq.
☎32.55.301/9. Map 2D4 ⅢⅡ AE
⊡ ⊡ VISA

An excellent French chef and maybe
the classiest service in Athens.

Chang's House
*Doiranis 15 (turn right at
Syngrou 190)* ☎95.95.191 ⅢⅡ AE
⊡ ⊡ VISA

160 varieties of Chinese dishes.
Closed for lunch on Sun.

China
*Efroniou 72, Ilissia (beyond the
Hilton)* ☎72.33.200 ⅢⅡ AE ⊡ ⊡
VISA

The best chefs from Taiwan and
Hong Kong. Luxurious decor.

Hlorofili
Soultani 12, Exarhia. Map 2C4 ⅢⅡ

Graceful vegetarian restaurant with
attached health-food store. Dinner
only.

Kublai Khan
*In Hotel Athenaeum
Intercontinental, Syngrou 89*
☎90.23.666 ⅢⅡ AE ⊡ ⊡ VISA

Mongolian cuisine: barbecue and
firepot. Also Chinese specialties.
Dinner only. Closed Sun.

Maralinas
Vrassida 11, near the Hilton
☎72.35.425. Map 2D6 ⅢⅡ ♫ AE
⊡ ⊡ VISA

Lebanese specialties. Live Arabic
music after 11pm.

The Plowman
*Iridanou 26, Ilissia (near the
Holiday Inn)* ☎72.10.244 ⅢⅡ AE
⊡ ⊡ VISA

English fare and ambience,
complete with dartboard and
lukewarm beer. Closed Sun.

Steak Room
Eginitou 6 ☎72.17.445 ⅢⅡ AE ⊡
⊡ VISA

Located between Hilton and the US
Embassy, and serving good, juicy
steaks — a rare delicacy in Greece.

Symposium
On Erechtheou. Map 1E3 ⅢⅡ AE

Considered by many to be the best
"international" restaurant in town.
Good bar, view of the Acropolis.

Da Walter
Anapiron Polemou 4, Kolonaki
☎72.48.726. Map 2D5 ⅢⅡ AE ⊡
⊡ VISA

Excellent Italian food. Closed Sun.

For a quick snack

There are cafés and snack bars galore in Athens; the following
are conveniently located and perform well as what the Germans
call a *Treffpunkt:* a good place to meet someone, or just to keep
in mind as a point of reference in a busy city.

Brazilian Coffee Shop   Voukourestiou 1, just off Syntagma.
Map 2D4 ⅠⅡ A stand-up coffee-shop with good pastries; a
perennial Athens favorite and meeting point of the literati.
Byzantine Room ⅢⅡ Fine cafeteria in the **Hilton** *(map 2 D6)*
with a pleasant, greenhouse décor.
GB Corner ⅢⅡ Very "English" coffee-shop of **Hotel Grande
Bretagne** *(map 2 D4)*, with separate entrance. Lunch fare.
Jimmy's Coffeeshop   Valaoritou 7, two blocks from
Parliament. Map 2D4 ⅠⅡ A permanently crowded café and snack
bar catering equally to students, businessmen and Foreign
Ministry personnel.
Orea Ellada   Located upstairs from the Center of Hellenic
Tradition *(entered through a passage at Pandrossou 36, map
1 D3)*. Truly pleasant cafe with superb view of the Acropolis.

Nightlife and entertainment

In general, "authentic" Greek entertainment seems to be reserved
for tourists, while Athenians themselves prefer Western music and
dance. The spirit of Zorba the Greek pervades **Plaka** at night. For a
somewhat more sophisticated, and darker, strain of the Greek soul,
try one of the *rembetika* clubs in **Exarhia**.

Greek nights

Plenty of tavernas in **Plaka**, notably those located on
Mnisikleous and at the edge of **Acropolis hill**, offer Greek
song-and-dance shows, often with the active participation of
patrons. Similar establishments of varying degrees of
sophistication exist on **Syngrou**, in **Piraeus** and along the
Saronic coast toward the airport. Some, notably those on the
coast and in outlying areas of the city, are frequented by locals as
well as foreigners; these tend to feature a greater proportion of
Europeanized tunes and semi-rock rhythms.

The categories of musical taverna, nightclub and *bouzoúkia*
(from *bouzoúki,* a stringed instrument) are used more or less
interchangeably; the Athenian colloquialism is *skillárika,* or
"doghouse." All serve full meals along with *ouzo* and other
alcohol — Greeks rarely drink without food and company —
although the food as a rule is irritatingly expensive. Bashing
china is no longer considered polite, but some establishments
provide supplementary plates made of light plaster for patrons
who wish to engage in this celebrated form of Greek merriment.

Dances include the *zeibékiko,* an intricate and expressive solo
dance performed by men; the *tsiftetéli,* a sort of male belly dance;
the *kasápiko,* where a string of people holding hands
synchronize their steps to a strongly rhythmical beat; and the
sérviko, a quick and lively dance. The first three are of Anatolian
origin; the fourth hails from Serbia.

The popularity of any given establishment is subject to the
vagaries of season and fashion and of the musicians featured.
Given here is a sampling of current favorites. Many places of
entertainment in central Athens close in summer; some maintain
seasonal branches on the coast or in hill suburbs such as Kifissia.

All of the following feature live Greek music and dancing; all
accept charge and credit cards. Typical hours are 10pm-3am.

Athinaia　　Posidonos 33 (on the coast) ☎94.23.089. Well
known and expensive.

Esmeralda　　Kefalinias 50, Kipseli ☎86.71.290. Off map **2**A5.
One of many musical tavernas in Kipseli frequented mostly by
Athenians. Popular *bouzoúki* singers, jolly atmosphere.

Neraida　　Vass. Georgiou B, in Kalamaki (near airport)
☎98.12.004. For many years one of Athens' most famous
nightspots; lively atmosphere.

Palace　　Syngrou 255 ☎94.24.267. Expensive and glitzy, very
often featuring the most popular stars of the season. Closed Tues.

Ravanastron　　Dimitsanis 60, Ambelokipi ☎64.49.534. Musical
taverna rarely visited by tourists, offering genuine and original
folk music from the islands and Anatolia.

Regina　　Syngrou 140 ☎92.28.902. The least expensive of the
bouzoúki joints along Syngrou. Closed Sun.

Rembetika clubs

Rembetika may be called the Greek counterpart of jazz. It was
invented in the 1920s in the down-and-out clubs of Piraeus
frequented by refugees from Asia Minor, and became the badge
of a bohemian subculture. Banned by the military regime of
1967-74, it became immensely popular among students and
intellectuals later in the 1970s. Its bleakly pessimistic themes and
expressive tunes are cherished by many as the most elegant form
of Greek music.

Rembetika clubs (often called *boites*) are concentrated in
Exarhia; the following is a small selection. Performances start
about 10.30pm, but things don't really start rolling before

midnight. Some places serve food, costing somewhere between 2,000-3,000dr. Reservations are recommended.

Frangosyriani   Arahovis 57, Exarhia ☎36.00.693. Map **2**C4. Closed Thurs.

Rembetiki Istoria   Ippokratous 181, Exarhia ☎64.24.937. Map **2**C5. Closed Mon, Tues, Wed.

Taksimi   Isavron 29, Exarhia ☎36.39.919. Map **2**C4. Closed Wed.

Bars
Western-style cocktail bars, very often featuring piano or guitar music, became all the rage in the 1980s with Athens' young urban professional classes. Most are to be found in **Kolonaki** and the area around the **Hilton hotel**. The following are currently very much "in"; those marked ⊨ offer full-scale dining as well.

To Kouti   Very nice little place hidden off lower Adrianou, near the Theseum. Map **1**D2.

Memphis   Near Hilton. Map **2**D6. Full of cute teenagers.

Mike's   Vass. Alexandrou 5, near Hilton ☎72.91.689. Map **2**D6.

Montparnasse   Haritos 32, Kolonaki ☎72.90.746. Map **2**D5 ⊨ Popular with theater people.

Radka   On Haritos St. Map **2**D5 ⊨ Excellent food, interesting people.

Remezzo   Haritos 6 ☎72.28.950. Map **2**D5. Intimate and very fashionable. Closed Sun.

Jazz, latin, rock'n'roll
Half Note   On Patriarhou Fotiou, Kolonaki ☎36.41.841. Map **2**C4. The principal jazz venue of Athens. Local and foreign bands.

Latin   Kalidromiou 69, Exarhia ☎36.45.978. Map **2**C4. Unique in Greece, offering Peruvian, salsa, tango, etc. on different nights.

Rock'n'Roll Cafe   On Loukianou, Kolonaki. Map **2**D5 ⊨ Best rock in Athens, but no dancing.

Discotheques
Popular discos in Plaka come and go with the seasons. Athenians themselves prefer places on the coast and near the airport.

Barbarella   Syngrou 253 ☎94.25.601 ⊨ Three dance floors, Barbarella girls.

9+9 (Enéa syn enéa)   Agras 5 (near the Stadium). Map **2**E5 ☎72.22.258 ⊨ So sure of its leadership among Athenian discos that the name isn't even displayed. Closed in summer.

Papagayo   Patriarhou Ioakim 38, Kolonaki ☎72.40.736. Map **2**D5 ⊨ A favorite with the gilded youth of Kolonaki.

Floor-show and striptease
A number of establishments in the vicinity of **Syntagma** offer strip shows and associated pleasures. The following are considered reputable places. Both open 11pm-3pm and welcome charge and credit cards. To find the less reputable ones, it is sufficient to hang around Syntagma late at night and look aimless; someone is certain to approach with a proposal.

Copacabana   Kallirois 4 (across the Temple of Olympian Zeus) ☎92.32.648. Map **1**E3.

Maxim   Othonos 6 (Syntagma Sq.) ☎32.34.831. Map **2**D4.

Gambling
The only casino in Athens is located in the **Mt. Parnes Hotel** (☎24.69.111/4), at the top of the funicular at an elevation of 1,100m (3,609ft).

Arts and festivals

Classical music and opera do not have an established tradition in Greece, despite such illustrious exports as Maria Callas and Dimitri Mitropoulos. The opening of the **Palace of Music** in May 1991, after nearly 30yrs in construction, may now breathe some life into the relatively placid concert scene.

Exhaustive **listings** of concerts, lectures, art galleries, exhibitions, theater and cinema is to be found in the monthly *Athenian*.

The **Acropolis Sound and Light Show** can be watched from the **Pnyx** in English from 9-9.45pm and in German or French from 10-10.45pm (☎ *92.26.210* ☎ *500dr*). The words are so corny that it may be advisable to choose a language you don't know.

Foreign **films** are as a rule shown in the original language with Greek subtitles. Several movie theaters in the central area change their films daily for the benefit of a clientele consisting mainly of tourists. Most theaters functioning in summer are in the open air.

Greek **TV** often broadcast English-language movies with Greek subtitles. The **US Armed Forces Radio** operates on 1484 and 1594 Khz AM, with news every hour. The **Olympic Action Radio** broadcasts 24hrs of news and entertainment in English culled from the BBC, VOA and CNN on 102.1 FM.

Festivals and special events

The **Blessing of the sea** is performed at **Piraeus** and other ports on Jan 6. A cross is immersed in the sea and retrieved by swimmers.

Carnival is celebrated throughout Greece with processions, costumes and dances during the eight days preceding Shrove Monday (Feb or Mar, usually later than Catholic countries). Lively shows at **Plaka**.

St George's Day is commemorated on Apr 23 in many places with picturesque folk festivals involving dances, buffoonery, and blessing of the cattle, notably at **Aharnes** outside Athens and at **Arahova** near Delphi.

Easter is by far the most important religious and popular feast for Greeks. The Greek Orthodox Easter does not usually coincide with the Western date, being set between 1 and 4wks later. On **Good Friday** bells toll and flags fly at half-mast. At night, Christ's funeral procession is carried through the main streets of every parish. Particularly impressive is the procession from the **Metropolis** round **Syntagma Sq**. in Athens. After the **Sat night** mass, the light of resurrection is passed from candle to candle, and taken home lit. In Athens there is a moving spectacle from the hill of **Lykavitos**, when one church after another in the darkened city bursts into light to the ringing of bells. The fast is broken with *magirítsa* (thick soup with lamb's innards). **Easter Sunday** is celebrated with lamb roasted on the spit; rejoicing and dancing continue on **Easter Monday**.

The **Athens Festival** runs from June to mid-Sept, during which period the ancient **Odeon of Herodes Atticus** on the s slope of the Acropolis becomes a stage for ancient Greek drama performed in the original tongue, as well as operas, ballets and concerts performed by both Greek and foreign companies. The setting is impressive, and you don't have to be fluent in Classical Greek: just read your Sophocles beforehand and you'll be quite able to enjoy the drama. *(Information and tickets from the Athens Festival box office, Stadiou 4 ☎ 32.27.944, map 2 D4).*

Plays ancient and modern are performed also at the open-air theater on **Lykavitos** hill.

Greek **folk dancing** is presented at the open-air theater on **Philopappos** hill by the Dora Stratou company at 10.25pm every summer night, with additional performances at 8.15pm on Wed and Sun (☎ *32.44.395*).

The **Assumption of the Virgin** is celebrated on Aug 15 by important festivities in many locations around Greece, though festivities in Athens are unimpressive. A major pilgrimage takes place on the island of **Tinos**.

Shopping in Athens

Anything that you would like to buy in Greece can be bought in Athens, and often easier, cheaper and better than elsewhere. Handicrafts, gold and silver jewelry, and furs are what most visitors find interesting.

Bear in mind that the export of antiquities and works of art is prohibited except by written permission from the **Department of Antiquities** at Polygnotou 13.

Souvenirs and handicrafts

Souvenir stores exist in great abundance in **Plaka** and **Monastiraki**, with **Adrianou**, **Pandrossou** and **Ifestou** forming the principal shopping axes. Museum copies of pottery, sculpture and icons predominate. Some of the earthenware looks quite nice but is not recommended for practical use.

Traditional handicrafts have declined to a uniform level of execrable kitsch, with lamentably few exceptions. Individual artists producing modernistic designs based on Greek themes occasionally come up with some fairly creditable work. Among traditional products the vividly dyed cotton *flokáti* rugs and *tagária*, the shopping bags made from coarse wool, deserve mention. These are made in the Vlah villages of central and NW Greece, important centers being Arahova, near Delphi, and Metsovo.

For detailed information about **folk art** it is worth applying to the **National Organization of Greek Handicrafts** (*Mitropoleos 9, on the s side of Ermou, map 1 D3*). This has a large, priced display, and will provide a list of stores where purchases at these set prices can be made.

A delightfully chaotic **flea market** operates along Ifestou, with its hub in the area around the **Avisinías** marketplace, in Monastiraki (*map 1 D2*), on Sun morning and to a lesser extent throughout the week. Everything from second-hand clothes and spare parts to ancient photographs and phonographs is touted. The likelihood of finding a secret gem is next to nil, but the rummaging and bargaining is nevertheless great fun.

Seekers of **curiosities** may discover interesting items in the stores for ecclesiastical paraphernalia, located on Filotheis St. between the Metropolis (cathedral) and the Archbishopric of Athens.

Jewelry

Gold jewelry forms a major category of interest because of the unique Greek designs, not because they have any claim to keen prices or superlative workmanship. The mother houses of two worldwide jewelry chains, **Lalaounis** (*Panepistimiou 6, map 2 D4, and many branches in town*) and **Zolotas** (*Panepistimiou 10, map 2 D4, and branch at the airport*), are both located near

Syntagma. Both carry a wide selection of museum reproductions, as do many lesser jewelers located in their immediate vicinity and in Plaka.

Silver filigree and turquoise jewelry, produced mainly in the town of Ioannina in Epiros, forms a separate category that features Oriental rather than Classical motifs. The main concentration of Ioannina silversmiths in Athens is in **Leka St**., off Ermou *(map 1 D3)*.

Fur

Furs are very much in a class of their own, for no animal ever wore such coats. They are made of scraps and snippets left over from cutting, sent from all over the world to the town of Kastoria in Macedonia, where they are pieced together with a skill perfected over centuries. They are sold by the meter like any other textile, and eventually end up as mink coats, leopard jackets or beaver hats, though they are much cheaper than the orthodox article.

A great variety of furriers are to be found on **Mitropoleos St**. *(map 1 D3)*, the heart of the fur trade in Athens. **Sistovaris** *(branches also at Ermou 4, map 2 D4, and Panepistimiou 9, map 2 D4)* is the leading establishment in Kastoria furs, sold by the meter or in every kind of clothing.

Clothing

Except for souvenir shirts and whimsical beachwear, there is little reason to buy clothes in Greece. Neither price nor quality is particularly attractive, and fashions echo the West — at a considerable distance. The more elegant shops are to be found along **Stadiou** and in the area from **Syntagma** to **Kolonaki Sq**., notably **Voukourestiou** and side streets. Cheaper clothes stores cluster together on **Ermou** between **Syntagma** and **Monastiraki**.

Minion *(28 Oktovriou and Veranzerou, map 1 C3)* is the best **department store** in the city, with a comprehensive selection of both local and imported labels, a fine food store and a roof cafeteria.

Leather goods, sold in abundance, are generally of above-average quality and reasonably priced. **Eleni** *(Kriezotou 14, off Syntagma, map 2 D4)*, **Skourletis** *(Ermou 28, map 1 D3)* and **Viennezikon** *(Stadiou 9, map 2 D4)* are among the better shops.

Books and records

The most extensive selection of **foreign-language books** is to be found at **Eleftheroudakis** *(Nikis 4* ☎ *32.21.231, map 1 D3)*, **Compendium** *(Nikis 28* ☎ *32.21.248, map 1 D3)* and **Pentelides** *(Amerikis 11, map 2 D4)*. Bookstores in all luxury hotels, as well as **Reymondo's** *(Voukourestiou 18, map 2 D4)*, stock a variety of periodicals, books on Greece and current paperbacks. **Turtle Bookshop** *(Patriarhou Ioakim 24, Kolonaki, map 2 D5)* has a charming collection of children's books.

The best place to look for **antique and out-of-print books** is the **flea market** along Ifestou. For specialized help, try **Pharos/Athens** *(P.O.B. 1826* ☎ *72.42.589)*.

Souvenir **cassettes** of Greek music are thick on the ground in Plaka. A more extensive and sober collection can be found at **Filodisk** *(Emm. Benaki, off Panepistimiou, map 1 C3)* or at the commendable **Eleftheroudakis Music Center** *(Tower of Athens* ☎ *77.96.589)*.

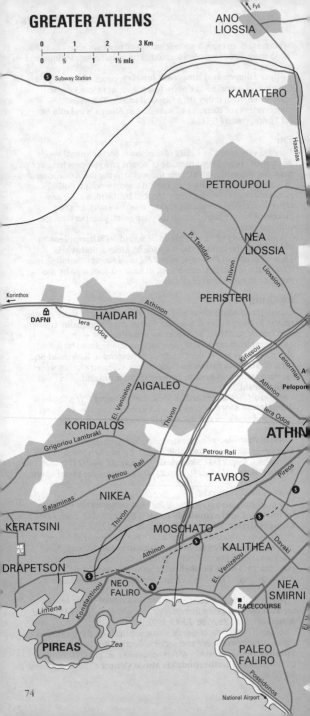

GREATER ATHENS

0   1   2   3 Km
0   ½   1   1½ mls

S Subway Station

↑ Fyli

ANO LIOSSIA

KAMATERO

Hassias

PETROUPOLI

NEA LIOSSIA

P. Tsaldari

Thivon

Liossion

← Korinthos

⌂ DAFNI

HAIDARI

Iera Odos

Athinon

PERISTERI

Kifissou

Lenorman

AIGALEO

El. Venizelou

Thivon

Iera Odos

Athinon

Pelopon

KORIDALOS

Grigoriou Lambraki

ATHIN

Petrou Rali

Petrou Rali

TAVROS

Pireos

S

Salaminas

NIKEA

Thivon

MOSCHATO

S

KALITHEA

Davaki

KERATSINI

Athinon

S

NEA SMIRNI

DRAPETSON

Konstantinou

NEO FALIRO

S

El. Venizelou

Limena

RACECOURSE

PIREAS

Zea

PALEO FALIRO

Possidonos

National Airport

74

Leisure, sports, ideas for children

Sea

Public beaches exist all along the sw and e coasts of Attica. The sea near Piraeus is polluted. It may at times get somewhat murky as far as Glyfada and Voula, though the periodic alarms about pollution in the Saronic Gulf seem vastly exaggerated. See COASTAL SUBURBS (opposite) for more details.

Information about scuba diving, water skiing, wind surfing, sailing and other water sports can be obtained from the respective sport federations; these may be contacted through the **GNTO**.

Walks and mountain sports

Athens has fewer parks than any European city of comparable size, and the absence of other natural promenades (riverbank, harbor walk) is at times acutely felt. The **National Garden** *(map 1 E4)* is just about the only option in town for a (relatively) quiet stroll amid greenery. The best place for a nature walk near Athens is **Mt. Parnes**, which offers a 14km (9-mile) loop around its summit through woods and bush.

The **Hellenic Alpine Club** *(Ermou 52 ☎ 32.12.429, map 1 D3)* maintains mountain refuges at a variety of places around Greece, including one at **Bafi** (alt. 1,150m/3,773ft) on Mt. Parnes.

Ski facilities exist on **Mts. Parnassus** and **Olympus**, though skiers should be warned that, apart from their association with gods, neither the snow nor the facilities afford overmuch pleasure.

Golf

There is an 18-hole course at **Glyfada** *(near the airport ☎ 89.46.820)*, and there is a 9-hole course at **Varibobi** *(21km/13 miles N)*.

Ideas for children

The **Lykavitos funicular** *(map 2 C5)* should fascinate children of all ages. The **Koutouki cave** at Peania (16km/10 miles E) is full of stalactites and stalagmites.

Three museums could be of particular interest to children: the **Goulandris Museum of Natural History** *(Levidou 13, Kifissia ☎ 80.80.254, open Sat-Thurs 9am-2.30pm, closed Fri and mid-July to mid-Aug)* contains a fascinating collection of nature's curiosities; the **War Museum** *(Vass. Sofias and Rizari ☎ 72.90.543, map 2 D5, open Tues-Sun 9am-2pm, closed Mon)* has a range of antique and modern airplanes parked in its courtyard; and the **Piraeus Maritime Museum** *(Akti Themistokleous, near Zea Marina ☎ 45.16.822, open Tues-Sat 8.30am-1pm, closed Sun, Mon)* displays model ships from ancient to modern times.

Outskirts of Athens

Located within less than an hour of downtown Athens and accessible by urban public transportation are a second city (**Piraeus**), a lively seacoast (**Piraeus** and the **coastal suburbs**), three grand mountains (**Hymettus**, **Pendeli** and **Parnitha**) and two important medieval monasteries (**Daphni** and **Kesariani**). There are, too, some badly polluted wastelands (Elefsina, for one).

COASTAL SUBURBS 🚇

6km (4 miles) to 23km (14 miles) s of Athens. Bus to Paleo Faliro, Agios Kosmas, Elinikon from Syntagma Sq. (map 2D4); to Glyfada, Voula, Vouliagmeni, Varkiza from Leof. Olgas (map 2E4).

The Saronic coast from Piraeus to the headland of Vouliagmeni is densely built with summer apartments, hotels, nightclubs, yacht marinas and beach and sport facilities. On summer weekends the area tends to get extremely crowded. The continuous din of the multilane highway that runs close to the shore and the noise of airplane traffic from the Elinikon Airport are equally disturbing factors.

The beaches at **Fáliro** and **Glyfáda** (8km/5miles and 18km/11 miles respectively) are not recommended, though they remain as popular as ever with Athenians. Both the setting and the sea get considerably better at **Voula** (22km/14 miles), while **Vouliagmeni** (24km/15 miles) is a highly attractive town with luxurious park-like vegetation, elegant hotels and excellent beaches. In addition, Vouliagmeni has a small sulfurous lake with dramatically overhanging rocks, where the last spurs of **Mt. Ímitos** come down to the sea; the baths are said to cure arthritis, rheumatism and gynecological ailments.

The best **public beaches** are those operated by the GNTO, which exist at **Voula 1** (☎ 89.53.248) and **2** (☎ 89.59.569), **Vouliagmeni** (☎ 89.60.906) and **Varkiza** (☎ 89.72.102). All are well-managed and have cabins, cafeterias, tennis courts and other sport facilities.

🛏 **Astir Palace** (L) at Vouliagmeni (☎ 89.60.211 or 89.60.602 ▥▥ *three separate compounds* ⇌ 🚇 ☐ ὁ Ⓐ 💿 🔲 🎴) is not only the most luxurious hotel of the area but possibly the best beach hotel in the whole of Greece.

Another **Astir Hotel** (L) exists at Glyfada (☎ 89.44.273 ▥▥ *bungalows* ⇌ 🚇 ≈ ☐ ὁ Ⓐ 💿 🎴).

Of the half-dozen class-A beach hotels at **Voula** and **Vouliagmeni**, **Armonia** (☎ 89.60.105 ▥▥ *80 rms* ⇌ 🚇 ≈ ☐ ὁ Ⓐ 💿 🔲 🎴) is the largest and best-established. **Costi** (☎ 89.61.007 ▥), a small, well-kept pension, **Greek Coast** (☎ 89.60.401 ▥▥) and **Margi House** (☎ 89.62.061 ▥▥) deserve mention.

A very large number of hotels in all categories is to be found at **Glyfada/ Elinikon**. Except in peak season, prices tend to be substantially lower than at comparable establishments in Athens or at major resorts elsewhere in Greece. Examples:

Emmantina (A) Vassilissis Georgiou 33 ☎89.32.111/5 ▥ ⇌ 🚇 ▦ 💿 🔲 🎴

Golden Sun (B) Metaxa 72, Glyfada ☎89.55.218/9 ▥ ⇌ 🚇 ▦ Ⓐ 💿 🔲 🎴

Beau Rivage (C) Vassilissis Georgiou 87 ☎89.49.292 ▥ ⇌ 🚇 ▦ 💿

⇌ The coast is popular with Athenians as a place to go out dining, and thus abounds in fine restaurants. Notable are various attractively located fish restaurants at **Vouliagmeni** (expensive) and a string of — for Greece — unusual cuisines (Arabic, Indian, Vietnamese, Korean) represented at **Glyfada/Kalamaki**.

Ithaki Apollonos 28, Vouliagmeni ☎89.63.747 ▥ Set in a lovely garden overlooking the sea. Excellent seafood; piano music.

Mooring's At the Vouliagmeni Marina ☎89.61.113 ▥▥ One of Athens' classiest restaurants, which is popular with yachtsmen and Sunday diners alike.

Singa Litous 1, Vouliagmeni ☎89.60.676 ▥ The only Melanesian restaurant in Greece. Sunday buffet lunch.

Viet Hy Posidonos 43, Kalamaki ☎93.35.666 ▥ 💿 Excellent Vietnamese fare.

DAPHNI MONASTERY ⛪ ☆

Located on Athens-Corinth highway 11km (7 miles) W of Athens ☎ 58.11.558. Map 7D1. 20mins by bus 026 from Syntagma Sq. (map 2D4) 🚌 200dr. Open Tues-Fri 8am-7pm, Sat-Mon 8.30am-3pm.

The monastery is considered the most important Byzantine monument in the vicinity of Athens on account of its brilliant but partially preserved **mosaics** of c.1100. A popular **wine festival** is held here every day from early July through late Aug.

The monastery occupies the site where ancient Athenians believed that the nymph Daphne, escaping the unwelcome attentions of Apollo, had metamorphosed herself into a laurel tree *(daphne).* A sanctuary of Apollo with a sacred laurel grove occupied the site until its destruction by the Goths in 395. An early monastery emerged in the 6thC, but the current edifice dates from 1080. The Cistercian order possessed the monastery in the Frankish epoch, and several Dukes of Athens including Othon de la Roche and Walter de Brienne are buried here. Reverting to Orthodox monks under Turkish rule, it was abandoned at the time of the war of independence.

Neither the site nor, strictly speaking, the architecture of the monastery is very attractive. However, its Byzantine mosaics, in a sparse, severe style, are the best in Greece and among the most important in the world after those of Ravenna and Istanbul.

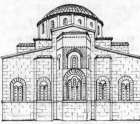

The 11thC church at **Daphni** typifies the single-dome cross-in-square plan.

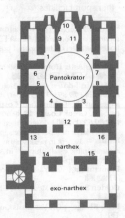

Key to mosaics
1 Annunciation; 2 Nativity; 3 Baptism; 4 Transfiguration; 5 Entry into Jerusalem; 6 Crucifixion; 7 Resurrection; 8 Thomas; 9 Michael; 10 Virgin with Child; 11 Gabriel; 12 Assumption of the Virgin; 13 Last Supper; 14 Judas' Betrayal; 15 Prayer of Joachim and Anna; 16 Presentation of the Virgin

The thematic arrangement of the mosaics follows standard late Byzantine practice. Christ Pantocrator (Almighty) occupies the central dome surrounded by Old Testament prophets (elsewhere: the 12 Apostles); the gold background signifies Heaven. On the dome of the main apsis is the Mother of God rising above the archangels. The area under the dome is reserved for the principal church festivals; in corners and lesser surfaces are the saints and martyrs. The arrangement reflects the heavenly hierarchies. The narthex (inner vestibule before the main hall) is the preserve of worldlier scenes from the New Testament; over the main gate stands the theme to which the church is dedicated, here the Assumption of the Virgin. Depictions of sin and hell are usually found in the exonarthex (outer vestibule at church entrance — here scrubbed clear of mosaics).

ELEUSIS *(Elefsína)* 🏛

20km (13 miles) w of Athens. Map 4H7. Population 20,000.
Bus from Eleftherias Sq. (map 1C2). Archeological area
signposted from the highway. Open Tues-Sun
8.30am-5pm. Closed Mon 💰*200dr.*

Elefsína is an industrial wasteland with a small archeological
area. It will principally interest the determined scholar, or the rare
romantic who is familiar with the pomp and beauty of ancient
Eleusinian Mysteries.

From the earliest (possibly pre-Greek) times, Eleusis was a
sanctuary of the cult of Demeter and Kore, whose rites became
one of the most important religious celebrations of Antiquity.
Unlike most ancient rites, the worship of Demeter was an *esoteric*
cult: that is, one in which only those initiated in its mysteries
could take part. The nature of these mysteries remains unknown
to the present day.

‡ *Demeter, the goddess of agriculture, had a daughter called*
Persephone or Kore (Girl), who was abducted by Hades while
picking flowers in a field. The goddess wandered around the
world in despair, but was taken in by the kindly king of Eleusis,
and here she taught mankind how to sow and reap the earth. By
special dispensation from Zeus, Persephone was allowed to
return to the earth for half of the year (time of growth and
fertility), but went back to the lord of the underworld for the rest
of the time.

The Mysteries were celebrated each year in March and October.
For the Greater Eleusinia in October a great multitude of the
initiates *(mystae)* arrived in Athens from around Greece. On the
sixth day a procession wearing myrtle branches and carrying
torches and farm implements set out for Eleusis. Here the
participants stripped off their clothes and took a ritual bath in the
sea. On the tenth day they were allowed into the *Telesterion,* the
inner sanctum of the goddess, where the sacred cult objects were
revealed to them, whose nature was a secret to be kept under
pain of death.

It was at the communal bathing at Eleusis that Praxiteles, the
greatest sculptor of the 4thC BC, was said to have first seen
Phyrne, a priestess of Aphrodite (in other words, a temple
prostitute), who inspired his *Bathing Aphrodite (the Aphrodite of*
Cnidus).

The Eleusinian mysteries remained popular through the Roman
centuries. Emperors Hadrian, Marcus Aurelius and Julian were
initiated, as was Cicero. Certain aspects of the rites (baptism by
water, death and rebirth of a divinity, revelation of sacraments)
appear to have been widely influential around the time of the
birth of Christianity.

The colossal cult statue of Demeter was still revered at the
beginning of the last century by superstitious peasants, who
pasted it with cow dung to ensure a fertile harvest. It was then
acquired by an English adventurer named E.D. Clarke, who
planned to remove it to Cambridge, but was lost with everyone
else on board when the ship carrying it sunk off the English
shore.

In the archeological area one can see sad, broken bits of the
Telesterion and associated buildings. The **museum** contains a
small number of quite interesting items, including a magnificent
7thC BC amphora (narrow-rimmed urn) illustrating the *Blinding*
of Polyphemus in a grandly stylized manner.

FÁLIRO   See COASTAL SUBURBS.

GLYFÁDA   See COASTAL SUBURBS.

HYMETTUS (Ímitos)   See KESARIANI.

KESARIANÍ MONASTERY ⛪ ☆
*8km (5 miles) E of Athens. Map 7D2. Trolley #2 from
Syntagma Sq. (map 2D4) to Kesariani district, then 40min
walk: easier by taxi. Open Tues-Sun 8.30am-3pm. Closed
Mon.*

The late Byzantine monastery of Kesariani is an intensely
charming and peaceful place with a fine distant view of the
Acropolis. Although long abandoned by the monks, the site
retains an intimate and monastic atmosphere.

The origins of the monastery are unknown, although the main
buildings date from the 11th-12thC. The name is also obscure:
one explanation refers to Hadrian, the Caesar, who built an
aqueduct here, another to a holy icon brought from Caesarea in
Cappadocia (Turkey). In 1456 the abbot of Kesariani was chosen
to present the keys of Athens to Mehmed the Conqueror, no
doubt reflecting the monks' predilection toward the Turks as
against their Latin masters, typical of the Orthodox monastic
establishment of the period. The Turks held the monastery in
high regard and exempted it from taxes. In the 16th-17thC it was
well known for its olive press, wine, and apiaries producing the
famous Hymettian honey.

The main church, dedicated to the Presentation of Mary, is
richly decorated with **frescoes** of the mid-16thC. The frescoes of
the narthex are dated 1682, while the poorly preserved ones in
the small side chapel go back to the 14thC. Other buildings
include the refectory, living quarters (in restoration) and a
Roman-type **bathhouse**, unique among Greek monasteries.
Numerous fragments, including an Ionic column near the church
entrance and a ram's head fountain outside, seem to have
belonged to a temple of Aphrodite known to have existed at this
site in ancient times.

A road continues from the monastery to the summit of **Mt.
Imitós** (Hymettus of Antiquity, 1,027m/3,369ft), passing by the
smaller Byzantine monastery of **Asteríou** (frescoes). The summit
is a military exclusion zone. Hymettus was known in Antiquity
for its marble and its honey, which formed a major export
product of early Athens. A statue of Zeus once stood on the peak
where a radar installation exists now.

KIFISSIÁ
*16km (10 miles) N of Athens. Map 7C2. Population 55,000.
Altitude 270m (886ft). 35mins by urban rail from Athens.*

Kifissia is the most elegant of several garden suburbs located on
high ground NE of Athens. It sports a number of sumptuous
19thC villas in Italianate style, various institutions of the Anglo-
American expatriate community, well-endowed shops selling
quality Western brands, and many young people who are
pleasant to look at. The rich greenery forms a welcome contrast
with the usual parched looks of Athens. The **Kefalari**
neighborhood at the foot of Mt. Penteli (a 15min walk E from the
train station) has the main concentration of soigné residences
and fine resort hotels. Some of the best villas are to be found
along **Tatoi St**.

Also notable are the homes of 19thC oligarchs Trikoupis
(Benaki 13), Deligiannis *(Levidou 19)*, Giorganda-Kolokotronis
(Kolokotroni 7) and Pesmazoglou *(Pesmazoglou 25)*.

The **Goulandris Museum of Natural History** (*Levidou 13,* ☎ *80.80.254, open Sat-Thurs 9am-2.30pm, closed Fri and mid-July to mid-Aug*) houses the private collection of a loving and enthusiastic amateur: plants, insects, stuffed animals, fossils and rocks.

≈ **Pentelikon** (L) (*Deliyanni 66* ☎ *80.12.837* ▥▥▥), **Cecil** (A) (*Xenias 7 and Trikoupi* ☎ *80.13.836* ▥▥▥) and **Grand Chalet** (A) (*Kokkinara 38* ☎ *80.84.837*) carry the memories and traditions of the *belle époque* of the turn of the century (*all* ▥▥▥ ⇌ ▣ ▣ ▣ ▨). There are also several class-C hotels.

The summit of **Mt. Pendéli** (◁⬱) — Mt. Pentelicon of Antiquity — can be reached via the village of Nea Pendeli (*bus from behind the National Archeological Museum; 1hr walk or taxi from Kifissia*). At the end of the road is the **Moni Pendeli**, the richest and one of the largest of the monasteries currently functioning in Greece. Signs mark the way to the **Rhododaphne Palace** (★), a sumptuous all-marble neo-Gothic villa that once belonged to the Duchesse de Plaisance (see page 59), where she is buried. The palace was later restored as a royal residence and is now sometimes used for concerts.

Several paths lead farther up to ancient and modern **marble quarries**, eventually reaching a **peak** (1,000m/3,281ft; the main summit is a restricted military zone) that offers an extraordinary view extending from Mt. Dirfis on Euboea to a large number of islands in the E and SE.

‡ *Pentelic marble was the chief material of Attic architecture and sculpture in the Classical age and constituted an important export product of ancient Athens. Its yellowish hue is due to the presence of iron, which slowly oxidizes when it comes in contact with air. The bluish Hymettian and the translucent white Parian marbles can easily be distinguished.*

MOUNT PÁRNITHA ◁⬱ ☆

35km (22 miles) N of Athens (to the hotel). Map 7C2. Bus 714 (to Agia Triada) and 736 (to the teleferique) from corner of Aharnon and Sourmeli (map 1B3).

A most spectacular view covering all of Greater Athens, most of Attica, Euboea, the Saronic Gulf and some of the Cyclades opens up at 1,100m (3,609ft), where **Grand Hotel Parnes** (A) is located. The hotel (☎ *24.69.111/15* ▥▥ ⇌ ⇌), which no longer maintains the high standards of its past, contains the only gambling casino in the Athens area and is served by a teleferique (*8am-3am daily except Wed*).

A road continues from Agia Triada (3km/2 miles before hotel) to the **refuge** of the Greek Alpine Club and on to the summit (1,413m/4,636ft) of **Karambola**.

PENDÉLI   See KIFISSIA.

PIRAEUS (*Piréas*)

8km (5 miles) SW of Athens. Map 4H7. 20mins by urban rail from Athens. Population 200,000 ℹ at Zea Marina ☎ *41.35.716 or 41.35.730.*

The port of Athens, although it has in practice fully merged with the city, is always thought of as a separate town; it has a separate mayor and fields its own soccer team (Olympiakos). Each of its three natural harbors is the focus of an urban area of very distinct character.

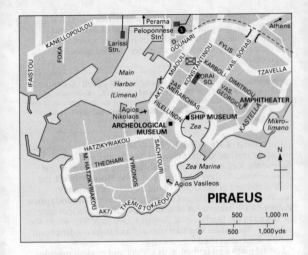

The **main harbor** (*Liména*) of Piraeus is the town's core and
raison d'être. From here passenger boats depart to more than 60
islands and a dozen countries; cargo ships representing the
world's third-largest merchant fleet (second if the various flags of
convenience used by Greek shipping magnates are counted in)
unload their wares. The embankment is full of a shabby and
aggressive worldliness, with endless travel and shipping
agencies, spend-your-last-penny-here stores, and, on more
discreet side streets, many bars and hotels of dubious flavor.

The **Zéa harbor** (until recently called **Pashalimani**)
accommodates the yachts of Athens' yachted classes and is the
hydrofoil terminal for the Saronic Islands, where the same classes
own summer property. It is surrounded by a wall of comfortable
apartment blocks, and the neighborhood possesses many shops
specializing in imported household goods.

Mikrolimano (★), popularly known by its traditional name of
Turkolimano, and the steep hill district of **Kastella** that rises
behind it, display a surprisingly cheerful small-town ambience.
The harbor is full of bright fishing boats and small craft, and
bristles with some two-dozen tavernas that manage to squeeze in
a prodigious number of tables at the water's edge. Many years
ago Turkolimano was where Athenians came to enjoy a simple
fisherman's fare. Now armies of uniformed waiters accost any
passer-by with invitations in six languages, the fish is more likely
to arrive by refrigerated truck than fisherman's dinghy, and the
bill is far from cheap. But under the limb-loosening southern sky
and sweet Aegean breeze, few people seem to mind all this, and
Mikrolimano remains a perfectly enjoyable place for a good meal
and a relaxing stroll.

Before 493BC, the Athenians simply parked their ships on the
beach at Phaleron (Fáliro). It was Themistocles who decided to
build a fortified harbor at Piraeus to underpin the new Athenian
policy of naval expansion. Pericles employed Hippodamus of
Miletus to create here the second city in the ancient world to be
laid out in a regular grid pattern (the first was the architect's own
Miletus). By 431 the Long Walls, two parallel lines of fortification
securing the Athens-Piraeus road, were completed.

Piraeus was sacked by Sulla in 86BC, and never fully recovered after this. It lay abandoned through the medieval and Turkish centuries, when the place was known as *Porto Leone* after the statue of a derelict lion lying among the rubbish. It was resettled by islanders in the 19thC, but received its real impetus for growth only with the arrival of Anatolian refugees after 1922.

The **Archeological Museum** of Piraeus *(Harilaou Trikoupi 31* ☎ *45.21.698, open standard hours)* merits a visit on sole account of the famous **Piraeus Kouros**, a splendid bronze statue of c.520BC discovered during canalization works in 1959.

✎ Most hotels in the immediate harbor area are not recommended for bona fide purposes. But several good B and C hotels exist on the streets joining the Main Harbor to Zea, others on Kastella hill. Examples:

Diogenis (B) Vass. Georgiou 27 ☎ 41.25.471 ⅢⅡ A large, modern hotel in central Piraeus.

Cavo d'Oro (B) Vass. Pavlou 19, Kastella ☎ 41.13.742 ⅢⅡ Good view of the sea and Mikrolimano.

Park (B) Kolokotroni 103 ☎ 45.24.611 ⅢⅡ A large hotel three blocks from the ferry docks.

The nearest luxury hotel is the **Athens Chandris** *(Syngrou 385, Paleo Faliro* ☎ *94.14.824* ⅢⅡ *)*.

≡ It would be pointless to list all the fish tavernas at Mikrolimano or to single out any one by name. More tavernas of the same type exist along Akti Themistokleous immediately s of Zea Marina, and on the skirts of Kastella hill between Zea and Mikrolimano.

Altogether in a class of its own is **Vasilenas** *(Etolikou 72* ☎ *46.12.457* ⅢⅡ *)*. This temple of epicurean delights counts magnates, monarchs and movie stars among its clients. Dinners consist of 16 to 24 courses served under the personal attention of the host, George Vasilenas.

≡ The seaside town of **Pérama**, about 6km (4 miles) w of Piraeus, owns an attractive harbor promenade with a lineup of fish tavernas that many Athenians consider to be superior to those of Mikrolimano.

VOULIAGMÉNI   See COASTAL SUBURBS.

Excursion 1: Attica

For Athenians, Attica equals beaches. Good beaches exist virtually everywhere along the E and sw coasts of the peninsula, and numerous sea resorts and summer colonies have sprung up to accommodate the summer crowds (see also COASTAL SUBURBS, page 77). The region offers one of the most dramatically situated ancient temples of Greece, at **Sounion**, as well as the historic battlefield of **Marathon** and several Classical sights of lesser importance.

A tour of Attica can easily be completed in one day provided you travel by car and put aside a limited time for lunch and a quick swim. It may even be possible to throw in a side trip to the peak of **Mt. Parnitha**, covered elsewhere under OUTSKIRTS OF ATHENS (page 81). A typical itinerary might then look like this:

Morning panorama at **Mt. Parnitha**, followed by side trip to **Amphiaraeum**. **Ramnous** and the **Marathon** tumuli for those especially interested in antiquities. Lunch at **Nea Mákri** or **Rafina**. **Brauron**. Beach at **Porto Ráfti** or **Kaki Thálassa**; or side trip to **Koutoúki Cave** (✱). Evening sun at **Sounion**. Back by the "Apollo Coast."

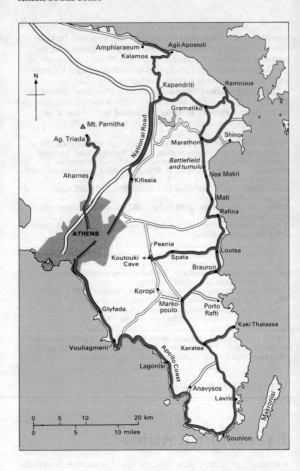

An alternative would be to combine the tour with a visit to the scenically impressive southern half of the island of **Euboea**, in which case two days should be reckoned with, choosing the pleasant harbor town of **Karystos** as a possible overnighting point. It is possible to drive onto the island by the bridge at **Halkida** and return by ferry from Karystos, or vice versa.

Length of proposed itinerary: c.230km (144 miles), excluding Mt. Parnitha, Koutouki Cave and Euboea. Note that particularly in the eastern half of the peninsula there are a great many local roads that do not appear on many maps and are very poorly signposted; so count on getting lost a few times if driving your own car.

THE SOUTH COAST

The s coast of Attica, which tourist brochures have for no apparent reason christened the **Apollo Coast**, has the more striking landscape: mountains drop quite steeply to the shore, becoming wilder toward the headland of Sounion. The land is

84

very arid, such that few villages existed here until recent times. The settlements that now dot the shore beyond the suburban limits of Athens are quite modest affairs consisting of a few hotels and clusters of summer housing. A great number of small but excellent beaches are found along the way and remain surprisingly unexploited even at the height of summer.

The best hotel along the coast is at **Lagonisi** (☎ code 0299): **Xenia Lagonisi** (L) (☎ *83.911* **IIIII** ⊒ ⌘ ≋ ♪ 🗌 ▥ 🖭 ⊙ ▣ 🚾).
Class-A hotels exist at **Anavysos** (☎ code 0299): **Saronic Gate** (☎ *53.711* **IIIII**) and at **Sounion** (☎ code 0292): **Belvedere Park** (☎ *39.102* **IIIII**); **Cape Sounion Beach** (☎ *39.391* **IIIII**); **Egeon** (☎ *39.200* **IIIII**). All ⊒ ⌘ ▥ 🖭 ⊙ ▣ 🚾
Adequate B and C hotels are located at frequent intervals.

▲ Pleasantly situated site at **Sounion** (on the way toward Lavrio).

SOUNION 🏛 📻 ★

69km (43 miles) SE of Athens. Map 7F3. Bus from Mavromateon and Leof. Alexandras (map 2B4); numerous organized tours. Temple open daily 10am-sunset 🖭*300dr* ☎*(0292) 39.363.*

The Temple of Poseidon on the barren promontory of Cape Sounion remains one of the most deeply moving sights of Greece despite the inescapable multitude of sightseers. The temple is built in the purest white marble and stands about 60m (200ft) above the sea at the edge of a cliff. About half its 34 Doric columns stand at full height (some re-erected), although the cella is gone. The view over the sea, particularly at sunset or moonlight, is striking. Byron rhapsodized it thus:

> "Place me on Sunium's marbled steep,
> Where nothing, save the waves and I,
> May hear our mutual murmurs sweep;
> There, swan-like, let me sing and die."

Cape Sounion was (and is) the last glimpse of the mainland for sailors departing from Athens and the first that would greet them on the journey home, so it made an obvious choice of location for a shrine to the god of the seamen. The present temple was erected c.440BC to replace an earlier one left unfinished by the Persian invasion.

For many centuries the secluded coves of Sounion were notorious as a pirates' haunt. As late as the end of the 19thC a group of English tourists were abducted by pirates at this spot, giving rise to the celebrated incident of the "Dilessi murders."

The temple ruins *(interior closed to visitors)* are completely covered with incised graffiti of visitors from the early 18thC to the present day. Some of the earlier inscriptions are elegant to the point of being worthy of the temple itself; but more recent efforts display a drastic and steady decline in the quality of the visitors. Among the famous signatures is that of Byron himself.

See above for hotels.

THE EAST COAST

The E coast of Attica is flatter, more fertile and more densely populated. The towns, although more substantial than on the S coast, are all of recent growth and lack any sense of traditional charm. The stretch of the shore between Brauron (Vravróna) and Marathon in particular, where the best beaches are, has begun to grow into one unbroken resort conglomerate displaying an increasingly suburban character. The landscape farther N becomes sharply mountainous, and here it is still possible to find some unspoiled corners of nature, notably at the minor historic sites of Amphiaraeum and Ramnous.

An excellent GNTO public beach exists at **Porto Ráfti.**

❧ Formerly a fishermen's hamlet, **Agii Apostoli** (☎ code 0295) has recently grown into a full-blown beach resort: **Kalamos Beach** (B) (☎ 81.339 ▥ ⯊ ☏); **Delphinia** (C) (☎ 81.202 ⬚ ⚲).

The E coast's only A hotel is near **Marathon** (☎ code 0294): **Golden Coast**, 3km (2 miles) E of town on the beach (☎ 92.102 ▥ 220 rms ▤ ⚲ ☏ ▤ ▦ ⚅ ⬭ ⬯). Many B, C and D hotels exist along the beach between the Golden Coast hotel and the tumulus.

A big concentration of good and moderate hotels exists around **Nea Makri** and **Mati** (☎ code 0294). In Mati: **Mati** (A) (☎ 71.511); in Nea Makri: **Marathon Bay** (B) (☎ 91.255), a modern, well-run beach hotel popular with European tour groups. Both ▥ ▤ ⚲ ☏ ▤ ▦ ⚅ ⬭ ▦

Rafina, surprisingly, has nothing but a few fairly run-down C hotels. There are adequate C hotels and private rooms at **Porto Rafti**, and private rooms and a nice beach at **Kaki Thalassa**

AMPHIARAEUM (Amfiaréo) 🏛 ⟨ ☆

49km (31 miles) N of Athens. Map 7B2. Bus to Kalamos from Mavromateon and Leof. Alexandras (map 2B4); then taxi or 25min walk. Archeological site open daily 8.30am-6pm. Free entrance ☎ (0295) 62.144.

The ruins of this ancient temple and spa complex dedicated to the hero-seer Amphiaraos are worth a visit less for their archeological value than for their strikingly beautiful natural setting at the foot of a forested ravine. Along the way, the **Kapandriti-Kalamos-Agii Apostoli** road offers magnificent unspoiled views toward **Euboea.**

The seer Amphiaraos of Argos fought as one of the "Seven against Thebes," and perished here when his chariot was swallowed up by the earth. A local cult associated with an oracle and a curative spa grew around his name. Pilgrims sacrificed a ram, wrapped themselves in its fleece for the night, and their dreams, interpreted by priests, advised them how to achieve a cure.

The very partially preserved **Doric temple** of the 4thC BC is a simple *prostyle* (one with only a row of columns in front of the entrance). Farther on are the remains of what must have been an impressive **colonnade** with the attached **thermal baths**, and a charming **theater** behind. Across the brook were patients' chambers and perhaps medical quarters.

6km (4 miles) down from Kalamos, the resort village of **Agii Apostóli** offers a good beach, hotels (B, C, D) and tavernas.

BRAURON (Vravróna, Vraóna) 🏛

38km (24 miles) E of Athens. Map 7D3. Bus to Markopoulo from corner of Mavromateon and Leof. Alexandras (map 2B4); then 8km (5 miles) taxi or walk. Archeological site open Tues-Sun 8.30am-3pm; closed Mon ▦200dr ☎ (0294) 71.020.

The sanctuary of Artemis Brauronia was one of the most ancient holy places of Attica, with many Archaic and violent myths associated with it. The heavily ruined remains lie on a pleasant knoll at the edge of a marsh.

The oldest Brauron myth concerned a bear, an animal sacred to Artemis, that killed a girl. Legend also said that Iphigenia, the daughter that Agamemnon wanted to sacrifice to the gods, came here with a sacred idol of Artemis and later died here. The most unusual aspect of the Brauronian cult was the company of little

Athenian girls called *arktoi* (she-bears) who lived in the sanctuary until puberty, wore saffron robes, and performed the bear-dance on certain occasions.

‡ *Peisistratus, the first nonaristocratic ruler of Athens, was a native Brauronian. He came to power by coup and ruled autocratically, but he was supported by the popular classes.*

The sanctuary consisted of a tiny **temple** and a large colonnaded enclosure containing the living quarters of the *arktoi*. A small late-Byzantine **church** was erected beside the temple ruins. The **museum** contains numerous nondescript articles and an interesting reconstructed model of the sanctuary.

500m (550yds) away on the road to Markópoulo one can see the ruins of a 6thC **church** of substantial size, one of the very few in Greece that date from the early Byzantine period. It appears to have been destroyed very shortly after its construction.

LÁVRIO
Map 7E3.

The otherwise undistinguished town of Lavrio was famous in Antiquity as the site of the most extensive lead and silver mines of the Mediterranean world. More than 2,000 ancient mine shafts are prominent on the hills behind the town. Lavrio now possesses a refugee camp for asylum seekers and undocumented aliens, which explains the Iranians, Turks, East Europeans, Africans etc. who are sometimes in evidence.

The barren island of **Makronísi** has gained notoriety for its prison camp where communist suspects, among them the great poet Yannis Ritsos, were detained during the civil war of 1944-49.

MARATHON 血
38km (24 miles) NE of Athens. Map 7C3. Bus from Mavromateon and Leof. Alexandras (map 2B4). Tomb and museum open Tues-Sun 8.30am-3pm; closed Mon ☎200dr ☎ (0294) 55.155.

In 490BC a small force of Athenians under Miltiades, aided by a unit of Plataeans, won a heroic victory at Marathon against a much larger Persian army. The runner Pheidippeides who brought the news of the victory collapsed and died on his arrival at the Athenian Agora. The "Marathon run" was revived at the first modern Olympics of 1896 with a Marathon-Athens race that was won by an itinerant Athenian water-seller named Louis.

‡ *The actual distance to the battlefield along the modern road is a little less than 42km (26 miles); the ancient road was somewhat shorter. The official marathon course of 42km 195m (26 miles 213yds) is in fact equal to the distance between Windsor Castle and the royal grandstand at Shepherd's Bush, the start and end points of the race as it was run at the London Olympics of 1908.*

The 12m/39ft-high **tumulus** where the 192 Athenians who died in the battle were buried rises amid orchards 4km (2½ miles) s of the modern town of Marathon. The smaller **tumulus of the Plataeans** (4km/2½ miles inland near the village of Vrana) is nearer the actual battlefield. Nearby, a concrete construction protects a **Bronze Age cemetery**, where the complete skeletons of remarkably small men and horses can be seen in open graves.

RAMNOUS 血 ☆
58km (36 miles) NE of Athens. Map 7B3. Bus to Agia Marina from Mavromateon and Heiden (map 2B4); then 6km/4 miles (3km/2 miles from road junction) taxi or walk. Archeological site open Tues-Sun 8.30am-3pm; closed Mon. Free entrance ☎ (0294) 63.477

The scant remains of a **Temple of Nemesis**, measurer of destiny and punisher of hubris, are situated at a lovely isolated site near a deserted shore accompanied by the even scantier ruins of a

Shrine of Themis, an Archaic earth-goddess. About 1km
($\frac{1}{2}$ mile) down the rocky valley is an overgrown **fort** (4thC BC)
enclosing some ruins on a steep hillock directly by the seashore.
The site has little history and lies undisturbed by tourist buses.
‡ *The fort is locally known as "Jew's Castle," a name it shares
with a great number of minor strongholds on both sides of the
Aegean. The origin of the term is obscure.*

THE MESÓGIA

The gently sloping land behind the Imitos is known as the
Mesógia (Inland), an agricultural district of olive groves and
vineyards producing the popular *rétsina* wine, with the
flourishing market towns of Peanía, Spata, Korópi and
Markópoulo forming its nodal points. Here in Antiquity the
Athenian aristocracy had its rural base. The native inhabitants
today are said to be of Albanian origin, though urban settlers are
rapidly eroding any lingering sense of ethnic particularity.

Numerous historic churches in the area deserve visits on
account of the vigorous frescoes of the 18thC artist Georgios
Markos of Argos, the single most noteworthy painter of the
Post-Byzantine era. Of greatest interest is the church of **Agia
Paraskevi** in **Markopoulo** *(off main square)*, whose frescoes
were judiciously restored in recent years. **Koropi** has several tiny
Byzantine chapels decorated by Markos.

The pleasantly wooded town of Liópesi, now renamed **Peania**
after its Classical predecessor, was the birthplace of the great
orator Demosthenes (c.384-322BC). The **Kanakis Taverna** *(▥
with garden)* is a well-known haunt of Athenian society. 5km (2$\frac{1}{2}$
miles) up from the town, the **Koutoúki Cave** *(▨ open daily
9.30am-5.30pm)* is small but nevertheless quite impressive, with
well-lit stalactites and stalagmites.

EUBOEA *(Évia)* ◁€ ☞

*Map 4. Island population: 170,000 ☎ code: 0221. Capital:
Halkída, 88km (55 miles) N of Athens; population 45,000.
Access: bridge at Halkida; car and passenger ferries
Rafina-Karystos (once daily, 1hr 40mins), Rafina-Marmari
(thrice daily, 1hr 10mins), Agia Marina-Nea Styra, Skala
Oropou-Eretria (20-25 times daily, 25mins), Arkitsa-Loutra
Edipsou, Glyfa-Agiokambos; bus to Halkida from KTEL
terminal at Liossion 260.*

Greece's second-largest island is wildly mountainous, and except
for the coastal area around Halkida remains comparatively
unaffected by the modern world — in marked and refreshing
contrast to neighboring Attica. Its towns are architecturally
uninteresting, but this is made up for by their calm pace and
often dramatic setting.

The three major cities of ancient Euboea, Chalkis (now
Halkida), Erétria and Cyme (Kimi), enjoyed a certain importance
in the early Archaic period, with colonies in Southern Italy and
the Black Sea. They declined under Athenian and Theban
dominance in later Antiquity. In the Middle Ages the island was
known as Negroponte, a corruption of *Euripos Bridge* (see
below). From 1210-1470 it was governed as a Venetian colony by
Italian and Frankish barons. Under the Turks the population
consisted mainly of Muslims, who were obliged to leave after the
annexation of Euboea by Greece in 1830.

SIGHTS AND PLACES OF INTEREST

Halkida is situated on both sides of the Euripos channel
separating Euboea from the mainland. A toy bridge, hardly 40m

(44yds) long, spans the narrowest point. The unique position of the town gives it an attractive aspect; lively promenades lined with some fine 19thC residences occupy both shores. The landward side is dominated by the **Karababa Fortress**, a Turkish structure of 1687. Also noteworthy are a handsome **mosque** and the medieval church of **Agia Paraskevi**.

‡ *The Euripos has been noted since Antiquity for its strong current, which abruptly changes direction several times a day. The phenomenon is still not adequately understood. Aristotle, who died in Chalkis in 322BC, is said to have drowned himself in despair over his inability to solve the puzzle.*

Erétria has some ancient ruins but, as a fast-growing though still pleasant beach resort, attracts rather more visitors. Farther S, the **road to Karystos** (128km/80 miles from Halkida) certainly qualifies as one of the most spectacular in Greece, notably along the **Styra-Marmari** stretch, which rises to 600m (1,968ft) above a deeply indented coastline. The landscape is dotted with small fortresses dating from the baronies of the Venetian period. **Kárystos** itself occupies a splendid location at the foot of **Mt. Ohi** (1,400m/4,593ft), with a small fertile plain and a fine beach. The town is modern but tidy; antiquities include the imposing **Castel Rosso** on the mountain and a smaller **fort** in town, both of Venetian origin.

The northern half of the island is much greener than the S, with dense forests of chestnut and plane. **Loutrá Edipsoú** is renowned throughout Greece for its thermal sulfur baths. **Mt. Dírfis** (1,743m/5,718ft) can be climbed with a relatively easy 1½ hr hike from the alpine refuge above Steni; the view covers all of Euboea, Attica and Boeotia, as well as a large sweep of the Aegean Sea.

In **Karystos** (☎ code 0224): **Venus Beach** (C) (☎41.226 💵 *bungalows* 🍴). Numerous C and D hotels in town including **Galaxy** (C) (☎22.600/3 💵), simple and charming. **Hironia** (D) (☎22.238 💵), simple and charming.

In **Marmari** (☎ code 0224): **Marmari Bay** (B) (☎31.301/3 💵 ⥵ ⍟ 📺 💻 📠), a large modern hotel.

In **Eretria** (☎ code 0221): **Eretria Beach** (A) *(4km/2½ miles W of town on the beach* ☎ 62.411 💵 ⥵ 🍴 ⍟ 📺 💻 📠); **Miramare** (B) *(short distance E of town* ☎ 61.112💵 ⥵ *with good homey food* 🍴).

In **Halkida** (☎ code 0221): **Lucy** (A) (☎23.831 💵 🍴), on the mainland; **Paliria** (B) (☎ 28.001/6 💵), at the heart of the harbor walk. Numerous moderate-to-good beach hotels exist along the coast to Eretria.

In **Loutra Edipsou** (☎ code 0226) a very large number of A, B, C and D hotels, and pensions, include **Aegli** (A) (☎22.215 💵 🍴), a large old hotel with a stately appearance but decaying plumbing, and **Galini** (C) *(on Ag. Nikolaou St.* ☎ 22.448 💵), smaller and more modern.

Excursion 2: Saronic Gulf islands

The five islands of the Saronic-Argolid Gulf are near enough to be regarded as part of the Athens metropolitan region. Fast and frequent hydrofoil services from Piraeus reduces travel time to **Spetses**, the farthest island, to 1hr 20mins. Many Athenians own or rent summer residences on the islands, and some even commute daily to work in the city. **Poros**, **Hydra** and **Spetses** in particular retain the delightful traditional atmosphere of the Aegean islands, so for visitors who do not have time to make a full sea trip they provide an excellent opportunity to enjoy their Greek islands at close range. **Aegina** offers the impressive ancient

temple of Aphaia as well as good beaches and a medieval ghost town. **Salamis** is interesting only in a historic sense.

Agencies in Athens offer day tours combining several islands, usually Aegina, Poros and Hydra. A typical tour will have enough time for temple and beach at Aegina, harborside lunch at Poros and afternoon stroll at Hydra. This, of course, merely scratches the surface, but it may still provide an ideal way to "sample" the archipelago with a view to returning later for a longer stay should any of the islands appeal. Tours usually cost the same or slightly less than the same itinerary followed independently by hydrofoil.

When traveling independently, remember that **"Flying Dolphins"** to Aegina depart from the main harbor of Piraeus, whereas those to Poros, Hydra and Spetses leave from the hydrofoil terminal at Zea Marina. Normal **ferries** to all islands depart from the main harbor; they cost about half as much and take approximately three times longer. The islands are interconnected with frequent boats, and connected to various mainland ports including Palea Epidavros, Methana, Galatas, Ermioni and Porto Heli. For "Flying Dolphins" information ☎ 45.36.107 or 45.37.107 in Athens.

Cars cannot be brought into Hydra, and they require special permission for Spetses. All points of interest in Poros are within longish walking distance, and there are taxis too. Aegina has bus, taxi and rental motorcycles to choose from.

AEGINA *(Égina)* 🏛 📻 🐚 ★

Map 4H7. Resident population: 12,000 (Aegina town: 6,000)
☎ *code: 0297 ℹ 22.391. Hydrofoil from: Piraeus main harbor 8-10 times daily, 30mins, 800dr; Palea Epidavros twice daily; Methana. Some direct boats from Agia Marina.*
Most visitors go to Aegina for the ancient temple of Aphaia, although the magnificently mountainous island also hides an abandoned medieval town and numerous Byzantine churches and monasteries that command extraordinary views. The main town with its busy harbor possesses considerable charm.

Aegina was the powerful and bitter rival of Athens until Pericles engineered the capture of "the eyesore of Piraeus" in 457BC. At the outbreak of the Peloponnesian war in 431, the Athenians deported the island's inhabitants in a disgraceful episode that Thucydides recounts as a parable in political cynicism.

After a long career in sea piracy under Venetian auspices, Aegina was captured and devastated by the Turkish admiral Barbarossa in 1537. The Venetians then made several attempts at recapture, and succeeded temporarily in 1687-1718. In 1826-28 the island served as temporary headquarters for the Greek independence movement under the presidency of Kapodistrias.
‡ *Pistachio cultivation forms the main source of income besides tourism and shipping, and Aegina counts after California and Turkey as one of the world's leading producers. The harvest, which takes place in August, is interesting to observe and gives a chance to buy the fresh nuts at a penny a pound. In recent years, however, the intensive irrigation required for the trees has drained the underground water and created an increasingly disastrous drought.*

SIGHTS AND PLACES OF INTEREST

Aegina town has a beach (beyond the archeological area), but the island's most popular beach resort is located at **Agia Marína** (12km/8 miles E) at the foot of the Aphaia Temple. Less crowded beaches exist at **Souvalá** (8km/5 miles NE) and at the pleasant fishing village of **Pérdika** (10km/6 miles S). With time to spare, it is worth making a trip to the steep and thickly wooded isle of **Móni** *(motorboat 10mins from Perdika),* where there is a campsite, a taverna and a pretty bay with crystal-clear water, often called the best beach within an hour's radius of Athens.

AEGINA TOWN 🐟 ☆

The harbor with its churches, narrow alleys, tavernas, horse-drawn carriages and colorful fishermen's boats forms the picturesque hub of the town. On a hill W of the harbor is the **archeological area** with the single standing column of a temple of Apollo and the floor mosaics of an early medieval synagogue. The town **museum** *(standard opening hours),* which originally housed the first high school of modern Greece, contains some interesting specimens of early pottery.

TEMPLE OF APHAIA 血 ◀€ ☆

12km (8 miles) E of town. Open daily 8.30am-sunset 📷*400dr.*
The temple of Aphaia, one of the most famous Classical sights of Greece, enjoys a matchless situation on a wooded mountaintop 200m (656ft) above the sea. The view takes in the Acropolis of Athens, the Acro-Corinth and several of the Cyclades. The Doric structure of undistinguished local limestone dates from the early part of the 5thC BC and remains in a reasonably good state with most of its 32 columns standing; colored fragments indicate that the temple was once fully painted.

Aphaia was a goddess worshiped under different names in Aegina and Crete alone, with apparently very ancient origins in the Minoan religion. Some later accounts made her a sister of Artemis and Apollo.

The superb sculptures of the temple were discovered nearly intact amid the rubble by the English architect Charles Cockerell and the German antiquarian Haller von Hallerstein on a weekend's digging trip in 1811. At the ensuing auction, the agent of the British Museum failed to arrive on time, and Crown Prince Ludwig of Bavaria, father of the future King Otto of Greece, was able to acquire the sculptures for 120,000 marks. Now at the Glyptothek of Munich, they count among the most important surviving works of Archaic Greek sculpture. Some fragments remain at Athens' NATIONAL ARCHEOLOGICAL MUSEUM.

PALEOHÓRA ▲ ☆

8km (5 miles) E of town, left turn on the Aphaia road. Contact tourist police in Aegina for access to churches.
To escape piratical raids, the main town of Aegina was moved to the mountain site of Paleohora ("Old Town") in the 8th-9thC, where it remained until the early 19thC. The site is now deserted. The houses were removed stone by stone, but some 30 churches still stand. They represent nearly every architectural period between the 13thC and the late 18thC; some have kept their frescoes. One is used occasionally for church services.

Below Paleohora on the Aphaia road is the **Monastery of Agios Nektarios**, commemorating the only canonized saint of modern Greece (died 1920). His tomb attracts many pilgrims, who put an ear to his sarcophagus to hear the holy man clatter inside. His feast is on Nov 9. Just outside Aegina on the road leading to Paleohora can be seen **Omórfi Eklésia** (Pretty Church), a charming edifice of 1282 built of Antique materials.

🍴 In Aegina town: **Nafsika** (B) (☎ 22.333 Ⅲ*bungalows* 🍽) and **Avra** (C) (☎22.303 Ⅱ), both on the beach on N; **Aktaeon** (D) (☎22.241).

In **Agia Marina**, a large number of hotels, nearly all C, include **Apollo** (B) (☎32.271/4 ⅢⅢ), **Aegli** (C) (☎32.221 Ⅱ) and **Argo** (C) (☎32.266 ⅢⅢ).

In **Perdika: Aegina Maris** (B) (☎ 25.130/2 ‖‖‖ ⇌ ≈ ⋔ 🖭 🖭 ⊙ 🖾 🖾), the largest and most modern hotel on the island; **Moondy Bay** (B) *(2km/1 mile outside the village ☎ 25.146/7 ‖‖).*

▲ Near the archeological site in **Aegina town** and on **Moni island**.

HYDRA (Ídra) 🖭 🖭 ★
Map 6/7. Resident population: 3,000 ☎ code: 0298
i 52.205. Hydrofoil from: Piraeus (Zea Marina) 8-10 times daily, 1hr, 2,100dr; Poros 5-7 times daily, 550dr; Ermioni 4-6 times daily, 700dr.

Hydra has a picture-perfect semicircular harbor, with the stately houses of 19thC seamen forming an amphitheater on the steep slopes. The town's enticing scenery made it popular with foreign — mostly English — artists and writers in the 1950s and '60s, and has attracted mass tourism (mostly young people) since the 1970s. In the competition for tourist money, peddlers of kitsch have replaced the artists, and simple fishermen's tavernas and cafés have been driven upscale, yet the pleasant harmony of Hydra's site and architecture remains unimpaired, outside the peak season. The car-less streets contribute hugely to the effect.

The barren island (the name, meaning "watery," is evidently ironic) was uninhabited in Antiquity and the Middle Ages. Albanian settlers arrived during the centuries of Turkish rule to profit from the great boom of Mediterranean piracy. A British connection cultivated during Napoleon's continental blockade (1806-14) put their buccaneering talents to good use in running the contraband trade to English ports. This brought the immense wealth and the overseas ties that made Hydriote captains such a crucial component of the Greek war of independence. Most of the naval chiefs whose names are now prominent on the streets and squares of Greece (Koundouriotis, Kriezis, Miaoulis, Tombazis, Voulgaris among others) were sons of Hydra. Their descendants included four prime ministers and one president of Greece. The "Hydriote cabal" was instrumental in forcing King Otto to accept the constitution in 1843 and in finally overthrowing him in 1862. The island itself declined from a population of 20,000 in 1821 to virtual desertion by the mid-20thC, when tourism engendered a rapid recovery.

SIGHTS AND PLACES OF INTEREST
The residences of the old merchant sailors are relatively simple on the exterior but sumptuously decorated inside. The finest are the two **Koundouriotis houses**, which can be toured on application to the owners. The **Tsamados house** has been converted into a merchant marine academy, while the **Tombazis house** accommodates a school of fine arts. In the district of **Kaló Pigádi** high above town there are several 18thC houses.

The coast around the town is steep and rocky, so the best way to go swimming is to rent a boat. A 40min walk E leads to a popular beach at **Mandráki**. Several monasteries are located in barely accessible parts of the mountain.

The major local event is the ***Miaoulia***, celebrated with naval parade and mock battles on June 20.

🕿 Accommodations in town consist mainly of pensions and private rooms in converted old buildings, which are generally delightful places, faulty plumbing and all. Finding a room in July-Aug is not easy: it might be better to try **Ermioni** or **Hydra Beach** on the mainland.
Typical of the mansions-turned-pensions in **Hydra town** are **Miranda** (B) (☎ 52.230), **Hydroussa** (B) *(formerly called Xenia ☎ 52.217)* and **Hydra**

(C) (☎ 42.597); all ▥▥. Also, **Sophia** (D) (☎ 52313 ▥▥).

Miramare (A), at **Mandraki**, is the top hotel on the island (☎ 52.300/1 ▥▥ 28 rms ⇥ ♨).

PÓROS 🏛 ♨ ☆

Map 4I7. Resident population: 3,500 ☎ code: 0298
i 22.462. Hydrofoil from: Piraeus (Zea Marina), 5-7 times daily, 50mins, 1,600dr. Frequent ferry from Galatas, 2mins, 25dr.

Poros town is located on the very narrow channel *(poros)* separating the island from the mainland, and its position helps to give it an immensely appealing, intimate look. The architecture of individual houses is undistinguished, but the ensemble cascading down the hill framed by pine forests forms an attractive sight. The long harbor promenade is lined with a great variety of boats and tavernas, but somehow maintains a sleepy feel that adds to the satisfaction of a long afternoon stroll.

The insignificant remains of a **temple of Poseidon** are located at a spot c.550m (1,804ft) high, with the usual extraordinary view. In this temple in 322BC Demosthenes committed suicide after having led Athens and Greece into disaster by inciting yet another fruitless revolt against the Macedonians.

The best beach is 4km (2½ miles) E of town below the pine-encircled monastery of **Zoodóhos Pigí** *(take a bus)*. From the mainland town of **Galatás**, effectively a suburb of Poros, it is possible to make an excursion to the ruins of ancient **Troezen** (8km/5 miles SW; see ARGOLID COAST, page 107) and the vast citrus plantations of the **Lemonodasos** (Lemon Forest).

📇 Accommodations in **Poros town** are limited to relatively simple hotels and pensions, such as **Latsi** (B) (☎ 22.392 ▥▥), or **Manessi** (C) (☎ 22.273 ▥▥), in a pleasant old building on the waterfront. A much larger number of hotels (C, D) exist in **Galatas**.

Sirene (B) occupies an excellent beach below the monastery of **Zoodohos Pigi** (☎ 22.741 ▥▥ 120 rms ⇥ ≈ ♠ AE ⊙ ● VISA).

Stella Maris (B)(☎ 22.562 ▥▥), on the beach 5km (3 miles) NE from **Galatas**, is the most adequate modern hotel in the vicinity.

SALAMIS *(Salamína)*
Map 4H7. Resident population: 20,000 ☎ code: 01.
Frequent ferry from Perama (bus from Eleftherias Sq., map 1C2).

Immortalized by the historic naval battle that turned the tide of the Persian invasion of Greece, Salamis today forms part of the industrial periphery of Athens and is heavily polluted by spillovers from the factories on the mainland nearby. Some good beaches nevertheless exist on the SE coast of the island and are popular with Athenian vacationers.

In Mycenaean times Salamis was the seat of an important kingdom. It took part in the Trojan war with a significant force under the dim-witted giant Ajax, son of Telamon.

In 480BC, after occupying most of mainland Greece and devastating Athens, Great King Xerxes attempted to deal the final blow to the Athenian navy gathered near Phaleron (Fáliro). The Athenians withdrew to the Gulf of Ambelakia, between Perama and the narrow headland of Cynosura on Salamis, and then annihilated the Persian armada with a gallant sortie. Xerxes is said to have watched the disaster from a throne set up in the (then forested) hills of Perama.

The battle vindicated Themistocles, who had advocated a policy of naval build-up with Churchillian tenacity. It marked the turning point of Persian expansion and the start of the age of Athenian supremacy. Deprived of naval support, the Persian army was defeated at Plataea the next year.

SPÉTSES 🏛 ⛴ ☆

Map 6l6. Resident population: 2,500 ☎ code: 0298
i 73.100. Hydrofoil from: Piraeus (Zea Marina) 5-7 times daily, 80mins, 2,700dr; Hydra 5-7 times daily, 950dr; Porto Heli twice daily. Ferry from Kosta, 4-5 times daily, 15mins, 60dr. Taxi boats available at Kosta.

The attractive island of Spetses, with steep hills covered by pine forest, is one of the favorite summer resorts of wealthier Athenian families. The main town, also called **Dapia**, is practically free of road traffic and maintains its well-proportioned traditional architecture. Several stately 19thC mansions and decorated pebble-mosaic streets complete a pleasantly low-key picture.

The pride of Spetses is the revolutionary war heroine **Laskaréna Bouboulína**. A cynic could hardly fail to note the similarity of her cult to that of the local goddesses of the ancients and the saints of the Christians. In real life, Laskaréna, the daughter of a Hydriote pirate, was born in prison in Constantinople, and became the widow of two captains who were either pirates, or were murdered by pirates, or both. During the war she fought the Turks with a private battle fleet of her own, engaging in various acts of reckless heroism. She was shot in her home in 1825 when a son seduced the daughter of a rival clan. Her statues in various heroic poses speckle the island. Her **home** is Spetses' main architectural landmark, and her ashes form the *pièce de résistance* of the local museum.

Each year on Sept 8, the anniversary of the Battle of Spetses is celebrated with fireworks, dance and music.

The most popular beach of Spetses is E of Dapia at **Agia Marina**, where much of the island's day and night life unfolds in summer. Magnificent and less crowded beaches are to be found at **Agii Anargyri** and **Agia Paraskevi** on the S coast, reached by taxi-boat or a highly scenic 2hr walk over the hill. In between these two is the interesting sea cave of **Bekiris**.

The islet of **Spetsopoúla** off the SE coast of Spetses belongs to the shipping magnate Niarchos, who is rumored to pursue there a life of unimaginable luxury.

≈ **Spetses** (A) (☎ 72.602 ▥▥ ≈ ▤ ▣ ✦ ▦ ▨), the top hotel on the island, in a nice building ; **Kasteli** (A) (☎ 72.311 ▥▥ *hotel and bungalows* ⛴ ▤ ▨ ✦ ▣ ▨); **Roumanis** (B) (☎ 72.244 ▥); **Faros** (C) *(on the main plaza* ☎ 72.613/4 ▯); **Acropole** (D) (☎ 72.219 ▯). **Pension Kardiasmenos** (☎ 73.741 ▭) is a lovely old mansion on the main plaza, simple but well kept.

Excursion 3: Delphi

Delphi is the most strikingly evocative of Classical Greek ruin sites, and justifies an excursion in its own right. The road from Athens passes through **Boeotia**, a land full of ancient memories, but what survives by way of actual sights is of limited appeal to the nonenthusiast. Along the way, the two great mountain masses of **Parnassus** and **Helicon** offer some extraordinary scenery to those with the time and means to explore their upper reaches.

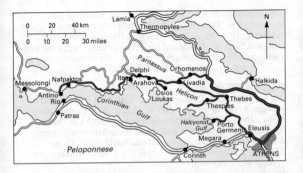

Delphi is connected to Athens by a fine highway of 167km (105 miles), with an alternative route of 184km (115 miles) via **Eleusis**, so that a day trip is perfectly feasible. On the other hand, an overnight stay at the lively tourist village near the site allows a more leisurely exploration of the sights along the way, with the bonus of an opportunity to visit the ruins during the less crowded early morning or evening hours.

Alternatively this excursion can be combined with a tour of the Peloponnese, using the Rio-Antirio ferry to cross the Corinthian Gulf on the way to or from Patras (see EXCURSION 4, page 129). In this case it is probably best to leave Delphi to the end as a fitting conclusion to a 3- to 10-day itinerary that would include (at least) Corinth, Nafplio, Mistra and Olympia.

Various tour operators in Athens organize one- or two-day excursions to Delphi, typical prices being about 7,000dr for a day trip including lunch and museum fees, or 15,000dr for a two-day tour including hotel, half-board and museum fees. Most tours feature stops at **Thebes** and **Arahova** and a side trip to the **Osios Loukas** monastery.

The same route can be followed slightly more inexpensively by public bus, but in peak season you should weigh this against the likelihood that finding either bus or hotel room could prove difficult indeed.

AIGÓSTHENA   See PORTO GERMENO.

ARÁHOVA ◁≣

8km (5 miles) E of Delphi. Map 3G5. Population 3,000. On Athens-Delphi bus route.

Arahova occupies a panoramic position (altitude 940m/3,084ft) on the flank of **Mt. Parnassus**, and forms the starting point of excursions into the mountain. The village has been famous for its hand-woven fabrics since Turkish times, although current products tend to be gaudy affairs of technicolor dye and crass design. They cover every wall and shop window along the main street, giving the town a distinctly psychedelic atmosphere.

A road (26km/16 miles) leads N, via Kalivía, to the **ski center** of Mt. Parnassus at 1,500m/4,921ft (≣ *no ski equipment available at Arahova*). From here it is possible to drive to within 1hr's walk of the summit (2,457m/8,061ft). The view from the top takes in nearly all of continental Greece from **Mt. Athos** in the N to **Mt. Taygetos** in the S.

The ancient Greeks believed the peak of Mt. Parnassus to be the abode of Dionysus, where he held orgiastic feasts with his wine-crazed Maenads. Later poetic tradition transferred the Muses from Mt. Helicon (see THEBES, page 103) to Parnassus, and in Latin and post-Renaissance literature the mountain came to represent both the source and perfection of artistic achievement. The frightfully barren, craggy peak bears little resemblance to the idyllic *Montparnasse* of 18thC painters and poets.

DELPHI ▥ ◖€ ★

167km (104 miles) NW of Athens. Map 3G5. Population of village: 2,000 ☎ code: 0265 ⅰ 82.220. Bus: 5 times daily from Athens (KTEL terminal at Liossion 260) via Thebes; 3 times daily from Lamia; 3 times daily from Nafpaktos. Museum and archeological site ▨500dr each. Open Mon-Fri 7.30am-6pm, Sat-Sun 8.30am-3pm (museum closed Mon morning).

Delphi holds an awe-inspiring position in the fold of two immense rose-gray cliffs, the **Phaedriades**, which climb toward the wild crags of Mt. Parnassus and command a majestic panorama over the aptly named "Sea of Olives" which stretches as far as the Gulf of Corinth below a drop of several hundred meters. The Sanctuary of Delphic Apollo was one of the most sacred places of ancient Greece, forming, like Olympia, one of the focal points of a common Greek cultural identity. The Delphic oracle played a prominent part in nearly every historic event from before the recorded era until the final victory of Christianity in the 4thC. Greek cities from Italy to the shores of the Black Sea vied with each other to win the oracle's favor by embellishing the sanctuary with costly gifts; they turned Delphi into a showcase of ancient art and architecture.

Legends

Delphi was originally a sacred place of Mother Earth (**Gaea**), who lurked in cracks and pits in the rock, protected by her son **Python**, the snake. Also here was the **Omphalos**, the Navel of the Earth (not the sculptured Omphalos now exhibited in the museum, which is evidently a much later cult object).

Apollo, who was born on the island of Delos in the Aegean, was brought here by some Cretans to whom he appeared in the guise of a dolphin *(Apollo Delphinios)*. He dispersed the underworld deities and killed Python, but thereafter adopted the snake as one of his symbols *(Apollo Pythios)*.

History

The arrival of the cult of Apollo implies Minoan origins and so must be placed sometime before 1500BC. By 1000BC a league comprising the representatives of all Greek tribes and cities (the Amphictyony) was entrusted with the administration of the site. The quadrennial Pythian Games were instituted early in the 6thC BC by the Athenian noble family of the Alcmaeonids, who were then influential at Delphi; they also built the early temple of Apollo and perhaps played a role in introducing the subordinate cult of Athena. The current temple of Apollo was erected in 366-329BC after an earthquake had destroyed the previous edifice.

The earliest recorded gift to the temple was that of the Lydian king Croesus c.550BC. By Roman times, the number of statues in the sanctuary alone exceeded 3,000. Some of these were carried off to Rome by Nero; the serpent column erected in 479BC to commemorate the Greek victory at Plataea was taken by Constantine to his new capital and now stands at the Hippodrome in Istanbul. The immunity of the holy site, however, was generally respected during the sundry wars and invasions of Antiquity, excepting an attack by the Gauls in 279BC, which was repulsed by an intervention of the god in person, reputedly in the form of a cataclysmic thunderstorm.

Delphi was abandoned after the outlawing of the oracle in AD391 and lay half-forgotten for 1,400yrs. The village of **Kastri** (Towers) emerged among the ruins; villagers put the ancient marbles to good use as building material, and the precinct of the Athena Temple (see below) now acquired the graphic name of **Marmária**, or "Where You Get The Marble." The investigations started in the 1860s by the French School of Archeology soon brought to light the **Naxian Sphinx** and the **Stoa of the Athenians**, thereby persuading the French government to put up the money needed to remove Kastri to its present location 1.5km (1 mile) w. Systematic excavations conducted in 1892-1903 by Th. Homolle recovered the ruins of Delphi more or less as they stand now.

The oracle

Pilgrims came to Delphi from all parts of the Mediterranean world to consult the oracle about marriages, business loans, voyages, elections, conspiracies and wars. The **Pythia**, the priestess of Apollo who was a peasant woman of over 50, drank from the Castalian spring to purify herself. She then inhaled the apparently hallucinogenic fumes that emanated from a chasm in the temple's crypt, took her seat on a tripod and delivered her advice in mumbled utterances. These were interpreted and put into hexameter verse by priests, who included such influential personalities as the historian Plutarch.

Lycurgus and Solon sought the oracle's advice about their constitutions of Sparta and Athens respectively. Colonies were never founded until it had been consulted. When Croesus wanted to know if he should go to war against Persia, he was told that if he did he would destroy a great kingdom; he did, and destroyed his own. In both the Persian and Peloponnesian wars the oracle tended to side with the enemies of Athens. Julian the Apostate (AD361-363) was the last pagan emperor to honor the Pythia. His messenger was told:

> "Go tell the king — the carven hall is felled;
> Apollo has no cell, prophetic bay,
> Nor talking spring; his cadenced well is stilled."

THE MUSEUM

It may be best to start a tour of Delphi with the museum, if only for the sake of the excellent graphic **reconstruction**, which gives a good idea of the splendor of the site as it must have appeared 2,000yrs ago.

The highlight of the collection is the bronze **Charioteer**, one of the great surviving masterpieces of Antiquity. This was part of a group marking a racing victory of Polyzalos, the tyrant of Gela in Sicily (473BC), and it is sobering to think that it constituted no more than a minor piece among more than 3,000 such gifts. The immense **Naxian Sphinx** was presented in 560BC by the people of Naxos. The primitive, almost "Egyptian" monument of **Kleobis and Biton** represent two priests of the Argive Hera who were deified after their death. The graceful statue of **Antinous**, the lover of Hadrian who was similarly deified posthumously, belongs to a different artistic era about 750yrs down the way.

Other noteworthy exhibits include fragmentary **friezes** of the Athenian, Siphnian and Sicyonian Treasuries, which the

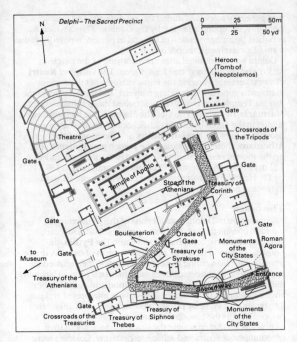

Delphi – The Sacred Precinct

respective cities built to house the gifts of their pilgrims, and the
Omphalos, which was kept in the crypt of the temple and
marked the center of the earth.

THE SACRED PRECINCT

The **Sanctuary** or **Temenos of Apollo** forms a rectangle
180m x 130m (197 x 142yds) in size, which contained, as well as
the temple itself, various administrative buildings, the treasuries
of the city-states, numerous votive monuments and a theater. The
stadium where the Pythian Games were held is located a short
distance above the sharply sloping enclosure.

The paved square in front of the main gate was the **Roman
Agora**, where pious offerings could be bought in the shops of
the stoa. Other Roman buildings outside the enclosure, mainly
baths, are recognizable by the use of brick.

The various **monuments** that survive in the form of bare
pedestals, if at all, commemorated a full spectrum of events and
personalities, sublime as well as workaday. There were trophies
marking the battles of Marathon and Plataea and the campaigns
of Alexander, while the **Bull of Corcyra** celebrated a particularly
good tuna catch, and the **Treasury of Siphnos** immortalized the
proceeds of a satisfying gold mine.

The **Temple of Pythian Apollo**, a Doric peripteral structure
with 6 x 15 columns, replaced the earlier temple of the 6thC at a
time of transition when the Classical Doric was already past its
prime, but the brilliant refinements of Hellenistic architecture
were yet unborn. Six of its strong, squat pillars have been
re-erected and give a sense of the temple's former majesty. Below
its front revetment, a pile of stones marks the site of the
prehistoric sanctuary of Gaea.

The **theater** (commands a marvelous view over the site, the olive-clad plains and the sea beyond. Here morality plays were staged re-enacting the battle of Apollo and Python, and musical performances honored the god of the lyre and the flute. Nero probably took this stage to display his talents in singing, playing instruments, heraldic speech and numerous other skills in which he earned the unanimous approval of the jury.

THE CASTALIAN SPRING AND MARMÁRIA

A short walk w along the Arahova road leads to the **Castalian Spring**, which wells up in the wild ravine between the Phaedriades. Here ancient pilgrims purified themselves before approaching the temple grounds.

Marmaria, consisting of a platform among olive groves below the road, holds the ruins of two **temples of Athena**, both erected by Athenians, the older one in the 6thC and the newer, smaller one in the 4thC. Beside them stands perhaps the most attractive of Delphi's monuments, the **Tholos**, or Rotunda, a circular structure of 20 Doric columns of which six have been re-erected. The original use of the building is obscure, although it may not be too far-fetched to think that sheer beauty may have been one inspiration.

🦐 The tourist village of **Delphi** has hotel capacity far exceeding its resident population. There are five A or B hotels, a great variety of C and D hotels, private rooms and a **youth hostel**.

Amalia (A) is the biggest hotel in the village, with 185 rms (☎ *82.101/5*), and **Vouzas** (A) the nearest to the archeological site (☎ *82.232/4* ✆*(01) 77.78.762* ▥ *terrace* ➡ *dramatic* ◀€). **Xenia** (A) is at an isolated spot at the w end (☎ *82.151* ▥). All ▦ ▣ ⊙ ▣ ▥ Also, **Iniohos** (C) (☎ *82.701* ▥) and **Parnassos** (C) (☎ *82.321* ▯ ◀€).

Additional hotels exist in abundance at **Itea**, a port and resort town of no special merit, but less crowded and less expensive than Delphi. **Nafsika** (B) (☎ *33.300/4* ▥ ➡ ▦ *no cards*) is the best.

🅰 At the campsite outside the w end of Delphi village.

MOUNT HELICON *(Elikón)*   See THEBES, Environs.

LIVÁDIA 🏰

122km (76 miles) NW of Athens. Map 4G6. Population: 18,000 ☎ code: 0261. Frequent bus from Athens (KTEL terminal at Liossion 260) or Thebes.

Livadia grew in importance during the Turkish era as Thebes declined, and the modern town keeps something of the spirit, if not the architecture, of a Turkish market town with busy narrow streets and diminutive shops. The **citadel** (Kastro), which was built by the Catalans after 1311 and used as the residence of the pasha later on, occupies a steep hill behind the town. At its foot, in a pleasant wooded area with a picturesque Turkish bridge and two springs, which apparently correspond to the ancient fountains of **Mnemosyne** (Memory) and **Lethe** (Forgetting), is the cave of the oracle of Trophonius. The method of consulting the oracle is described in fascinating detail by Pausanias.

🦐 **Levadia** (B) (☎ *28.266* ▥); **Helikon** (C) (☎ *28.520* ▯). The **Xenia** restaurant and guesthouse located over the springs of Memory and Forgetting provide a nice spot to stop for lunch on the Athens-Delphi route.

ENVIRONS

Livadia lies at the edge of what used to be **Lake Kopáis**, which was drained between 1887 and 1931 by the British Lake Copais

Co. The reclaimed fertile plain is planted with cotton fields.

Along the former lakeshore, 13km (8 miles) NE, is **Orchomenós** (population 5,000), where in 2000-1700BC flourished the civilization of the Minyans, a Middle Helladic people who may or may not have been Greek. They were distinguished for a special type of pottery (Minyan ware), and successfully drained Lake Kopais — a technical feat that eluded the repeated efforts of later Antiquity. Besides numerous Neolithic, Bronze Age and Classical traces, the site also possesses the monastery **Church of the Dormition**, possibly the oldest standing Byzantine edifice in Greece, dating from the year 873.

On the Lamia road 14km (9 miles) NW of Livadia, a giant lion marks the site of the **Battle of Chaeronia**, where in 338BC the Macedonian army under the 18-year-old Alexander put a definitive end to the ancient Greek system of independent city-states. In the town of **Chaeronia** (which has a small rock-carved theater), the historian Plutarch (c.AD46-125) was born.

NÁFPAKTOS 🏙 🕾

97km (60 miles) w of Delphi; 264km (165 miles) w of Athens. Map 3G4. Population: 9,000 ☎ code: 0634. Bus: 3 times daily from Athens via Delphi; 4 times daily from Patras.

Nafpaktos is a pleasant small town with a tiny circular harbor enclosed by the crenelated walls of a Turkish naval fort and a mighty Venetian-Turkish citadel looming on the hill above. A few attractive back streets and a fine beach E of town make this a worthwhile stopover on the Patras-Delphi route. The town is better known in the West by its medieval name of **Lepanto**.

‡ *The naval battle of Lepanto, in which an allied fleet led by Don Juan of Austria smashed the Turkish navy (Oct 7, 1571), is a turning point in modern European history comparable in scope to Salamis in Antiquity. The Ottoman Empire was late to develop as a marine power, but the navy created in the 1520s by Suleyman the Magnificent was soon strong enough to establish its mastery over the Mediterranean. After Lepanto, it never recovered. One ironic side effect of this was the power vacuum and the resulting proliferation of piracy that devastated the Mediterranean for the next 250yrs.*

Cervantes, the author of Don Quixote, *lost an arm at Lepanto and was taken captive by the Turks.*

🍽 **Xenia** (B) (**☎** 22.301/2 **Ⅲ⎕**) by the beach E of town. There are also C and D hotels in town.

Reasonable beach hotels exist at convenient intervals along the beautiful Nafpaktos-Itea stretch; notably at **Paralia Tolofonos**, **Agii Pantes** and on lovely **Trizonia island**.

▲ By the beach 3km (2 miles) w of Nafpaktos town.

ENVIRONS

11km (7 miles) w of Náfpaktos, another substantial Turkish fortress stands at the ferry point of **Antirio**, dating from the year 1499 like its twin at **Rio**, across the narrowest point of the Gulf of Corinth. (*Continuous ferry service, passage 15mins, 615dr per car.*)

ORCHOMENÓS   See LIVADIA, Environs.

OSIOS LOUKAS MONASTERY ⛪ 🕊 ☆

35km (22 miles) sw of Livadia, 10km (6 miles) from road

junction. Map 4G6. Occasional bus from Distomo. Included in most sightseeing tours of Delphi.

At the Triple Way where Oedipus slew his father, a road branches through the village of **Distomo** to the W slopes of Mt. Helicon. The valleys are still as lonely as they were in the 10thC when Blessed Luke, a local monk, retreated to them to weather the darkest days of Slav migration and Bulgar oppression. His solid faith in the Byzantine cause did not go unnoticed, his hermitage grew into a monastery, and a church bearing his name was erected c.1030. Its Byzantine **mosaics**, probably the work of imperial artists from Constantinople, are the most important in Greece after those of DAPHNI.

The **main church** (★) is similar in structure to that of Daphni: a cross-in-square plan round a central dome. Between the arched windows of the drum stand 16 mosaic prophets; the subordinate arches have fine mosaics of angels, saints and the languages and nations, while the recesses contain scenes from the life of Christ; the Virgin occupies her usual space in the apse. The adjoining **Church of Theotokos** is still used for church services by the few remaining monks. The broad terrace with ancient plane trees and partly ruined monks' cells can be a delightfully pleasant place when not overrun by bus-loads of sightseers.

MOUNT PARNASSUS   See ARAHOVA.

PORTO GERMÉNO *(Aigósthena)* ⤧ ⥹ ▥
65km (41 miles) E of Athens. Map 4H6. Bus from Thisio subway station (map 1D2).

The **Halcyonid Gulf** (Kólpos Alkyonidón), the extremely indented and mountainous NE branch of the Gulf of Corinth, is an area of great beauty that remains quite undeveloped despite its nearness to Athens. A half-dozen rather long and curvy but highly scenic roads descend to the coast at various points. Of these, Porto Germeno (renamed **Aigósthena** to conform with Classical precedent) has a couple of hotels, a string of fish tavernas and a lovely pebble beach fringed by olive groves. The mighty square towers of a 4thC BC **fortress**, considered the best-preserved example of Classical defense architecture in Greece, dominate the site.

To the N is the 1,409m (4,623ft) peak of **Mt. Kythairon**, which features prominently in mythology. Here the seer Tiresias was blinded for seeing the goddesses bathe naked, Pentheus was torn to pieces for observing Dionysius in orgy with his Maenads, and the infant Oedipus was left to die so he would not grow up to kill his father.

Other roads lead down to **Ag. Vasílios**, **Alikí**, **Ag. Ioánnis** and **Paralía Pródromou**, little hamlets with deserted beaches and a taverna or two which may not always be open. A boat may be rented at Porto Germeno to explore the coast with greater ease.

⤩ **Egosthenion** (C) (☎ *(0263) 41.226* ▯▢).

THEBES *(Thíve)*
77km (48 miles) NW of Athens. Map 4G6. Population: 18,000 ☎ code: 0262. Bus: frequently from Athens (OSE terminal at Larissis train station, map 1B2; KTEL terminal at Liossion 260). Train: 10 times daily from Larissis station.

Thebes, the hometown of Oedipus and Antigone, one of the great cities of Greece during both the Mycenaean and Classical ages, is today a busy provincial center with almost nothing to show for its long history. The **Archeological Museum** has a superb 6thC BC *kouros* and some interesting Mycenaean items.

History and legends

The city was founded in mythic times by Kadmos, a Phoenician, who sowed the dragon's teeth from which Thebes' noble families sprang. His descendants included Laios, who was told by an oracle that his son would grow up to kill him and marry his mother. The infant Oedipus was sent to die, was saved, grew up unaware of his identity, killed his father in a quarrel, saved Thebes from an evil sphinx, was elected king and married the widow of Laios, Jocasta, his own mother. When the truth came out, he put out his own eyes and went into voluntary exile. His sons Eteocles and Polynices quarreled, bringing about the disastrous siege of the Seven Against Thebes. His daughter Antigone was sentenced to be buried alive when she honored the dead body of Polynices against the wishes of the tyrant Creon. Various episodes of the saga formed the subject of the greatest tragedies of Aeschylus and Sophocles.

In Classical times Thebes was the dominant power of the Boeotian League and a bitter enemy of Athens. It sided with the Persians during the Persian invasion, and was an ally of Sparta during the Peloponnesian Wars. In 371BC, Epaminondas of Thebes shattered Spartan hegemony at the Battle of Leuctra, and for a decade afterward his city was the sole master of Greece. In 338BC it joined forces with Athens to resist Macedonian hegemony, but was defeated at Chaeronia, and was totally destroyed by Alexander the Great when it tried to make a comeback a few years later. In Roman times, according to Strabo, there was hardly even a village of respectable size left at the site. A brief revival as the capital of Othon de la Roche's duchy ended with defeat and destruction by the Catalans at the Battle of Lake Kopais in 1311. The city was rebuilt from scratch after 1830.

The *Vláhikos gámos*, a parody of a highland peasant wedding, held on Shrove Monday, attracts enormous crowds. The Vlahs (Vlach, Wallachian) are a Romanian people who settled much of central and NW Greece toward the end of the Middle Ages. Their language is now nearly extinct. The town of Metsovo is considered the center of Vlach culture.

❧ **Dionyssion Melathron** (B) *(Metaxa & Kadmou* ☎ *27.855 |||☐)*; **Meletiou** (C) *(Epaminonda 58* ☎ *27.333 |||☐)*.

ENVIRONS

At **Plataea** (13km/8 miles S of Thebes, then 5km/3 miles W) the Persians under Mardonius and their Theban allies were defeated by other Greeks in the concluding phase of the Persian wars in 479BC.

Thespiae (now Thespiés, 13km/8 miles W of Thebes, then 7km/4 miles S; minor ruins) was famed in Antiquity as the only city that had a temple and cult of Eros, god of love. People would go to Thespiae to see the statue of the god that Praxiteles gave as a gift to a "servant of Eros" (some say courtesan) named Glycera. Nero carried the statue off to Rome.

Nearby **Ascra** was the birthplace of Hesiod, perhaps the earliest of Greek poets (8th-7thC BC). It was his work that helped popularize a group of local deities called the *Muses*. Calliope, Clio, Erato, Euterpe, Melpomene, Polyhymnia, Terpsichore, Thalia and Urania were originally forest and water spirits who were seen by shepherds to sing and dance to the music of Apollo in a sacred grove deep in a high valley of **Mt. Helicon** (Élikon). Later they gained fame as the inspirers of various branches of the arts; to them we owe museums, music and the act of musing. A few bits of a sanctuary, believed to be of the Nine Sisters, can be seen some distance W of Ascra. Farther up near the E summit (1,526m/5,006ft) of the Helicon, the **fountain of Hippocrene**, now called **Krío Pigádi**, was a source of poetic inspiration.

Excursion 4: The Peloponnese

No other part of Greece can rival the Peloponnese, the huge, hand-shaped almost-island in the south, in either grandeur of landscapes or wealth of historic sights. In physical character it is Greece's Greece: uncompromisingly mountainous, crisscrossed with the most abrupt changes of scenery, and always within sight of the sea.

Located within easy reach of Athens in the northern half of the peninsula are **Corinth** and **Olympia**, the two most substantial and interesting ruin sites of Greece besides Athens and Delphi, as are the memorable Bronze Age citadel of **Mycenae**, the spectacular ancient theater of **Epidauros** and the lonely mountaintop temple of **Bassae**. Also here is **Nafplio**, perhaps the most attractive town in mainland Greece.

The southern half is far less touristically developed, and so retains that more direct and spontaneous charm which is so often a victim of organized mass travel. Yet its sights are no less impressive: the fantastic medieval towns of **Mistra** and **Monemvasia**, the bizarre fortified villages of **Mani** and the seductive landscape of **Messenia** must be reckoned among the top priorities of any serious itinerary through Greece.

The seven modern provinces (*nómoi*) of the Peloponnese (*Pelopónisos*) copy the seven or eight "countries" of Antiquity, each of which had its distinct ethnic and political identity. Each forms a physically and in part historically separate region, and it is useful to have some familiarity with their outlines. (See the map on page 104.)

Achaea and Corinthia

The northern seaboard of the peninsula owes its worth to its control over the most important waterway of Greece, the Gulf and Canal of Corinth. CORINTH flourished in Antiquity on this basis, as PATRAS does today. The pompous monuments of the former form a nice contrast with those of nearby NEMEA, which already lay in ruins when the Romans made Corinth the capital of their Greek province. Of the celebrated "hundred gorges of Achaea," the Vouraikos Gorge, leading up to KALAVRYTA, may be the most impressive.

Argolis

The fertile plain of Argos is carpeted with citrus orchards, which make a visit in spring, when the trees are in bloom, a most memorable experience. This plain was the hub of the Bronze Age civilization of the Greeks: ARGOS was the leading city of Greece for centuries, while Agamemnon, the supreme leader of the Trojan expedition, was king of MYCENAE, the royal citadel that has given its modern name to that prehistoric culture. Near the ruins of prehistoric TIRYNS stands the reminder of another age of

The Peloponnese

prosperity: NAFPLIO, under the name of Napoli di Levante, was the capital of the short-lived Venetian dominion in the Peloponnese (1687-1715), and retains its delightful mix of Italian and Turkish architecture from that period.

The ARGOLID PENINSULA forms a wild and extraordinarily scenic contrast to the placid plain (and, incidentally, provides an alternative springboard to visit the Saronic Islands). Hidden among its pine forests, the ancient medical complex of EPIDAUROS owns the best-preserved Classical theater in Greece.

Arcadia

Arcadia was inhabited in Antiquity by pastoral nomads who did not take to city life until forced to do so in the 4thC, and then did so only reluctantly. The Greeks, who had a sober opinion of country life, viewed them as uncouth brutes. The Roman poet Virgil first romanticized the singing shepherds of this land in his *Georgics,* and "Arcadia" has been a synonym for pastoral idyll ever since. It is possible to rediscover that idyll when the treeless hills and pastures break forth in a profusion of wild flowers in springtime, but otherwise Arcadia presents few interesting sights to the tourist. The two major towns, TRIPOLI and MEGALOPOLIS, seem designed to confirm the ancient Arcadians' dislike of cities.

The ARCADIAN COAST, which in Antiquity formed a separate region called Cynuria, is a beautiful stretch of mountainous seashore where hardly any roads existed until recently.

Laconia

A land of harsh, vast mountains with the lovely valley of the Eurotas tucked in between, Laconia has a scenery ideally suited to the martial culture of SPARTA, whose domain it was in Antiquity. Classical monuments are all but nonexistent, but their absence is more than compensated for by several of the most striking medieval sites of Greece. The walled towns of MISTRA and MONEMVASIA and the ghost village of GERAKI date from a brief interlude at the end of the Middle Ages when a semi-independent Byzantine principality wrested this part of Greece from the Frankish baronies and produced the swan song of Byzantine art before succumbing to the Turks.

After the Turkish conquest, some of the warlike inhabitants of Laconia withdrew to the inhospitable mountains of MANI, the middle "finger" of the Peloponnese, from where they marauded Turk and Greek alike until well into the last century. The strange fortified villages of this pirate republic are among the strangest sights of Greece, and the underground lake of the Glyfada Cave is perhaps its single most extraordinary natural prodigy.

Messenia

Nothing could be more pronounced than the contrast between wild Laconia and the soft, smiling hills and orchards of Greece's most southwestern province. The Messenians were subjected by

Sparta from early on, and never really broke loose despite a regular succession of revolts. Ancient MESSENE, their beautifully situated capital, remains the least tourist-swarmed of major ruin sites in Greece. The region also boasts some of the country's best beaches, which are punctuated by pleasant old seaside towns (PYLOS, METHONI and KORONI among others), each under the shade of a historic fortress bearing the marks of countless captures and recaptures by the Venetians and the Ottomans.

Elis

The landscape of Elis is reminiscent of northern Italy, with an intensively cultivated coastal plain and dense leafy forests in the foothills of the interior. In Antiquity it was regarded as a holy land and kept free of arms on account of the sanctuary of Zeus at OLYMPIA, the holiest site of the ancient Greek religion and the venue of the Olympic Games. The park-like setting of the ruins of Olympia contrasts with another Classical site nearby, the temple of Apollo at BASSAE, which crowns a barren mountaintop in the middle of wilderness, and formed perhaps the single most stirring ancient monument of Greece before it was condomized some years ago in an ill-advised protection scheme.

Planning

Packaged tours from Athens generally include only the northern half of the peninsula. A typical **4-day tour** would be: Corinth, Mycenae, Epidauros, Nafplio (overnight), Tripoli, Bassae, Olympia (overnight), Patras, Delphi (overnight), Thebes, Athens.

Alternatively: Corinth, Mycenae, Epidauros, Nafplio (overnight), Leonidio, Sparta-Mistra (overnight), Bassae, Olympia (overnight), Patras, Corinth, Athens.

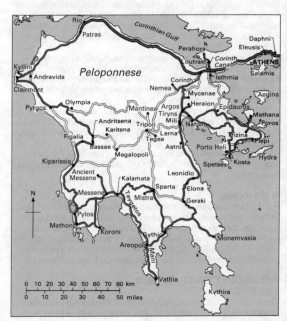

The following **7-day itinerary** would be hectic by most people's standards. It assumes a private or rented car and makes no provision for unplanned delays, laziness, lovely beaches, etc.

Day 1: Corinth and Acrocorinth; Nemea; Mycenae; Nafplio; Epidauros. Overnight at Nafplio (210km/131 miles from Athens, including Nafplio-Epidauros and back).

Day 2: Arcadian coast to Leonidio; Geraki; Monemvasia (189km/118 miles; slow driving most of the way).

Day 3: Gythio; tour of the Mani; night at Gythio (211km/132 miles; leave enough time for the Diros Caves and stopovers in villages).

Day 4: Sparta; Mistra; Kalamata; then either visit ancient Messene and spend the night at Kiparissia (201km/126 miles), or choose one of the following: Koroni (164km/103 miles), Pylos (160km/100 miles) or Methoni (175km/109 miles).

Day 5: Up to Bassae by the (partly bad) w road via Figalia; down via Andritsena; night at Olympia (198km/124 miles from Pylos).

Day 6: Fast drive to Patras; ferry from Rio to Antirio; Nafpaktos; night at Delphi — see EXCURSION 3, pages 96-99 — (225km/141 miles).

Day 7: Back to Athens (167km/104 miles).

Total distance: About 1,350km (844 miles).

Gain a day by cutting off Messenia: drive from Sparta to Megalopoli (direct route via Perivolia, slow but scenic), catch the sunset at Bassae, and arrive in Olympia after dark. Alternatively, **add a day** for a tour of the Argolid Peninsula, with visits to one or two islands: day one, continue from Epidauros to Poros; day two, visit Hydra, return to Nafplio at night.

Transportation

Buses to all points in the Peloponnese leave Athens from the KTEL terminal at Kifissias 100. As a rule, take the bus to the provincial capital (Corinth, Patras, Argos, Tripoli, Pyrgos, Sparta, Kalamata; direct buses also to Nafplio, Gythio and Pylos), then change to the local bus.

Ten trains a day run from Stathmos Peloponnisou in Athens to Corinth, then direct or via a connection to Patras-Pyrgos-Kiparissia-Kalamata *(7 trains a day)* and Argos-Tripoli-Kalamata *(4 trains a day)*. Nafplio and Olympia are served by local spurs from Pyrgos and Argos, respectively.

"Flying Dolphin" hydrofoils serve Leonidio and Monemvasia twice a week *(Tues and Sat 9am)* from the Zea Marina at Piraeus. For hydrofoils to the Saronic islands and mainland points across, see EXCURSION 2.

Car rental is available at Patras, Nafplio, Porto Heli, Olympia, Monemvasia and Gythio. A daily Olympic flight links Athens with Kalamata.

Sightseeing

For the best beaches, choose from the Messenian towns of Pylos, Methoni and Koroni. For grand scenery, drive the Argolid and Arcadian coast routes. For unspoiled and pretty Classical ruins, try Nemea and Messene. In any event, never contemplate missing any of the following: Nafplio, Mistra, Mani, Olympia. For points on mainland Greece, N of the Corinthian Gulf, see EXCURSION 3.

ARCADIAN COAST 〈⊱ 🐎 ☆

Map 6|5-6.

The E coast of the Peloponnese between the Argolid Plain and **Leonídio** is a wild, sparsely inhabited region with several pretty villages and many deserted beaches. Before the construction of the road in the 1960s, it was one of the least accessible parts of Greece. An ethnological curiosity still exists in the upper valley of the Vrassiótis Stream, where the **Tsakon** villagers (six villages accessible by poor road from Astros or Ag. Andreas) speak a Slavic language apparently descended from the early medieval Slav invasions.

The coast has a handful of beach resorts in the earliest stages of development, the beaches of **Ástros** and **Tirós** being the main ones. Astros (population 2,500) also owns the beautiful and little-visited 11thC Monastery of Christ the Savior, or **Loukoús** (4km/2½ miles NW).

With a population of 3,500, **Leonídio** *(hydrofoil from Piraeus and Monemvasia)* is an attractive town with many medieval buildings and narrow lanes. Driving down from the N, it strikes the visitor as being the first pleasant town in Greece not entirely to subsist on tourism.

The road farther S to GERAKI follows the extraordinary gorge (◀€) of the Dafnon Stream and climbs to over 1,000m (3,300ft) at the lovely village of **Kosmás**.

◇ **Astros beach** (☎ code 0755): **Paralia** (C) (☎ *51.412* ▯). **Tiros beach** (☎ code 0757): **Blue Sea** (☎*41.369).* **Leonídio** (☎ code 0791): **Kamaria** (C) (☎*22.757* ▯ *to* ▰), furnished apartments. Private rooms at Astros, Ag. Andreas and Tiros Beach, Leonídio town and beach.

▲ 7km (4 miles) S of **Ag. Andreas**.

ARGOLID PENINSULA ◀€ ℞ ☆
Map 6|6.

The drive from EPIDAUROS to Methana may be the most dramatic in Greece, with a magnificent island-speckled sea bursting unexpectedly into view at a height of 600m (1,950ft). The N coast is especially attractive, with rich vegetation and extensive citrus orchards. Although the peninsula is ringed with several rapidly growing beach resorts, the spaces between them remain surprisingly unspoiled.

Some ancient and medieval ruins are visible at the unexcavated site of **Troezen** (Trizína, near the village of Damala; turnoff S 7km (4 miles) W of Galatas), more interesting for their peaceful rustic setting than anything else. The city was important in Mycenaean times but played a secondary role in later Antiquity.

The small port of **Ermióni** is the subject of Strabo's curious remark that, the passage to Hades from this country being a short cut, the inhabitants did not put passage-money in the mouths of their dead. The passage in question remains undiscovered.

The principal resorts, **Paleá Epídavros** (not the ancient ruin site, which is 13km/8 miles inland), **Néa Epídavros**, **Galatás**, **Plépi** (Hydra Beach) and **Porto Héli/Kósta** offer precious little beyond beaches and acceptable hotels. They are unremarkable as towns, particularly the last four, which grew only recently to accommodate the spillover from the Saronic Islands. **Méthana**, which is older and nicer, is very popular with Athenians because of its hot sulfur baths.

◇ **Palea Epidavros** (☎ code 0753): more than 20 B, C and D hotels, such as **Stratos** (B) (☎*41.535* ▰) and **Apollon** (C) (☎*41.295* ▯). **Methana** (☎ code 0298): about a dozen B, C and D hotels, including **Avra** (B) (☎*92.382* ▯) and **American** (C) *(92.285/7* ▯).

Galatas: see POROS under SARONIC ISLANDS.

Ermioni (☎ code 0754): a few spartan hotels on the quayside, and two large resort hotels on the beach (E): **Costa Perla** (B) (☎ *31.112/8* 🏠) and **Lena-Mary** (B) (☎ *31.450/1* 🏠🏠).

Plepi (☎ code 0754): the two biggest, classiest and most modern resort complexes of the coast are **Hydra Beach (Kappa Club)** (A) (☎ *41.080* 🏠🏠🏠) and **Porto Hydra** (A) (☎ *41.112* 🏠🏠 *to* 🏠🏠🏠). See also HYDRA under SARONIC ISLANDS).

Porto Heli and Kosta (☎ code 0754): nine substantial A-B beach hotels and more than a dozen more modest ones, such as **Porto Heli** (A) (☎ *51.490/4* 🏠🏠), **Galaxy** (B) (☎ *51.271/3* 🏠🏠) and **Alcyon** (C) (☎ *51.161/3* 🏠 *to* 🏠🏠).

ARGOS 🏛

140km (88 miles) SW of Athens. Map 6I5. Population: 20,000 ☎ *code: 0751.*

Argos is one of the oldest cities of Greece and one of the very few that has had a more or less continuous history under the same name, but its historic sights are few and not of great interest. The town thrives as the chief market of the fertile plain of the same name, which yields a large part of Greece's orange product; the central produce market and "bazaar" streets are worth a visit for their colorful commotion.

HISTORY AND LEGENDS

Argos was the chief city of Greece in the Heroic Age, and Homer uses "Argive" as a synonym for Greek. It was established by the semilegendary **Pelasgians**, a pre-Hellenic people who introduced the cult of Hera. The royal line was founded by **Danaos**, an Egyptian who was a son of Io, the Holy Cow. His 50 daughters (the Danaids) murdered their husbands on the night of their collective wedding and threw their heads in the marshes of Lerna, for which ghastly act they were condemned by the god of the underworld to carry water forever in a leaking vessel.

The successors of Danaos included **Perseus**, king of Mycenae and Tiryns, who slew the snake-haired Medusa and married the Ethiopian princess Andromeda, and **Amphitryon**, who was the father of Heracles. The kingdom then fell to the descendants of Pelops, the eponymous ruler of the Peloponnese, who ruled from the citadel of MYCENAE; **Agamemnon** was his grandson.

In historic times Argos came under the sway of the Dorians, who invaded the Peloponnese c.1200BC, and was generally overshadowed by Sparta. In 272BC, the Macedonian king Pyrrhus, he of the Pyrrhic victory, was killed in Argos after being hit by a tile thrown by an old woman from a rooftop. The city maintained a degree of importance through Roman, Byzantine and Frankish rule, and only lost primacy to Nafplio during the Venetian-Turkish centuries.

SIGHTS AND PLACES OF INTEREST

There is a rather fine Hellenistic-Roman **theater** at the SW edge of the town; with a capacity of 20,000 spectators, it is one of the largest in Greece. More interesting is the **Kastro** (◀€), a Byzantine-Frankish-Venetian-Turkish citadel enclosing **Larissa**, the ancient acropolis of Argos.

✿ **Telessila** (C) (☎ *28.351* 🏠); but with NAFPLIO only 13km (8 miles) away, there is little reason to stay in Argos.

ENVIRONS

The massive but completely destroyed ruins of the Argive **Heraion** (temple of Hera) occupy a bald solitary hilltop 6km (4 miles) NE of town. They are certainly worth a visit for the splendid view. Not a trace has been found of the famous paintings of Polyclitus, which Strabo tells us were the most beautiful in the world.

Hera, the jealous wife of Zeus, was the principal deity of the Argives and thus the main protector of the Greeks during the Trojan War. She was born at the **Stymphalian Lake** (35km/22 miles NW, near NEMEA), whose waters were believed to communicate by an underground channel with the **Erasinos Spring** (in the village of Kefalari, 5km/2½ miles s of Argos).

BASSAE (Váses) 🏛 ⊲⋵

47km (29 miles) from coast (mostly unpaved road); 14km (9 miles) from Andritsena. Map 5I4. No public transportation (only tour buses). Free entrance.

The road climbs through a forested valley to increasingly barren and desolate mountains. Each turn reveals a higher range of gray cliffs, with only a few stray goats and a solitary hovering eagle to accompany the wild oaks. Joachim Bocher, who in 1765 was the first Westerner to get this far, was overwhelmed to discover on top of the highest peak of the range, at 1,150m (3,773ft), a nearly intact **Temple of Apollo** from the finest era of Classical architecture. The modern experience is somewhat less stirring: at the end of the gruelling drive the visitor is regaled with the sight, gleaming in the distance, of a vast, white circus tent.

It was the idea of some benighted archeologist, eager to protect his little domain against the depredations of sun and wind, to clothe the temple of Apollo in a plastic sack. The temple itself, which is as good as any other temple (Doric, 6 x 15 column peristyle, stylobate of three steps, etc.), once derived its tremendous majesty from a setting that inspired divine awe. It now looks like the skeleton of a dinosaur trapped in a sterile museum.

The temple is described by Pausanias as a work of Ictinus, the architect of the Parthenon, although modern opinion places it to a somewhat earlier date. The frieze of the cella, which had survived wholly intact, was removed by Ch. Cockerell in 1811-12 and forms one of the prize exhibits of the British Museum.

There is no food or shelter at the site. 14km (9 miles) down the way is the attractive mountain village of **Andritséna**, which has adapted itself to tourism in a so far pleasant way; there are several tavernas.

🍴 **Theoxenia** (B) *(at Andritsena ☎ (0626) 22.219 ||||)* rents rooms.

CORINTH (Kórinthos) 🏛 🏰 ★

Town 80km (50 miles) w of Athens. Map 6H6. Population 22,000 ☎ code: 0741. Archeological site 6km (4 miles) sw of town; open daily 8.30am-3pm 🎟500dr.

The modern town of Corinth was founded in 1858 after an earthquake destroyed the older site, which had grown among the ruins of ancient Corinth. It is a colorless place overshadowed on the one hand by the popular beach resort of **Loutraki** (5km/2½ miles N) and on the other by the lively touristville that has again sprouted near the ruins.

HISTORY AND LEGENDS

The name of Corinth indicates a pre-Greek origin. In the 7thC BC, under the enlightened rule of the tyrant Periander, the city became one of the leading maritime powers of Greece, with colonies as far afield as Corcyra (Corfu) and Syracuse (Sicily).

Overshadowed by Athens for several centuries, it returned to prominence in the 3rdC BC as the leader of the Achaean League, which was the last independent Greek power to emerge during the decline of the Macedonians. Its tense relationship with Rome finally led to its complete eradication by L. Mummius in 146BC.

Corinth was rebuilt in 44BC by orders of Julius Caesar and repopulated with Roman legionnaires and freedmen who, according to Strabo, looted an incredible amount of art among the rubble, swamping Roman markets with Corinthian antiquities. In 29BC Augustus created the Roman province of Achaea, comprising all of southern Greece except the "free" cities, with Corinth as its proconsular seat. The city was richly embellished by various emperors.

St Paul arrived in Corinth after Athens and lived here for 18mths plying his trade as tent-maker *(Acts 18.1-17)*. His epistles to the Corinthians contain one of the most famous and moving passages of the New Testament, the so-called Hymn to Love *(I Corinthians 13)*:

> "If I speak with the tongues of men and angels, and have not love, then I am become as sounding brass or a tinkling cymbal. And if I have the gift of prophecy, and understand all mysteries, and all knowledge; and have all faith so that I could remove mountains, and have not love, I am nothing. And though I bestow all my goods to feed the poor, and have not love, it profiteth me nothing.... For now we see the world through a glass darkly; but then we shall see it face to face."

The magnificent fortress of the Acrocorinth, being a key to the control of the Peloponnese and of the trade route through the Isthmus, allowed the city to maintain some importance during the Middle Ages. Under Frankish-Venetian rule it was the principal export point of Greek products to the West, including a type of raisin that obtained the name currant from its port of shipment.

ANCIENT CORINTH

The archeological area excavated by the American School comprises the **Roman Agora** (Forum), a vast and monumental space with the ruins of numerous public buildings surrounding it. The heavily ruined shells of a Greek-Roman **theater** and an **odeon**, the latter a gift of the ubiquitous Herodes Atticus, are seen outside the site. Soon after the main entrance, note the **Corinthian capitals** placed on the re-erected columns of an unidentified temple, recalling the architectural order that the city pioneered in the 4thC BC.

The agora is dominated from a prominence on the N by the 6thC BC Doric **Temple of Apollo**, whose seven standing columns are not only all that remain of the pre-Roman city, but the only relatively well-preserved specimen of an Archaic Greek temple as well. Several **stoas**, which in their own day must have been a glorious sight indeed, surround the marketplace, interspersed with the memorials of various Roman worthies, Mummius and Caesar among them. The ceremonial **Lechaion Road** was, as customary in wealthier Hellenistic and Roman cities, lined with marble colonnades to either side surmounted by rows of statues.

Some of these statues, mostly Roman works with the characteristic mixture of pomp and realism, can be seen at the site **museum**. The museum also contains interesting late Roman mosaics and a wealth of Latin inscriptions.

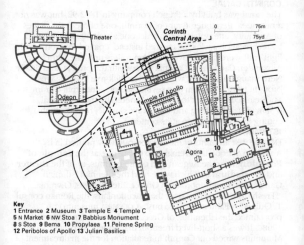

Key
1 Entrance 2 Museum 3 Temple E 4 Temple C
5 N Market 6 NW Stoa 7 Babbius Monument
8 S Stoa 9 Bema 10 Propylaea 11 Peirene Spring
12 Peribolos of Apollo 13 Julian Basilica

The attractive village of **Arhéa Kórinthos**, with its old rustic
houses set among orchards, derives its livelihood exclusively
from tourism. A derelict mosque and several old churches are
reminders of the town's history before 1858.

ACROCORINTH

The acropolis of Corinth was famous in Antiquity for its **Temple
of Aphrodite**, which owned more than 1,000 sacred prostitutes,
slaves dedicated to the goddess by both male and female
citizens. According to Strabo, the city was crowded with visitors
and grew rich on account of these women. Sailors freely spent
their money on them, whence the proverb, "Not for every man
the voyage to Corinth."

Acrocorinth was besieged without success for 5yrs by
Guillaume de Champlitte, Geoffroi de Villehardouin and Othon
de la Roche before it fell to the Franks in 1210.

The dizzying 575m-high rock (1,886ft) says a lot for the vigor of
those men of ancient times who came to pay their respects to the
goddess. The top is enclosed by a **triple fortification**; the first
gate through is Turkish, the second Venetian, the third, with
flanking towers, from the 4thC BC, when a Macedonian
stronghold was erected here as one of the key supports of
Philip's hegemony over Greece. The remains of an old Turkish
quarter (mosque, minaret, baths) are prominent within the
citadel. Traces of the Temple of Aphrodite are visible at the
highest point — and one of the most memorable views in Greece.

☞ In **Arhea Korinthos** there are numerous private rooms and
inexpensive hotels in a pleasant setting. **Xenia** (A) (☎ 31.208 ▥) is
mainly a restaurant with a few guest rooms.
 Korinthos: a dozen C and D hotels, such as **Ephira** (C) (*Vass.
Konstantinou 52* ☎ 22.434 ▯).
 Isthmia: King Saron (A) (☎ 37.201/4 ▥ ⇌ ⫷ ⩜ ⋒ ♫ ▤ ▣ ◉
◉ ⱽᴵˢᴬ) is the best and largest in these environs; **Isthmia** (B) (☎ 23.454
▥ ⫷ ⫸).
 Loutraki has an extraordinary wealth of hotels in all classes, including
nine A and over 20 B: **Paolo** (A) (☎ 48.742 ▥); **Barbara** (B) (☎ 45.258
▥); **Elpis** (C) (☎ 48.263 ▯).

CORINTH CANAL

The canal was built by a French company in 1882-92, but was not a new idea: Periander, tyrant of Corinth, one of the Seven Sages of Antiquity, attempted to construct one about 600BC. Defeated by technical obstacles, he created instead a paved road on which light craft were hauled over wooden rollers until the 12thC. Alexander, Caesar and Caligula toyed with the project, and finally Nero inaugurated work with a golden pick-axe. 6,000 slaves brought from Jerusalem dug several sectors, until civil war in AD68 caused the work to be abandoned. The modern canal, 6.3km (3.9 miles) long and 23m (25yds) wide, runs through a cutting 87m (285ft) deep at its center.

ISTHMIA

Despite vast amounts of money and publicity poured in by the American School, little remains to excite one at the **Temple of Poseidon**, near the Aegean end of the isthmus, or of the **theater** and the **stadium** in which were held the biennial Isthmian Games, the most important in Greece after those of Olympia.

Fresh from his victory over the Macedonians, the Roman consul T. Quinctius Flamininus (see bust at OLYMPIA museum) proclaimed the Liberation of Greece at the Isthmian Games of 196BC. It was a short-lived freedom that ended 50yrs later when Mummius wiped out Corinth in retaliation for the maltreatment of Roman envoys, who were showered with excrement in the streets of the city. Nero, not one to be outdone by precedent, announced the independence of Greece again at the Isthmian Games of AD67. No one took him seriously.

HERAION OF PERACHORA

The remote and wild site of the **Temple of Hera**, situated in an olive grove on the steep headland NW of Corinth, makes it a worthwhile excursion for lovers of dramatic sights. Not much is left of the temple, but there is a delightful deserted cove nearby with transparent waters, and the views along the way, especially at sunset, are spectacular.

DIROS CAVES See MANI.

EPIDAUROS (Epídavros) 🏛 ☆
28km (18 miles) E of Nafplio. Map 6I6. Local bus to Ligourio (3km/2 miles) or tour bus. Open Mon-Fri 8.30am-6pm; Sat-Sun 8.30am-3pm 🔁*500dr.*

The sanctuary of Asclepius, one of the most famous medical centers of Antiquity, was set in the tranquil atmosphere of pine- and oleander-clad hills not far from the coastal city of Epidauros. The sanctuary itself now consists of a heap of jumbled stone, but its 14,000-seat theater has been preserved almost intact, and as such forms one of the foremost Classical attractions of Greece. In size or architecture it will not exactly overwhelm a visitor who is familiar with Verona or Aspendos; but the site is truly pleasant, and the performances of Classical drama mounted at the theater evoke an extraordinary sense of Antiquity.

The cult of Asclepius probably originated in Thessaly, although its most important sanctuary was at Epidauros. The god of healing was born of Apollo and a mortal Thessalian woman by the name of Koronis (Crow), who was slain for sleeping with another man while pregnant with Apollo's son, bringing eternal disgrace upon the bird of her name. The boy was trained by Chiron the Centaur, and eventually wound up at Epidauros, where he incurred the displeasure of Hades by going so far as to raise men from the dead.

The Asclepian method of treatment involved an elaborate mixture of ritual, suggestion and psychological care besides baths, medicinal plants and surgery. The sick would perform ritual purifications, and wait for the god to prescribe a cure in their dreams. Artistic and intellectual pursuits were considered essential to the treatment, hence the theater, the odeon and the profusion of (now vanished) works of art. Payment was through the sacrifice of a cock and the presentation of a votive offering, usually a replica of the part of the body that was cured.

The **theater** dates from the 4thC BC, the earliest date when theaters were built of stone, and seems to have maintained its original structure without later alterations. The shape of the auditorium is designed for maximum acoustic effect, which can be tested by standing on the top row and listening to tourists' chatter some 25m (27yds) down on the stage.

The only noteworthy structure among the ruins of the sanctuary itself is a **tholos**, a large circular colonnade rather like the one at Delphi and similarly obscure in its original use.

Some ruins of the ancient city of Epidauros are visible beneath the transparent sea at **Paleá Epídavros**, 13km (8 miles) E (see ARGOLID PENINSULA).

The only accommodations at the site itself are in **Xenia** (B) (☎ (0753) 22.003 ▮▮▮), 24 stone bungalows hidden among the pines. People more normally stay at either NAFPLIO or Palea Epidavros.

GERÁKI ▲ ▥ ☆
42km (26 miles) E of Sparta. Map 6J5. Population: 1,600.
On a bare hill almost untouched by tourism stand the deserted, half-destroyed shells of medieval Geraki (locally Pírgos, or "Tower"), topped by a crumbling fortress that was once the seat of one of the 12 Frankish baronies of the Peloponnese. The fort was built in 1254 by Jean de Nivelet, a knight from the Franche Comté. The ruins include more than a dozen late medieval churches, some of which (notably the **Ag. Georgios** within the fortress) retain considerable frescoes. The site is particularly attractive in springtime when **Mt. Taygetos** rises snow-capped on the W horizon. The newer village of Geraki is a pleasant place, 2km (1 mile) to the W, with some tavernas. Those wishing to see the interior of the churches should apply here for keys.

GYTHIO ▨ ☞ ☆
47km (29 miles) S of Sparta. Map 6J5. Population: 4,000.
☎ *code: 0733.*
Gythio is a very attractive port town with much old architecture as yet unspoiled by modern encroachments. Until a decade ago it was practically untouched by tourism, though the recent popularity of the MANI, for which Gythio forms the best base of exploration, has begun to bring in a steady stream of visitors.

The town offers few specific sights. A tour of reconnaissance should include the harbor promenade, the first parallel street up (with many old houses) and the ruined castle (◀◗). On the islet of **Kranai** (reached by causeway), where Helen and Paris are said to have spent their first night together after eloping from Sparta, there is a Mani-style **tower house**, which has now been converted into a museum of Mainote folklore *(invariably closed)*.

10km (6 miles) W of town is the ruined castle of **Passava**, built in the 13thC under the name of *Passe-avant* by barons of the de Neuilly family.

The twice-weekly ferry to **Crete** via the island of **Kythera** departs from Gythio Wed 11am and Thurs 11pm.

≈ **Gythion** (A) (☎ *23.523* IIIⵏ), the best in town, is housed in a fine 19thC building on the harbor. Next door, in a similarly charming but slightly rundown house, is **Aktaion** (D) (☎ *22.294* ⵏⵏ), doubling up as the studio of the local artist and poet N. Zografakis.

On the beaches on either side of town: **Lakonis** (A) (☎ *22.666* IIIⵏ); **Belle Helene** (B) (☎ *22.867* IIIⵏ); **Laryssion** (C) (☎ *22.021/6* ⵏⵏ).

▲ On the beach NW of town.

KALAMÁTA
260km (163 miles) SW of Athens. Map 6J5. Population: 40,000 ☎ *code: 0721. Air connection daily at 7.50pm from and at 9.10pm to Athens, with added flight Sat-Sun, 7,000dr one-way (* ☎ *22.376 or 22.724).*

Kalamata is mostly uninteresting except as the producer of the excellent olives that have made its name famous around the world. Its broad main avenue shows the hand of the French engineers who laid it out after 1829. Traces of the 1981 earthquake, which caused extensive damage in Kalamata, are still very much in evidence, with fascinatingly graphic if unfortunate examples of the destructive mechanics of how a quake affects buildings.

The town has a somewhat prosaic 13thC **citadel** with several fine 19thC houses, and a Byzantine church nearby. A coastal boulevard continues E of the port to a mini pleasure port with tavernas, and on to a long pebble beach lined with hotels.

≈ **Elite** (A) (☎ *25.015* IIIⵏ ≈); **Filoxenia** (B) (☎ *23.166/8* IIIⵏ), considered the best, isolated site at the far end of the beach; **Haikos** (C) (☎ *82.886* ⵏⵏ). Several inexpensive hotels are near the railroad station.

KALÁVRYTA ◁≡ ☆
78km (49 miles) SE of Patra (28km/18 miles from coast). Map 6H5. Population: 2,000 ☎ *code: 0692.*

This pleasant summer resort is worth a visit for the spectacular scenery of the **Vouraikos Gorge**, through which a quaint 19thC toy train huffs and puffs its way up to a green and watery spot at 750m (2,460ft). The town was rebuilt after being wiped out by the Nazis in reprisal for partisan activities during World War II.

Near the N end of the gorge (9km/6 miles N of Kalavryta) is the **Monastery of Mega Spileo**, an astonishing complex perched at the edge of a cavern at the foot of an immense perpendicular cliff. The history of the monastery is lost in medieval lore, and the current buildings date from only 1934. Pride of place among the monastic possessions goes to an icon of the Virgin painted by St Luke the Evangelist himself, and the skull of St Euphrosyne, who discovered the aforementioned icon miraculously preserved in this cavern.

Another monastery nearby, the **Agia Lavra** (7km/4 miles SW of Kalavryta), occupies an important place in modern Greek history as the place where on March 25, 1821, Germanos, Archbishop of Patras, raised the banner of revolt against the Turks. The otherwise attractive site is marred by too much gushing patriotism.

≈ **Filoxenia** (B) (☎ *22.422* IIIⵏ); **Maria** (C) (☎ *22.296* IIIⵏ).

KORÓNI ☷ ☜ ☆

53km (33 miles) s of Kalamata. Map 5J4. Population: 2,000
☎ *code: 0725.*

Koroni is a pleasant little port town of whitewashed houses with
pink roofs surrounded by a generous landscape of vineyards and
olives. Its **Venetian castle** stands out of all proportion to the
village, a reminder of the time (1206-1500) when Coron, as it was
then called, and nearby Modon (METHONI) were the chief
strategic assets of the Italian city-republic in the Peloponnese.

The citadel was occupied by the Turks, by the Venetians again
(1687-1715), and then by the Turks again; it still contains some
inhabited houses and semiruined churches. Beyond it, a tawny
sand beach extends for miles, with only a decent number of
locals and some independently traveling tourists around to enjoy
its pleasures.

☞ Practically every other house in Koroni rents rooms. The only hotel
with any pretensions is **Auberge de la Plage** (B) (☎ *22.401* 〓).

KYLLÍNI ☷ ☜

Map 5H3.

The western "spur" of the Peloponnese is formed by the fertile
alluvial deposits of the Peneios River. **Andravída**, the chief
market of the district, retains few clues of its mighty past as the
seat of the Frankish Princedom of Achaea. The rich and proud
medieval port of **Clarence** (Glaréntsa), which once stood at the
NW tip of the peninsula, is now reduced to a few indefinite bits of
stone at the western edge of the nondescript beach resort of
Kyllini. On a lone prominence dominating the entire plain, 5km
(2½ miles) inland, is the **Castle of Clairmont** (Hlemoútsi, or
Castel Tornese), the best-preserved Frankish monument in
Greece, a building of huge size and barbaric splendor. It contains
a little Gothic church, and a maze of parapets and bastions
pervaded by a melancholy air.

The plain belonged in heroic times to the kings of Elis, who
were famous for their innumerable herds of cattle. One of the
twelve labors of Heracles (see NAFPLIO) involved cleaning the
stables of Augeias, King of Elis, which had grown so thick with
manure that the land could no longer bear fruit. The hero
accomplished his task by bringing the rivers Alpheios and
Peneios together to flush the plain clean, and "cleaning the
Augean stables" has been proverbial ever since for a bold attack
on a long-neglected sore.

The Principality of Achaea (or Morea) was created in 1205 by
Geoffroi de Villehardouin, a knight of the Champagne, and held
suzerainty over the 12 Duchies of the Frankish Peloponnese. It
was later conquered by Mahiot de Coquerel and the Chevalier de
San Superan, acquired by the Kingdom of Navarre, sold to the
Counts of Cephallonia, and finally abolished by the Despots of
MISTRA in 1432.

‡ *The Duchy of Clarence was the allodial (absolutely owned)
domain of the Princes of Achaea, from whom it passed by
marriage to the family of Hainault. The title was revived by
Edward III of England and his Queen, Philippa of Hainault, in
favor of their second son, Lionel, and remains one of the most
illustrious titles of the English nobility to this day.*

☞ Numerous beach hotels at **Loutra Kyllinis**, 9km (6 miles) s of Kyllini
on the opposite shore of the peninsula. Some simple hotels in **Kyllini** itself.

LEONÍDIO   See ARCADIAN COAST.

MANÍ ⛰ 🏨 🏮 ⟨⟨ 🦐 ★

*Areopoli (main village) 82km (51 miles) SE of Kalamata,
28km (18 miles) SW of Gythio. Map 6J-K5. Population of the
peninsula: c.2,000 ☎ code: 0733. Bus from Kalamata to
Areopoli; from Gythio to all villages.*

The mountain fastnesses of the middle "finger" of the
Peloponnese, called Mani after the Frankish castle of Le Grand
Maigne or Maine near Cape Tenaro, were the refuge of Laconian
fugitives during the centuries of Turkish rule. After
independence, much patriotic mileage was made out of the claim
that Mani constituted the only part of the Greek fatherland never
to have been subjected to the Turk; the prosaic truth seems to
have been more like certain parts of the Bronx that New York
police write off as beyond saving. Unlike the Bronx, however,
the Mainote bandits had the esthetic sense to dot their eyries with
incredibly picturesque fortified villages, so that their strange and
eerie land is now one of the most rewarding to tour in Greece.
To be sure, Mani is no longer the lost world so lyrically described
by Patrick Leigh Fermor in the 1960s; there is no shortage of tour
buses that ply its precipitous lanes; but they have not yet fully
eradicated that awesome sense of crossing the farthest edge of
the continent.

SIGHTS AND PLACES OF INTEREST

The only substantial village in Mani proper, that is, the only one
with more than two shops, is **Areópoli**, which must constitute
the beginning and end of a tour (86km/54 miles) of the peninsula.
‡ *Areopoli was renamed after Ares, the god of war, in memory of
its most famous son, Petrobey Mavromichalis, hereditary
chieftain of Mani during the War of Independence. Of godlike
beauty with black bushy eyebrows, and armed to the teeth with
scimitar and carbine, he took part in 49 battles, not all of them
against the Turks. Imprisoned by the revolutionary government,
he responded by having Kapodistrias, the first president of
Greece, assassinated. On his mother's side, he descended from a
mermaid.*

There are some 40 villages in the shadow of the **Kakovoúnia**
(Evil Mountain, 1,214m/3,983ft), consisting mostly of a few
tower-houses huddled together. Nearly all bear the stamp of the
Middle Ages, and it is hard to pick one that is more picturesque
than others: **Kíta** (population 100), which was the stronghold of
the notorious Nicli clan, and **Váthia**, which was deserted by its

inhabitants before the GNTO
restored it as a rustic hotel-
hamlet, yield the best
photographs. **Tsikaliá** and
Lágia have memorable
settings. The little gloomy
port of **Geroliménas** is the
only village set directly on
the shore. A dozen or so
villages own quaint little
late-Byzantine churches, and
the **Ag. Iannis** of Areopoli
contains some naive wall-
paintings of vivid imagination.

   In all, some 800 tower-
houses have been counted.
Their architecture testifies to

the exigencies of warding off not only the forces of law but the no less dangerous rapacity of neighbors, rivals, kinsmen and blood-foes. Most are more or less abandoned, but some of the few that remain in use are veritable museums of folk art, and people who do own such houses (such as in Areopoli and Kita) will usually be eager to show them off to curious visitors.

Cape Tainaron (Ténaro), the tip of the peninsula, was known in mythology as the spot where Heracles descended into the underworld to steal Cerberus, the three-headed dog of Hades. The ride across the ridge from Gerolimenas to **Kokála** offers the most extraordinary scenery.

Small beaches of dazzling white pebble exist all around the peninsula, notably near the **Diros caves** (see below), at **Mezapos**, below **Vathia** and at **Kotronas**.

DIROS CAVES ★
📧 *1,100dr.*

The **Glyfáda Cave**, at the seashore below Pirgos Dirou, must count as the most extraordinary natural sight of Greece and is bound to impress even the most jaded cave-goer. The cave in fact an underground lake 5km ($2\frac{1}{2}$ miles) long and 5 to 25m ($5\frac{1}{2}$ to 27yds) wide, with an enormous wealth of stalactites. Visitors are taken on a 45min rowboat ride through a scenery of terrifying beauty, which cannot fail to evoke images of Charon and the Styx. Even the silliest tourists are reduced to awed silence even after the first few minutes of the ride.

Located about 200m (220yds) from the entrance of the Glyfada along the seashore, the **Alepótrypa Cave** is reputedly as impressive, although in order to safeguard the numerous Paleolithic and Neolithic finds inside, it remains closed to visitors.

EXO MANI ◁

The W slopes of **Mt. Taygetos** along the coast between Areopoli and KALAMATA, known as the Outer Mani, are traversed by a magnificent road with fabulous views. The scenery changes rapidly from the scrub-covered gray hills of the S to a delectably lush environment of vineyards, palms and dark cypresses. Instead of the grim pride of Mani proper, villages present the smiling countenance of agreeable little squares with cafés set under ancient plane trees, pergolas of climbing rose, and pomegranate trees of dazzling color. There are deserted inlets for swimming, and the usual complement of Byzantine churches in practically every village. The pleasant fishing port of **Kardamyli** is a good place to stop for lunch or a beach break.

‡ *In 1675, the inhabitants of Oitylo (or Ítilo) emigrated en masse to Corsica. There is a persistent legend that the family of Napoleone Bonaparte descended from these emigrants, and that its name was a literal translation of Kalomeris, Greek for "Goodland."*

☙ **Inner Mani:** The GNTO have restored tower-houses in **Areopoli**, **Gerolimenas** and **Vathia**; they are wonderfully atmospheric places to stay, but the villages do become somewhat lonely at night, so many will prefer to set up base at GYTHIO. In addition, some basic hotels or pensions exist at **Itilo**, **Areopoli**, **Pirgos Dirou**, **Gerolimenas** and **Kotronas**.

GNTO guesthouses *(all class-A* ▮▮▮ *no cards)*: **Pirgos Kapetanakou** *(Areopoli* ☎ *51.233)*; **Pirgos Tsitsiri** *(Gerolimenas* ☎ *54.297)*; **Vathia Traditional Village** *(* ☎ *54.244)*.

Outer Mani: **Lefktron** (B) *(on Neohori beach at Stoupa* ☎ *(0721) 54.322* ▮▮▮*)*; **Theano** (C) *(Kardamyli* ☎ *(0721) 73.222* ▮▯*)*. Some basic accommodations also exist at **Ag. Nikolaos**.

▲ At **Stoupa**.

MEGALÓPOLI

37km (23 miles) SW of Tripoli. Map 6I5. Population: 5,000
☎ *code: 0791.*

The only sight of moderate interest in Megalopoli is the half-ruined ancient **theater**, which was once the largest in Greece, with a seating capacity of more than 20,000.

The city owes its outsized name and appointments to the grandiose concept of Epaminondas, who herded together the inhabitants of 40 Arcadian communes in 371-368BC to create Megali Polis (Great City) as a strategic bulwark against Sparta. A hundred years later the place lay dead and deserted. Its one famous son was Polybius the historian (204-122BC), the man who gave the Romans their first taste of Greek civilization.

≈ Leto (C) (☎ *22.302* ▯□).

MESSENE *(Arhéa Messíni)* ▥ ☆

26km (16 miles) N of Messini town (37km/23 miles NW of Kalamata). Map 5J4.

The ruins of ancient Messene lie scattered in a beautiful countryside against the imposing backdrop of Mt. Ithomi (800m/2,625ft); the village of **Mavromáti** occupies part of the ancient site. Much of the old buildings lie half-buried in soil and overgrown with vegetation, and the absence of overt archeological activity forms a welcome contrast with other Classical locations.

The city was built after 370BC at the instigation of Epaminondas, who liberated Messenia from its long subjection to Sparta and encouraged its inhabitants to build cities. Pausanias called its walls the most powerful he had seen, not excluding those of Babylon. Messenians believed that Zeus was reared on Mt. Ithomi by a nymph. A hymn referred to —

> "Zeus of Ithomi whose heart the muse pleased,
> With her pure strings, with her free sandals."

The ruins are to be found in a wide arc below the village. They include a substantial portion of the walls that so impressed Pausanias (the **Arcadian Gate**, about 1km/½ mile NW of the village), a large and a small **theater**, and an **agora** containing traces of a sanctuary of Asclepius.

On the peak of **Mt. Ithomi** (20min climb), some abandoned monastic buildings occupy the site of the former Temple of Zeus, with extraordinary views over the surrounding country. The **Vourkano Monastery**, on a SE spur of the mountain with buildings dating from the 18thC, provides room for travelers. Further accommodations and a railroad station exist at the village of **Meligalás** (Milk-and-Honey), 13km (8 miles) NE.

METHÓNI ▥ ☜ ☆

65km (41 miles) SW of Kalamata. Map 5J4. Population: 1,750 ☎ *code: 0723.*

Of the Messenian ports of Methoni, KORONI and PYLOS, each having the similar attractions of a pleasant village, Venetian castle and beach, Koroni boasts the quaintest village, Pylos the best beach and Methoni the finest castle. The harbor has been sanded up, and where Venetian galleys once dropped anchor, small numbers of Northern Europeans enjoy the sun.

The **castle**, a magnificent structure with moats and drawbridges and parapets, has traces of the pre-independence town (ruined baths, mosque, church) within its vast enclosure. The two bastions on either side of the main landward gate bear the proud Venetian names of Bembo (15thC) and Loredan (1714); beyond them is a Gothic inner gate from the 13thC. The graceful fortified tower (**Boúrtsi**) on an islet at the seaward entrance is a Turkish addition (16thC). Cervantes was kept in the fortress as a prisoner after his capture at Lepanto (see NAFPAKTOS); otherwise it shares the history of its twin at Koroni.

The uninhabited islands of **Sapiénza** and **Schíza** are within rowing (or long swimming) distance of the coast.

✑ Methoni is much better equipped with adequate hotels than Koroni.
Methoni Beach (B) (☎ *31.455 or 31.544* ▥*compulsory half-board* 🚗 ▨ *12 rms*) has a prime location between the castle and beach; **Alex** (C) (☎ *31.219* ▥ *18 rms); **Phoenix** (D) (☎ *31.390* ▯).

▲ On the beach SE of town and at **Finikounda**, 14km (9 miles) E.

MISTRÁ ⛰ 🏨 ◁€ ★
8km (5 miles) W of Sparta. Map 6J5. Site open daily 8.30am-3pm, sometimes until 6pm 🎫*500dr.*

On a nearly vertical mountain face in the eastern foothills of Mt. Taygetos stand the spectacular ruins of the medieval walled city of Mistra, where for a brief Indian summer in the 15thC the Byzantine civilization experienced its last and in some ways most interesting flowering. The churches, monasteries and palaces are unique in Greece in that they surpass the unambitious scale usually associated with Byzantine buildings in this part of the empire; they reflect the taste and wealth of the Constantinopolitan court, which briefly took refuge in this wild mountaintop before being swept away under the Turkish wave.

The fortress of Mistra was built by Guillaume de Villehardouin in 1249. After changing hands several times in the following 100yrs, it became in 1349 the seat of a semi-independent Byzantine governor by the title of Despot (Lord) of Morea, who managed to retake the Peloponnese from the Franks piecemeal over the next 80yrs. The despotate was usually held by a brother or son of the reigning Byzantine emperor, and reached its apogee under Theodore II Paleologue (reigned 1407-43). The Despot Constantine Dragazes (reigned 1443-48) later ascended the imperial throne as Constantine XI, last emperor of Byzantium.

The most famous resident of Mistra was **Gemistus Plethon** (c.1360-1450), who has been called the originator of Platonic studies in the West. Born in Constantinople, he spent some time in the Ottoman court in Edirne before taking residence in Mistra. Here he all but renounced Christianity, devoting himself to Platonic philosophy and to the idea of reviving the ancient Greek spirit. He had enormous influence in the courts of Renaissance Italy: inspired by Plethon's lectures during the Council of Florence (1439), Cosimo de Medici went on to found the celebrated Platonic Academy, which revolutionized European philosophy. Sigismondo Malatesta, the famous *condottiere* who attempted to capture Mistra from the Turks in 1464 on behalf of Venice, transferred Plethon's mortal remains to Rimini.
‡ *Faust, transported to medieval Sparta in Part II of Goethe's play, imagines a Germanic revival of Greece with Mistra at its vanguard.*

Mistra came under Turkish rule in 1460. It experienced a period of revival during the Venetian occupation of 1687-1715, but was sacked by the Mainotes in 1770 and by Turkish troops during the War of Independence, and gradually abandoned after the refounding of Sparta in 1834. Remaining families were expelled by the archeologists in 1952.

SIGHTS AND PLACES OF INTEREST

Sightseeing involves a very steep climb between the lower entrance (360m/1,181ft) and the citadel (620m/2,034ft). There is an upper entrance below the citadel. The six major churches and the Despots' Palace deserve full attention; numerous minor churches, a mosque, and the ruins of both patrician and humble houses lie scattered over the rest of the space.

The **Metropolitan** (Cathedral) was built in 1309, with frescoes executed at that time, but the domes were added in the 15thC. A lovely courtyard containing an ancient sarcophagus and a 19thC fountain commands a good view over the Eurotas Valley.

The **Vrontochion Monastery** contains two churches, the **Ag. Theodore** and the architecturally unique **Panagia Odigitria** (Virgin Guiding the Way), built in 1310. The frescoes of the latter, notably those in the narthex depicting the miracles of Christ, compare in quality with the best work of the contemporary early Florentine and Sienese masters. Theodore II, who is buried in a side chapel, is represented in one mural in the habits of despot and monk.

The delightful **Pantánassa Monastery**, founded in 1428 by John Frangopoulos, the chief minister of the Despotate, whose house survives a short distance below the monastery, is still occupied by some elderly nuns, who sell their intricate embroideries. Among the frescoes is a fine 15thC portrait.

The **Perivléptos Monastery** is a 14thC edifice, although its architecture recalls the tiny 11thC churches of Athens. Its frescoes are among the most complete and expressive of any Byzantine church in the world.

The **Agia Sophia**, in the upper town, was built in 1350 and used as the palace chapel. Theodora Tocco and Cleopa Malatesta, wives of two successive despots, are buried here.

The impressive **Despots' Palace** is a rare specimen of Byzantine secular architecture. The E wing, dating from the 13thC, is probably Frankish and shows Gothic influences; the w wing was built in the 15thC and is preserved in its three stories.

℞ There is one small but fine hotel — **Byzantion** (B) (☎ (0731) 93.309 IIIⱭ) — and several pensions in the pleasant village below the ruins. For more accommodations, see SPARTA.

MONEMVÁSIA ⛰ ⛺ 🍴 🏛 ⇤ 🚢 ☆
100km (63 miles) SE of Sparta. Map 6J6. Population: 600 ☎ code: 0732. Hydrofoil from Piraeus, Tues and Sat 9am. Bus from Sparta.

Monemvasia, the walled medieval town whose name means "Single Exit," occupies a seaside ledge at the foot of a huge rock, on account of which it has often been called the Gibraltar of Greece. Once a famous city from which the Malmsey wine obtained its name, it was reduced to obscure penury in modern times, until less than 100 inhabitants remained to live among its decaying houses. More recently, tourism has created a modern hodgepodge town (called **Géfira**) on the mainland across the rock, while the strange ghost town within the walls has slowly begun to return to life with restored tourist stores, replanted gardens and reconsecrated churches. The pace of revival, however, has not been so fast nor so rash as to destroy the evocative, melancholy atmosphere of the place.

A stupendous **fortress** rises vertically above the town to the summit of the rock, where the fine 12thC church of **Agia Sophia** stands at the edge of a vertiginous terrace. There are four historic churches within the town itself, though none of great distinction.

The history of Monemvasia echoes that of Mistra. The city grew in significance as a Greek redoubt during the medieval Slavic invasions of the Peloponnese. It was taken by Villehardouin and retaken by the despotate. It became a Venetian property after the rest of Greece had fallen to the Turks, and remained so until 1540, whereafter the Turks and the Venetians changed place several times again.

‡ *Yannis Ritsos (1909-90), perhaps the greatest poet of modern Greece, was a native of the old village of Monemvasia. Members of his immediate family still live there.*

In ancient mythology the wild peninsula s of Monemvasia was known as the last home of the centaurs, men with horses' bodies.

🗫 There are for now only three hotels in the **historic area**, all in judiciously restored old buildings, all equally lovely: GNTO-operated **Kellia** (A) (☎ *61.520* **III ▯**); **Malvasia** (A) (☎ *61.323* **III ▯**); **Vizantino** (A) (☎ *61.351* ⊛*61.331* **III ▯**). Other hotels are expected soon.

A great number of C-D hotels, and pensions, have emerged recently in **Gefira**, across the causeway.

▲ **Paradise**, on the beach 5km (3 miles) s of town.

MYCENAE *(Míkines)* 🏛 ⧏ ☆
12km (8 miles) N of Argos. Map 6H6. Bus from Argos and Nafplio. Site open daily 8.30am-3pm, sometimes until 6pm ☎*500dr.*

The imposing hilltop stronghold of the Bronze Age kings was already a vaguely noticed ruin in Classical times. Its discovery by Schliemann in 1874-76 and the unearthing of the various royal treasuries buried within were among the finest hours of modern archeology. The grim splendor of the site cannot fail to impress the modern visitor.

The legendary history of Mycenae is inextricably confused with that of ARGOS. The citadel was said to have been founded by Perseus, and appears to have controlled the Peloponnese toward the end of the "Mycenaean" era. Its last important ruler was **Agamemnon**, who led the Greek armies against Troy in a war that was precipitated by the abduction of Helen, the wife of Agamemnon's brother Menelaus, the king of Sparta. He returned from the war with a mistress, Cassandra; his wife Clytemnestra had in the meanwhile also taken up a lover, Aegisthus by name, and contrived to murder the king at his return banquet. She was in turn despatched by her son Orestes, aided by Electra, his sister.

Archeological evidence suggests that Mycenae was inhabited from c.5000BC, with a time of highest civilization around 1600-1200BC. The culture of this period shows clear Egyptian influence, according with the Egyptian origins of Danaos, the legendary founder of Argos, and with various Homeric references to relations with Egypt. The royal palace was destroyed by fire c.1200BC, the supposed era of the Dorian invasions.

SIGHTS AND PLACES OF INTEREST
The **citadel**, a mighty structure of irregular "Cyclopean" masonry, is entered through the **Lion Gate**, its massive lintel supporting a slab with a relief of two rampant lionesses. Immediately past the

15thC BC gold death mask

gate is the **First Circle of Royal Tombs** where Schliemann discovered six graves containing the royal death masks and the spectacular gold jewelry now displayed at the Athens National Archeological Museum. Schliemann thought he had found the grave of Agamemnon, but the tombs, which date from the 16thC BC, are in fact much older than he suspected.

The **Palace**, which is based on the design of the Minoan palaces of Crete, consisted of two terraces connected by stairways which gave access to the *megaron*, the throne-room, whose form later provided the basis for Greek temple architecture. The E spur of the citadel yields a good view over the site, with a panorama extending over the Plain of Argos.

A **Second Circle of Royal Tombs**, located outside the citadel near the entrance to the archeological site, was discovered by accident in 1951. Its contents, dating from the 17thC BC, are also in Athens.

By far the most interesting tomb architecturally is to be found beside the road about 1km ($\frac{1}{2}$ mile) below the site. This so-called **Treasury of Atreus** consists of a massive underground chamber *(tholos)*, 14m (46ft) high and 15m (49ft) in diameter, which was topped by a colossal stone block weighing 120 tonnes. The inhabitant of the tomb, whose identification with the father of Agamemnon has no basis in fact, lived in the 14thC BC; most of his belongings are at the British Museum. Eight other *tholos* tombs have been discovered in the vicinity of the citadel.

A tourist-trap village, though not unpleasant, has grown up some distance below the site.

☞ There are about a dozen simple hotels and pensions in the village. **Agamemnon**, **Menelaus**, **Helen**, **Clytemnestra**, **Electra** and **Orestes** are all represented; so is **Schliemann**. A cut above is **La Petite Planete** (B) (**☎** (0751) 66.240 **🏚** 13 rms **🚌**).

NÁPLIO ▮ 🏛 🍴 ★

153km (96 miles) SW of Athens; 13km (8 miles) SE of Argos. Map 6I6. Population: 10,000 ☎ code: 0752 i 24.444. Hydrofoil daily in summer from Zea Harbor, Piraeus. Frequent bus from Argos; some direct routes from Athens (KTEL terminal at Kifissias 100). Train from Corinth and Argos.

With its color-washed, balconied houses and flower-filled back streets, Nafplio is one of the most beautiful towns in Greece. On a vertical rock behind the town rises the dizzying 18thC Venetian fortress of Palamidi. An islet facing the port is occupied by the pretty 15thC bastion of the Bourtzi. The attractive setting of the Argolid Gulf, surrounded by high mountains, and the presence of excellent beaches nearby make Nafplio a good place to spend an extended vacation.

The ancient history of Nafplio (Nauplion) is marginal except for the hero Palamedes, a clever fellow who was credited with the discovery of dice, navigational instruments and certain letters of the alphabet, and who was stoned to death at Troy on false charges of treachery concocted by Ulysses.

The city remained in Venetian hands until 1540, 80yrs after the rest of Greece had come under Turkish dominance. It acquired prominence as a seaport during the second Venetian occupation (1687-1715). It was Greece's main town at independence, and as such became its first capital (1828-34) until Athens was resuscitated to fulfill that duty.

SIGHTS AND PLACES OF INTEREST

A walking tour of Nafplio reveals street after street of pure visual delight. Many of the buildings populating the old town are of Venetian origin, with perhaps a more generous share of Turkish contributions than official guides would admit. The **Venetian Arsenal** on the main square dates from the prolific governorship of Agostino Sagredo (1711-14), and now houses the **museum** (▣ *standard opening hours* ☎ 27.502), which has unusual Mycenaean idols from Tiryns. In the larger of the two **mosques** on the same square, the first National Assembly met in 1825-28, and met again to confirm Otto's election as king in 1832. Before the gate of the church of **Ag. Spyridon** (built 1702), John Kapodistrias, the first president of the transitional government of Greece, was assassinated in 1831.

‡ *John Kapodistrias was born in Corfu, entered the Russian diplomatic service, and served as the Czar's Minister at the Congress of Vienna. He was elected president by the National Assembly in 1827, and struggled in vain to impose some discipline over the various bandit chiefs and warring clans that constituted the independence movement. He was assassinated by the henchmen of Petrobey Mavromichalis (see* MANI, *page 116), whom he had imprisoned.*

Across the street from Ag. Spyridon, a fountain bears an inscription in Turkish, dated 1734-35, inviting whoever drinks to pray for the soul of the founder, a certain Bektash. The Byzantine church of **Ag. Nikolaos** contains frescoes by an 18thC Italian painter. A fine **mosque** of white stone, farther uphill, was converted into a Catholic church in 1840 for the benefit of Otto, who was a Catholic; it contains a Raphael copy that was presented to the young king by Louis Philippe of France.

The **Palamídi Fortress** is accessible by a discreet back road, although some may prefer to take up the challenge of the 857 steps, which Otto's Bavarian courtiers had to negotiate daily to visit the king-elect at his modest residence within the fort. The **Lower Fortress**, also called *Its Kale* or *Acro-Nafplio*, now enclosing the luxury bungalows of Hotel Xenia (see below), is of much older construction and displays the proud Lion of St Mark.

≈ Located within the citadel of Acro-Nafplio, **Xenia** (☎ 28.981/5 ☎ 28.987 ▥▥▥ *51 rms, 54 bungalows, small* ☜ *within walking distance* ≈ ◀€) is the only class-L hotel in the Peloponnese. There is also a class-A **Xenia** next door.

Amfitryon (A) (☎ 27.366/7 ▥▥▥), a beautiful modern hotel with a lovely harbor view; **Agamemnon** (B) (☎ 28.021 ▥▥); **Helena** (C) (☎ 23.888 ▯ to ▥▥); **Amymoni** (☎ 27.219 ▯), an inexpensive hotel in a stately but decaying 19thC house.

ENVIRONS

The archaeologically important but visually unexciting ruins of the Mycenaean citadel of **Tiryns** (Tiryntha) lie directly by the Argos road 4km (2½ miles) N of Nafplio (▣ *open daily 8.30am-3pm).*

Tiryns figures prominently in legends of the Heroic Age, where it appears to have been as powerful a place as Mycenae and Argos. **Heracles** inherited the kingdom of Tiryns from his mother, but was cheated out of his inheritance by Eurystheus, who then set up a series of impossible tasks for the hero.

‡ *The Twelve Labors of Heracles were slaying the Nemean lion and the many-headed Hydra, capturing Artemis' stag, the Erymanthian boar and the Cretan bull, cleaning the Augean stables, hunting the Stymphalian birds, taming the man-eating horses of Diomedes, stealing the girdle of Hippolyte the Amazon and the cattle of the three-bodied Geryon, finding the apple of the Hesperides, and bringing Cerberus, the black dog of Hades, back to earth. He also sailed with the Argonauts to capture the Golden Fleece, held the earth up to give Atlas a break, and helped Apollo and Poseidon build the walls of Troy. He was made immortal, but his end was tragic: his wife Deianeira gave him a poisoned mantle, which once worn could never be taken off. In agony, Heracles built a funeral pyre on top of Mt. Oita, and perished in the flames.*

1.5km (1 mile) outside Nafplio on the Tolo road, the monastery of **Agia Moní**, with a 12thC Byzantine church, occupies a pretty site beside the **Kánathos spring**, in which Hera, to the envy of mortals and immortals, annually renewed her virginity.

Farther SE, past the insignificant ruins of ancient **Asine**, is the long sandy beach of **Toló**, 11km (7 miles), lined by a string of hotels and fish tavernas.

☙ A large number of hotels, mostly C, in Tolo, including **Sophia** (B) (☎ 59.567 *III*), **Epidauria** (C) (☎ 59.219 *III*) and **Minoa** (C) (☎ 59.207 *II*).

NEMEA 🏛 ☆
32km (20 miles) SW of Corinth. Map 6I5. Site and museum open daily 8.30am-3pm; restricted hours on Sun; other hours on Sat. Museum closed Mon, sometimes Tues. Different schedules for off-season and half-season ☎200dr.

The three slender columns of the **Temple of Nemean Zeus** stand in a peaceful, evocative valley, surrounded by hills and rarely disturbed by the torrents of tourism flowing between CORINTH and MYCENAE. In this corner of apparent rural calm, Heracles once slew the ferocious Nemean lion (see above), who was in fact a creature of Hera and was therefore translated to the heavens to form the constellation Leo. The temple was built in 340-320BC in a solitary sacred precinct of Zeus, which hosted the biennial Nemean Games, the fourth most prestigious in ancient Greece after those of OLYMPIA, DELPHI and ISTHMIA.

The **stadium** of the Games is visible on a hillside some distance from the temple site. The local **museum** is certainly worth a visit for its well-organized and well-documented displays, the work of the American School. A few attractive tavernas exist some distance farther on at modern **Nemea**, formerly the Turkish village of Kuçuk Vadi ("Little Glen").

OLYMPIA (Olímbia) 🏛 ★
278km (174 miles) SW of Athens; 18km (11 miles) E of Pyrgos. Map 5I4. Population of village: 500 ☎ code: 0624. Train 5 times daily from Pyrgos. Site open weekdays 8am-5pm; Sat-Sun 8.30am-3pm ☎500dr. Museum open Tues-Sun as site hours; Mon 11am-5pm ☎500dr.

Olympia, set amid the pastoral gentleness of Elis, makes a striking contrast with the dramatic grandeur of DELPHI, the only other site to which it compares for importance. The beautiful lichen-gray ruins of the Sanctuary of Olympian Zeus, the most important holy site of ancient Greece and the home of the Olympic Games, cover a wide park-like area shaded by venerable pines, plane trees and evergreen oaks.

THE OLYMPIC GAMES

In one account Zeus himself instituted the Games after he had overthrown his father Cronos to become lord and master of the gods in a wrestling match here at Olympia. The height flanking the sanctuary was known as Cronos Hill (Kronion), pointing to a very ancient tradition. The more common account honored Pelops, the Lydian hero who conquered Elis and became the master of the Peloponnese, as the founder of the Games.

From 776BC, when written records began, the Games were held on the August full moon of every fourth year for over 1,000 uninterrupted years. The Olympiad formed the basis of the Greek calendar. A truce was declared during the games to allow participants to travel freely from all parts of the Greek world. The territory of Elis, which administered the Games, enjoyed permanent neutrality; those who violated it were placed under a curse and suffered eternal ignominy; armies entering it had to lay down their arms and received them back only after they left.

Only men whose native tongue was Greek could compete (Nero was the first non-Greek to take part), although barbarians were allowed in as spectators. Slaves and married women were excluded from the precinct under penalty of death. The principal event was the "stadium" race over 204m (223yds), the name of whose winner became the designation of that particular Olympiad. Other competitions were held in wrestling, boxing, *pankration* (an all-out fight), horse and chariot racing, and the pentathlon, which in turn comprised the stadium run, wrestling, long jump, discus throw and javelin. Winners were crowned with a wild olive branch, feasted at public expense, praised by famous poets (such as Pindar's *Odes*), and given the option of erecting a statue at the sanctuary (Pliny counted 3,000 of those in the 2ndC AD). There were never second prizes. Many famous political careers were launched by an Olympic victory: the earliest written record about Athens concerns one Cylon, winner of the Olympic foot race, who attempted a coup d'etat c.640BC.

The Games were erratically recorded in the 3rdC AD, and were banned by the Edict of Theodosius in 391. The modern Olympic Games were initiated by Baron de Coubertin at Athens in 1896.

THE SANCTUARY *(Altis)*

The sacred precinct, which had been overlaid with sand and debris up to a height of 6m (20ft), was excavated in 1874–81 and 1936–41 by, successively, Ernst Curtius, Wilhelm Doerpfeld and Emil Kunze under the auspices of the German Archeological Institute. The trees, which form one of the site's attractions, were planted by the Germans.

The present entrance is across the stoa of a 3rdC BC **gymnasium** adjoined by the double colonnade of a **palaestra**, a broad courtyard that was used for athletic training. The **Prytaneion** was the banqueting hall where the victors were entertained. In front of it, a small circular structure with Ionic columns was erected by Alexander the Great to commemorate the victories of his father Philip.

The **workshop** where Phidias created his spectacular statue of Zeus between 456 and 447BC was described by Pausanias some

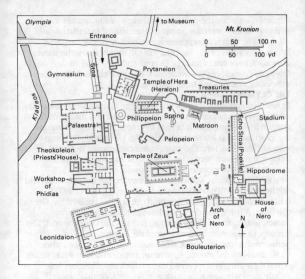

600yrs later and has been identified with certainty by the discovery of a jug bearing the sculptor's name and the molds he used for Zeus's cloak. The **Leonidaion** was built by a certain Leonidas of Naxos as a residence for distinguished guests, and later accommodated the Roman governors of Greece. The **Bouleterion**, dating in part from the Archaic period, was the meeting place of the Olympian senate, elected from the aristocracy of Elis. The **Arch** and **House of Nero** commemorate the scandalous extra Olympiad ordered on the occasion of the emperor's visit in AD67.

As at Delphi, Nero competed in all regular and several irregular events, and was declared the winner in all; his name was later expunged from the Olympic records.

The **Temple of Zeus**, occupying the center of the Altis, was built in the Doric style by Eleians in 470-456BC; its foundations and the lower drums of the 6 x 13 columns survive.

The temple's chief claim to fame was Phidias's colossal **statue of Zeus**, which was considered one of the Seven Wonders of the World, the only one to be so distinguished in mainland Greece. The statue was in gold and ivory, and painted in bright color by the sculptor's brother Panaenus. Pausanias, who saw it in its original position in the temple, confessed that merely to note its measurements could give no idea of its awe-inspiring scale, and Quintilian reported that to gaze upon it enhanced men's understanding of religion. Strabo, on the other hand, thought that Phidias had gotten his proportions wrong, as the god's head almost touched the roof and seemed ready to hit it if Zeus wanted to stand up. A few fragments said to belong to the god's throne wound up in Rome, and are now at the Hermitage Museum of Leningrad.

The **Temple of Hera** is better preserved than that of her husband, despite being the oldest structure in the Altis. It was erected in the early 6thC BC with wooden Doric columns, which were gradually replaced with stone over the centuries.

Next to this temple, Herodes Atticus erected a **Nympheum**, or public fountain, in the sumptuous style of the 2ndC AD (see drawing of reconstruction, in the museum); ranged beside it are the remains of the **treasuries** of various Greek cities, and the foundations of a small **temple** dedicated to Cybele, the Mother of the Gods. A small excavation in front of the fountain reveals the signs of Neolithic occupation found beneath the Classical level of the sanctuary, perhaps going back to the age when the low hill flanking the Altis at this point received the name of Cronos, the ruler of the pre-Olympian generation of gods.

The **Olympic Stadium** is a large open space where excavations undertaken on Hitler's personal orders revealed the start and finish lines of the races, as well as a wealth of trophies now exhibited in the museum. The **Echo Stoa**, so called because of its famous sevenfold echo, separated stadium and Altis.

THE MUSEUM

Instituted by the German archeologists, the museum is next only to the Archeological Museum of Athens in the wealth and quality of its collection. The most memorable displays include the colossal **pediments** of the Temple of Zeus, and the statue of **Hermes** attributed to Praxiteles. The *Hermes*, if it indeed belongs to the 4thC master as Pausanias claims, is the only surviving original work of a great sculptor of Antiquity. The pediments, which are well-preserved and extremely powerful, represent the horse-race of Pelops and Oinomaos (E) and the battle of Centaurs and Lapiths (w).

Hermes of Olympia, attributed to Praxiteles

‡ *Pelops was the son of Tantalus, the king of Lydia in Asia Minor. He sought the hand of Hippodamia, the daughter of Oinomaos, king of Pisa in Elis, whose father challenged suitors to a chariot-race between Olympia and the Isthmus against his invincible horses, and nailed the heads of the losers to his palace gate. Pelops won with the help of Hippodamia, killed the nefarious king, instituted the Games, and gave his name to the Peloponnese ("Pelops' Island"). His children and grandchildren (who included Agamemnon and Menelaus) ruled Mycenae, Tiryns, Troezen and Sparta, as well as Elis.*

Perithoos, king of the Thessalian tribe of Lapiths, invited the Centaurs, the race of half-horse half-men, to his wedding. The Centaurs got drunk and attempted to abduct Lapith women, unleashing a famous war.

Other interesting items at the museum include a remarkable Archaic terra cotta **statue** of *Zeus Abducting Ganymede*, and numerous memorial statues spanning the 1,000yr history of Olympia. A fascinating 3-D reconstruction of the **Altis**, a gift of Kaiser Wilhelm II from his postwar exile, and another one incorporating the latest archeological evidence, are displayed in the entrance hall.

OTHER PLACES OF INTEREST

The **International Olympic Academy**, a short distance beyond the museum, and the **Olympic Museum**, located in the village, are quaint relics of the era when modern Olympics had yet to grow into the media and business extravaganza they are today.

The **village** of Olympia, consisting of some two dozen blocks of hotels, pensions, tavernas, discotheques and souvenir stores amid profuse flowers and greenery, comes alive each summer evening with a multitude of tourists from every Western country.

The densely forested hills of the vicinity are ideally suited for nature walks.

☞ There are two A, seven B, nine C hotels and scores of pensions and simple accommodations in the village. **Amalia** (A) (☎ 22.190/1 █████) has a fine setting in the woods; **Europa** (A) (☎ 22.700 Ⓢ 23.166 █████ 《€ ▒▒ ▦▦) overlooks the village from high up on a hill; **Xenia** (B) (☎ 22.301/2 ███) offers excellent value in its price range; also **Apollon** (B) (☎ 22.522) and **Ilis** (C) (☎ 22.547 ███).

A dozen C and D hotels exist in **Pyrgos**, 18km (11 miles) w, including **Letrina** (C) (☎ 23.644 █).

▲ On the hillside behind the Olympic Games Museum and a short distance w of town on the Pyrgos-Patras road.

PATRAS *(Pátra)*

208km (130 miles) w of Athens. Map 3G4. Population: 140,000 ☎ code: 061 ℹ 420.304. Bus from Athens (OSE and KTEL, frequent), Pyrgos, Nafpaktos, Tripoli (twice daily) and elsewhere. Train from Corinth and Kalamata. Terminal for most ferries from Italy, Corfu, Ithaki, Kefalonia.

The third-largest city and second-largest port of Greece has practically nothing to show for its pre-independence history except for a meager citadel (**Kastro**) of Byzantine-Frankish-Venetian-Turkish lineage and a rather attractive Roman **Odeon**. The **harbor**, which is the only part of the city that most visitors see, is a busy international ferry port cum bus terminal cum railroad station. A short walk inland, however, reveals unexpectedly pleasant, even elegant, sections around **Vassileos Georgiou Sq**. and at the edges of the Kastro.

The principal monument is the church of **Ag. Andreas**, a devotional, if not architectural, masterpiece that was completed in 1979 to house the relics of St Andrew, returned by the Pope shortly before that date to the town of their origin. An important pilgrimage takes place here on Nov 30.

‡ *The Apostle Andrew is said to have traveled to Patras, where he was martyred in the reign of Nero by being crucified on an X-shaped cross, which explains the origin of the St Andrew's Cross. His relics were removed to Constantinople in the 4thC to buttress that city's claim to apostolic blessing; they were also removed by St Regulus to the monastery of St Andrews in Fife, furnishing Scotland with its patron and protector. Still undiminished in either quantity or efficacy, the saint went on to save Patras from a Slavic invasion, and was finally carried off to Rome when Thomas Paleologue, the last despot of Mistra, fled before the Turks in 1460.*

☞ Many hotels in all price categories exist around the port. Examples: **Astir** (A) *(Agiou Andrea 16* ☎ *276.311* ███ *120 rms* ▤ ▒▒on roof ▦▦ ▦ ◉ ◐ ▨ *)*; **Galaxy** (B) *(Agiou Nikolaou 9* ☎ *275.981/3* ███ ▦ ▦▦ ◉ ◐ ▨ *)*; **Mediterranee** (C) *(Agiou Nikolaou 18* ☎ *279.602* █ *)*.

The coast to either side of Patras is peppered with middle-range beach resorts, notably **Bozaika** and **Lakopetra** in the s and **Río** and **Arahovitika** in the NE, each with numerous adequate hotels.

The best beach hotel in the vicinity is **Porto Rio** (A) *(in Rio* ☎ *922.212* ███ *all amenities).*

ENVIRONS

The fast-growing beach resort of **Rio**, 9km (6 miles) NE of Patras *(continuous ferry to Antirio)*, has a powerful **Turkish fortress**, built in 1499 to guard the entrance of the Gulf of Corinth. It is still used as a prison.

PYLOS 🏨 🍴 ☆

50km (31 miles) W of Kalamata. Map 5J4. Population: 3,000
☎ *code: 0723.*

The capital of Homer's "wise old Nestor" commands the Bay of Navarino, one of the most beautiful natural harbors of Greece. Gently rising hills form a vast amphitheater around it with as many as 20 villages smiling from afar among the rich vineyards and olive groves of the Messenian landscape. The attractions of the town itself include warm and sleepy streets full of whitewashed houses and little tavernas, a quaint fortress, and a spectacular 6km/4-mile-long beach lying between the mirror-straight sea and a lagoon.

‡ *At the Battle of Navarino on Oct 20, 1828, an allied British-French-Russian fleet annihilated the Turkish navy of Ibrahim Pasha, which was lying at anchor in the bay, in a surprise attack not unlike Pearl Harbor in conception and result. This action marked the formal entry of the European Powers into the fray of the Greek revolt, and forced a Turkish capitulation within a short time. Some of the 53 Turkish ships sunk at Navarino are still visible under the surface of the water.*

The substantial **fortress**, at the southern edge of the town, is a Turkish structure of 1573 with modifications carried out by the French in 1829. The interior *(open 8.30am-3pm, closed Mon)* has a mosque converted into a church and excellent views of the bay.

The steep, uninhabited island of **Sfaktíria**, which hems in the bay in almost completely, contains monuments to various heroes of Navarino and the tomb of Paul-Marie Bonaparte, a nephew of Napoleon. At its southern end, a great hollow rock known by the unusual name of **Tsishli Baba,** or Isle of the Blessed Pisser, blocks the harbor entrance. At the N end, where the deserted far end of the beach comes within wading distance of the island, a ruined Venetian **castle** *(Paleókastro)* marks the medieval (and possibly Mycenaean) site of Pylos.

🛏 Pylos has five B and C hotels and numerous pensions. **Karalis Beach** (B) (☎23.021/2 ▣22.970 ▥▦ ⬛ ▨ 🍴) is on an isolated site between the fortress and the sea at the edge of town. **Neleus** (B) (☎22.518 ▥▢) is a charming pension. **Karalis** (C) (☎22.960 ▥▥ ▣ ⬛ ▢▢ ▨▨) has a nice site overlooking the harbor.

▲ Lovely spot near the beach at **Gialova**, 6km (4 miles) N.

ENVIRONS

The so-called **Palace of Nestor** *(open 8.30am-3pm, closed Mon* ▨ *200dr)*, located by the roadside 13km (8 miles) N of Pylos, is considered the second most important Mycenaean find after Mycenae itself. What remains of its foundations will not overwhelm the casual visitor, though the ground pattern is decidedly curious.

The palace, whose superstructure was built of wood, was occupied c.1300-1200BC and burned down at the end of that period. The single largest cache ever found of tablets containing the Mycenaean "Linear B" script were baked into brick in that fire and were thus saved for posterity. The association of the palace with the legendary king Nestor of Pylos has no basis in fact.

Nestor, the amiably long-winded old warrior, appears in the *Iliad* as the commander of the second-largest Greek fleet and a ruler whom Agamemnon respects in his own right. In the *Odyssey,* Telemachus visits Pylos to find out the whereabouts of his father Ulysses, and is treated by the old king to a banquet on the beach — perhaps that at the N end of Navarino Bay.

The road continues N through a beautiful land of farms and orchards, which yield the largest share of Europe's dried raisins. The market town of **Gargaliáni** has its assured niche in history as the ancestral home of former US Vice-President Spiro Agnew, né Agnostopoulos. **Kyparíssia**, a pleasant oldish town with an excellent beach, perches on a hillside with a ruined Franco-Venetian castle.

SPARTA *(Spárti)*
*230km (144 miles) SW of Athens. Map **6**J5. Population: 12,000* ☎ *code: 0731.*

"The sober, hard,/ and man-subduing city, which no shape/ of pain could conquer, nor of pleasure charm," was abandoned at the end of Antiquity in favor of the eagle's nest of MISTRA, nearby. Modern Sparti was raised on empty ground after 1834; its broad avenues, the lush green of the Eurotas Valley and the looming presence of **Mt. Taygetos** conspire to make it a more attractive place than most other Greek towns of comparable newness. But there is hardly any trace of the city's past greatness, fulfilling Thucydides' prediction that future ages would be puzzled that Sparta once counted as an equal of Athens, for while Athens would leave splendid monuments in marble, Sparta, whose buildings were all of wood, would vanish completely.

Sparta, also called Lacedaemon, was already an important city in the Mycenaean epoch, when Menelaus ruled and Helen was called the most beautiful of mortal women. The Dorians who invaded it c.1200BC enslaved the local population *(helots)* and developed the proverbially frugal culture of their small warrior aristocracy. Spartan boys were taken from their families at the age of 7 and raised in harsh conditions designed to instil physical courage and contempt of luxury. Those who failed were left in a gorge of the Taygetos to die; those who passed the initiation rites of adulthood were expected to kill or die without flinching.

In a series of wars between 461 and 403BC, Sparta successfully checked Athens' ambition to be the dominant power in Greece. Its own era of de facto mastery was brought to an end in 371BC by Epaminondas of Thebes. The city was nevertheless highly regarded by the Romans, and maintained an important position through the imperial period.

⌖ Menelaion (B) (☎ *22.161/5* **Ⅲ▢**), a fine Neoclassical building in the center of town; **Sparta Inn** (C) (☎ *21.021/6* **Ⅱ▢**).

ENVIRONS
6km (4 miles) S of Sparta, a few dressed stones and a small isolated church on a low hill commanding a lovely landscape of orange and banana groves mark **Amyklai** (Amiklés), the ancient cult site of Apollo's lover Hyacinth.

Hyacinth was a mortal youth of untold beauty with whom Apollo fell in love; theirs was the first love between man and man. Zephyr, the west wind, was jealous; when she blew, a discus that the god had hurled went off and killed the youth. Out of his blood grew the flower that bears his name, and Apollo ordained the annual feast of the Hyacinthia in his memory.

TIRYNS *(Tyrintha)*   See NAFPLIO, Environs.

TRÍPOLI
166km (104 miles) SW of Athens. Population: 22,000
☎ *code: 071.*
The capital of Arcadia is a rather dreary place. Near it are the
equally uninteresting ruins of **Tegea** (5km/3 miles S) and
Mantinea (11km/7 miles N), the latter remembered as the site of
two famous battles in which the Spartans defeated the Athenians
(418BC) and were defeated in turn by the Thebans of
Epaminondas (362BC).

☜ **Arcadia** (B) (☎ *22.25.51* Ⅲ◻); **Galaxy** (C) (☎ *22.51.95* Ⅰ◻);
Menalon (C) (☎ *22.24.50* ◻).

Greek in a nutshell

The Greek alphabet

Letter		Name ancient/ modern	Romanized form
A	α	alpha	a
B	β	beta/vita	b
Γ	γ	gamma	g
Δ	δ	delta	d
E	ε	epsilon	e
Z	ζ	zeta/zita	z
H	η	eta/ita	i
Θ	θ	theta	th
I	ι	iota	i
K	κ	kappa	k
Λ	λ	lambda	l
M	μ	mu/mi	m
N	ν	nu/ni	n
Ξ	ξ	xi	x
O	ο	omicron	o
Π	π	pi	p
P	ρ	rho/ro	r
Σ	σ, ς	sigma	s
T	τ	tau/taf	t
Y	υ	upsilon/ipsilon	y or i
Φ	φ	phi	ph or f
X	χ	chi/hi	ch or h
Ψ	ψ	psi	ps
Ω	ω	omega	o

Pronunciation

Vowels

A, E, I present no problem. O and Ω are both pronounced *o*.
H and Y, which used to be long *e* and *y* in Classical Greek, are
now both pronounced *i* as in *pizza*.

Diphthongs

AI — *e* as in *bed*	AU — *av* or *af*
EI — *i* as in *pizza*	EU — *ev* or *ef*
OI — *i* as in *pizza*	OU — *u*

Double dots on a vowel indicate that it is not part of a
diphthong, and is voiced separately.

Consonants

Z, K, Λ, M, N, Ξ, Π, P, Σ, T, Φ, Ψ present no problems.
B, which used to be *b* in Classical Greek, is now *v*.
Δ is a soft *th* as in *this*.
Θ is a hard *th* as in *thing*.
Γ is tricky. Before E or I, it is pronounced *y* as in *yet*. Elsewhere
it is never a hard *g* as in *go*, but halfway between *g* and *h*.
X is a hard *h*, but not quite a *kh*.

Double consonants

NT — *d* or *nd*	MΠ — *b* or *mb*	ΓK — *g* as in *go*.

The *d, b, g* sounds only occur in borrowed foreign words.

ΓΓ — *ng*	ΓΞ — *nx*

Grammar

Nouns

Greek nouns are masculine, feminine or neuter in gender.
Typically, but not always, **masculine** nouns end in -os,
feminine nouns end in -i or -a, and **neuter** nouns end in -o.

Depending on their position in the sentence, nouns can be in
one of three cases: **nominative** (subject of the action),
accusative (object of the action, or any word following a
preposition), or **genitive** (possessor of another noun). In the

sentence, "John took Jack's wife to the movies," John is nominative, Jack is genitive, wife and the movies are accusative.

Greek **adjectives** agree in gender and case with the nouns they modify.

	masculine	feminine	neuter
	(man)	(day)	(water)
Nom. singular	o andros	i mera	to nero
Acc. singular	to andro	ti mera	to nero
Gen. singular	tou androu	tis mera	tou nerou
Nom. plural	i andri	i meres	ta nera
Acc. plural	tous androus	tis meres	ta nera
Gen. plural	ton andron	ton meron	ton neron

Verbs

Greek verbs take on suffixes indicating person and tense. Here are the present tenses of the verbs *to be* (I am, you are, he is, etc.), *to want* (I want, etc.) and *to go*.

		be	want	go
I	ego	ime	thelo	pao
you (sing.)	esi	ise	thelis	pas
he, she, it	aftos, afti, afto	ine	theli	pai
we	emis	imaste	theloume	pame
you (plur.)	esis	isthe	thelete	pate
they	afti, afti, afta	ine	theloun	paoun

Reference words

Monday Deftéra	Friday Paraskeví
Tuesday Tríti	Saturday Sávvato
Wednesday Tetárti	Sunday Kyriakí
Thursday Pémpti	

January Ianouários	July Ioúlios
February Fevrouários	August Ávgoustos
March Mártios	September Septémvrios
April Aprílios	October Októvrios
May Máios	November Noémvrios
June Ioúnios	December Dekémvrios

1	éna	11	éndeka	21	ikossiéna
2	dyo	12	dódeka	22	ikossidío
3	tría	13	dékatria	30	triánda
4	téssera	14	dékatéssera	40	saránda
5	pénde	15	dékapénde	50	penínda
6	éxi	16	dékaéxi	60	exínda
7	eptá	17	dékaeptá	70	evdomínda
8	októ	18	dékaoktó	80	ogdónda
9	ennéa	19	dékaennéa	90	enenínda
10	déka	20	íkossi	100	ekató

First prótos	Quarter past.... ....ke tétarto
Second défteros	Half past.... ....ke missí
Third trítos	Quarter to pará tétarto
Fourth tétartos	Quarter to six.... ....éxi pará tétarto

Mr kyrios	Ladies ginekón
Mrs kyría	Gents andrón
Miss despinís	

Red kókkino	Blue blé
Yellow kítrino	Black mávro
Green prássino	White áspro

133

Words and phrases

Basic communication

Yes	ne	Straight ahead	issia embrós
No	óhi	Near	kontá
Please	parakaló	Far	makriá
Thank you	efharistó	Above	apó páno
I'm very sorry	lipáme polí	Below	apó káto
Excuse me	signómi	Front	embrós
Not at all/you're welcome	parakaló	Behind	písso
Hello	yiá sou	Early	norís
Good morning	kaliméra	Late	argá

Yes ne
No óhi
Please parakaló
Thank you efharistó
I'm very sorry lipáme polí
Excuse me signómi
Not at all/you're welcome parakaló
Hello yiá sou
Good morning kaliméra
Good afternoon kalispéra
Good night kaliníhta
Goodbye adío
Morning proí
Afternoon apógevma
Evening vrádi
Night níhta
Yesterday htés
Today símera
Tomorrow ávrio
Next week tin álli evdomáda
Last week tin perasméni evdomáda
....days ago prin apó....méres
Month mínas
Year hrónos
Here edó
There ekí
Big megálo
Small mikró
Hot zestó
Cold kryo
Good kaló
Bad kakó
Beautiful oréo
With me
And ke
But allá
Open aniktó
Closed klistó
Entrance íssodos
Exit éxodos
Free tzámpa
Left aristerá
Right dexiá

Straight ahead issia embrós
Near kontá
Far makriá
Above apó páno
Below apó káto
Front embrós
Behind písso
Early norís
Late argá
Pleased to meet you. Hárika pou sas gnórissa/héro poly.
How are you? Pos íste?
Very well, thank you. Polí kalá, efharistó.
Do you speak English? Miláte Anliká?
I don't understand. Den katalavéno.
Please explain. Parakaló exigíste.
Please speak more slowly. Parakaló milíste pió argá.
My name is.... To onomá mou íne....
I am American/English. Íme Ánglos/Amerikanós.
Where is/are...? Poú íne...?
Is there a...? Ypárkhi éna...?
What? Ti?
When? Póte?
How much? Pósso?
That's too much. Íne pára pollá.
Expensive akrivó
Cheap fthinó
I would like.... Tha íthela....
Do you have...? Éhete...?
Where is the toilet? Poú íne i toualéta.
Where is the telephone? Poú íne to tiléfono?
That's fine/OK. Poly oréa/O.K.
I don't know. Den xéro.
What time is it? Ti óra íne?
I feel ill. Den esthánome kalá.

Shopping

Where is the nearest/a good...? Poú íne to plisiéstero/éna kaló...?
Can you help me/show me some...? Boríte na me voithíssete/na mou díxete meriká...?
I'm just looking. Aplós kyttázo.
Do you accept charge/credit cards....travelers checks? Pérnete credit cards....travelers checks?
Can you deliver to...? Boríte na to meteférete sto...?
I'll take it. Tha to páro.
I'll leave it. Tha to afísso.
Can I have it tax-free for export? Boró na to páro aforológito gía exaghí?
This is faulty. Can I have a replacement/refund? Aftó éhi elátoma. Boró na to alláxo/na páro tá leftá písso?
I don't want to spend more than.... Den thélo na xodépso perissótera apó....
I'll give you....for it. Tha sas dósso....gi'aftó.
Can I have a stamp for...? Boró naého éna gramatóssimo giá...?

Shops

Antique store antíkes
Art gallery gallerí érgon téhnis
Baker foúrnos
Bank trápeza

Beauty parlor instítouto kallonís
Bookstore vivliopolío
Butcher (and variants) kreopolío
Cake shop zaharoplastío

Clothes store katástima idón rouhismoú
Dairy galaktopolío
Department store megálo katástima
Fish store psarádiko
Florist anthoplío
Greengrocer manáviko
Grocer bakáliko
Haberdasher psilikatzídiko
Hairdresser kommotírio
Jeweler kosmimatopolío
Market agorá

Newsstand efimeridopólis
Optician optikós
Pharmacy/chemist farmakío
Photographic store fotografío
Post office tahidromío
Shoe store katástima ypodimáton
Supermarket super market
Tailor rafío
Tobacconist kapnopolío
Tourist office touristikó grafío
Toy store katástima pehnidion
Travel agent touristikos práktor

Some useful goods

Antiseptic cream antisiptikí kréma
Aspirin aspirínes
Bandages epídesmi
Band-Aid/sticking plaster lefkoplástis
Cotton (wool) vamváki
Diarrhea/upset stomach pills diárria/hápia giá stomahikí diatarahí
Indigestion tablets hápia gia dyspepsia
Insect repellant ygró giá éntoma
Sanitary napkins serviétes ygías
Shampoo sampouán
Shaving cream kréma xyrísmatos
Soap sapoúni
Sunburn cream kréma giá engávmata apó ton ílio
Sunglasses gialiá ilíou
Suntan cream/oil kréma/ládi mavrísmatos

Tampons tampón
Tissues hartomándila
Toothbrush odontóvourtsa
Toothpaste odontókrema
Travel sickness pills hápia giá naftía

Bathing suit mayó
Bra soutién
Coat paltó
Dress fórema
Jacket sakkáki
Pants/trousers pantelóni
Pullover poulóver
Shirt poukámiso
Shoes papoútsia
Skirt foústa
Socks káltses
Stockings/tights káltses nylon/kalson

Film film
Letter grámma
Money order émvasma

Postcard kart postál
Stamp grammatósimo
Telegram tilegráfima

Driving

Gas/service station stathmós venzínis
Fill it up. Gemíste to.
Give me....drachmes worth. Válte moú venzíni....drahmón.
I would like....liters of petrol. Tha íthela....lítra venzíni.
Can you check the...? Boríte na kittaxete to...?
There is something wrong with the.... Káti den pái kalá me to....
Battery bataría
Brakes fréna
Engine mihaní
Exhaust exátmissi
Lights fóta
Oil ládia
Tires lástiha
Water neró
Windshield par-bríz
My car won't start To aftokínito dén xekinái.
My car has had a puncture. Émina apó lástiho.
How long will it take to repair? Se pósso keró tha íne étimo?

Other methods of transportation

Aircraft aeropláno
Airport aerodrómio
Bus leoforío
Bus stop stássi leoforíou
Coach poúlman
Ferry/boat ferry/plío
Ferry port limáni ferry boat
Hydrofoil yptámeno delfíni
Station stathmós
Train tréno

Ticket issitírio
Ticket office grafío isstiríon
One-way/single monó
Round trip/return met' epistrofís
Half fare missó issitírio
First/second/economy próti/ défteri/tríti
Sleeper/couchette me krevváti/ kousétta

135

Words and phrases

Food and drink

Have you a table for...? Éhete éna trapézi giá...?
I want to reserve a table for....at.... Thélo na klísso éna trapézi giá....stis....
A quiet table. Éna íssiho trapézi.
A table near the window. Éna trapézi kondá sto paráthiro.
Could we have another table? Boroúme na éhoume állo trapézi?
I only want a snack. Thélo káti elafró.
The menu, please. Ton katálogo parakaló.
I'll have.... Tha páro....
Can I see the wine list? Tón katálogo tón krassión parakaló?
I would like.... Thélo....
What do you recommend? Tí moú synistáte ná páro?
What do you want to drink? Tí thá píite?
I did not order this. Den to parángila aftó.
This is bad. Avtó íne halasméno.
Can this be changed? Boríte ná tó alláxete?
Lunch/dinner gévma/dípno
Bring me another. Férte moú állo éna.
The bill please. Tón logariasmó parakaló.
Is service included? To servís perilamvánete?

Restaurant estiatório	Oil ládi
Taverna tavérna	Vinegar xídi
Hot zestó	Bread psomí (ártos when written)
Cold kryo	Butter voútyro
Glass potíri	Cheese tyrí
Bottle boukáli	Egg avgó
Half-bottle missó boukáli	Milk gála
Beer/lager bíra/láger	Pastry store zaharoplastío
Orangeade/lemonade mía porto	Coffee house kafenío
kaláda/lemonáda	Coffee kafé
Water neró	Greek (Turkish) coffee ellinikó
Iced.... ....pagoméno	kafé
Mineral water emfialoméno neró	without sugar skéto
Carbonated/noncarbonated me	moderately sweet métrio
anthrakikó/horís anthrakikó	very sweet vary glykó
Flask/carafe karáfa	Ice cream pagotá
Red wine kókkino krassí	Chocolate sokoláta
White wine áspro krassí	Honey méli
Rosé wine kokkinéli krassí	Sugar záhari
Cheers! Stín ygiá sas!	Tea tsái
Sweet glykó	Steak filéto
Salt aláti	well done kalopsiméno
Pepper pipéri	medium métrio
Mustard moustárda	rare senián

Menu decoder

Kouvér cover charge	Tyriá cheese
Orektiká appetizer	Froúta fruit
Psária fish	Glyká dessert
Kymádes minced meat	Potá drink
Salátes salad	Byres beer
Psomí bread	Anapsyktiká soft drink

Arní lamb
Avgolémono chicken broth with rice, lemon and egg
Bakaliáros fried salt cod usually served with *skordaliá*
Baklavá thin pastry layers stuffed with nuts and spices, doused in syrup
Bourekákia tiny stuffed flaky pastry pasties
Fasólia beans
Galaktoboúreko flaky pastry with a custard filling, doused in syrup
Kotópoulo chicken

Kreatópitta triangular flaky pastry containing minced meat
Melitzánes eggplant/aubergines
Moskhári veal
Moussaká mince and eggplant/ aubergine layers topped with béchamel and cheese sauce
Mydia mussels
Pagotá ice cream
Stifádo meat stew with tomatoes, onions, herbs and red wine
Taramosaláta cod's roe purée
Tyrópitta flaky pastry cheese pasties
Yaoúrti yogurt

136

Index

Bold page numbers refer to main entries. *Italic page numbers* refer to illustrations and maps. See also the LIST OF ATHENS STREET NAMES on page 144.

Index

Index

Index

Athens street names

All streets mentioned in the book that fall within the Central
Athens area covered by our map **1-2** are listed here, with a map
reference. Map numbers are printed in **bold type**.

Not every street can be labeled on the map, although of course
all major streets and most smaller ones are named. To help you
find your way when streets are not named on the map, their map
references are also given both in this list and in the main text.

Street names

ATHENS AND THE CLASSICAL SITES

1-2 CENTRAL ATHENS
3-4 CENTRAL GREECE
5-6 PELOPONNESE
7 ATTICA

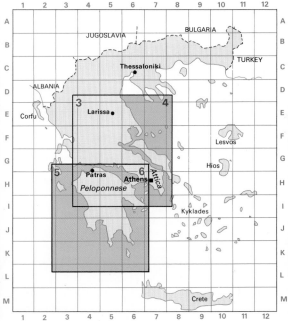

LEGEND

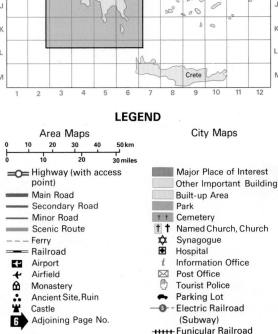

Area Maps

```
0   10   20   30   40   50 km
0        10        20   30 miles
```

- **=O=** Highway (with access point)
- Main Road
- Secondary Road
- Minor Road
- Scenic Route
- - - - Ferry
- Railroad
- ✈ Airport
- ✈ Airfield
- ⛪ Monastery
- ∴ Ancient Site, Ruin
- 🏰 Castle
- **6** Adjoining Page No.

City Maps

- Major Place of Interest
- Other Important Building
- Built-up Area
- Park
- † † Cemetery
- † † Named Church, Church
- ✡ Synagogue
- ✚ Hospital
- *i* Information Office
- ✉ Post Office
- ✋ Tourist Police
- ☎ Parking Lot
- —S— Electric Railroad (Subway)
- +++++ Funicular Railroad
- → One Way Street

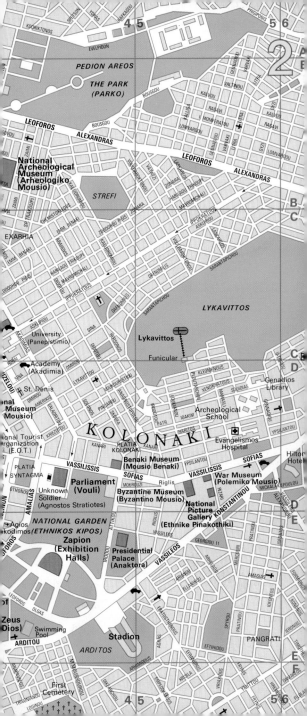

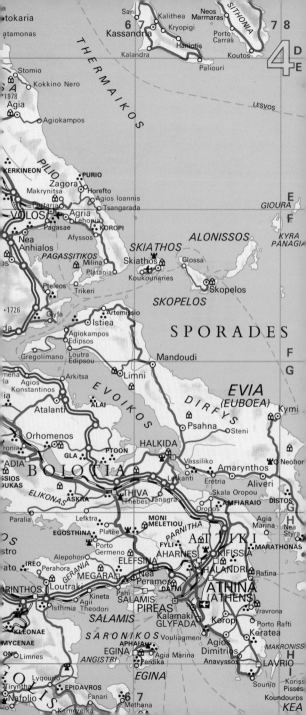

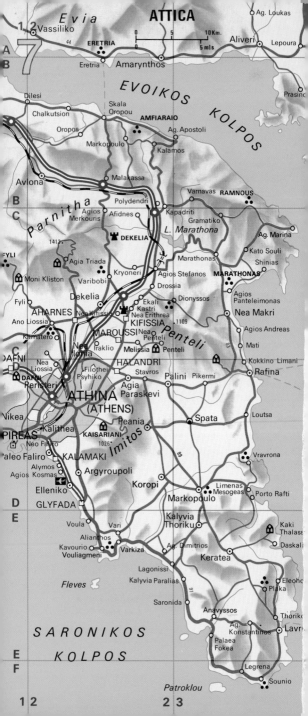